D0810371

Readings in
Russian Philosophical
Thought

Edited and translated with preface and
introductory chapter and notes
by
LOUIS J. SHEIN
McMaster University

1968 · MOUTON · THE HAGUE · PARIS

© Copyright 1968 in The Netherlands.
Mouton & Co. N.V., Publishers, The Hague.

*No part of this book may be translated or reproduced in any form, by print,
photoprint, microfilm, or any other means, without written permission from
the publishers.*

197
Sh 42r

LIBRARY OF CONGRESS CATALOG CARD NUMBER: 68-15528

Printed in The Netherlands by Mouton & Co., Printers, The Hague.

Dedicated to my wife Margaret
and the children,
Brian, David, Elizabeth and Fraser

69— 65441

PREFACE

The present work is the result of a practical need that arose in connection with a course I introduced some five years ago on *The Development of Russian Thought*. Since most of Russian philosophical works were unavailable in English translation, I decided to meet this need, at least partially, by providing in English translation some representative selections of Russian philosophic writings.

This volume contains selections of representative philosophic writings of the second half of the nineteenth century and the first quarter of the present century. This material to my knowledge (with three exceptions) has not hitherto appeared in English translation. Most of the selections were chosen from the Russian philosophical journal, *Voprosy filosofii i psikhologii* (1888-1917) [Problems of Philosophy and Psychology]. One selection is from Berdyaev's *Subjektivism i Individualism v Obschestvennoi Filosofii* [Subjectivism and Individualism in Social Philosophy] (Chapter I, abridged) (St. Petersburg, 1901). Two selections from Lossky's writings. One from *Tsennost' i Bytie* [Value and Existence] (Chapter III, abridged, YMCA Press, Paris, 1931) and a selection from Lossky's *An Epistemological Introduction into Logic* (published in brochure form in English by the Russian Free University, Prague, 1939). Transliteration of Russian titles is based on the new Russian orthography as shown on the transliteration table in the back of the book.

The material is arranged in three philosophic problems, namely, epistemology, metaphysics and ethics. A subsequent volume will contain selections from works on logic, aesthetics and philosophy of history. I hope that the present volume will meet a partial need and will stimulate further interest in Russian philosophy.

Among the many to whom I am deeply indebted, I wish particularly to thank: Professor George L. Kline of Bryn Mawr College for invaluable suggestions; Mrs. Lorraine Mazur for typing the manuscript and compiling the bibliography and index, and Miss Gail Kellett for proof-reading the manuscript; the staffs of the New York Public Library and Columbia University library for their help and co-operation. I am especially grateful to McMaster University and the Canada Council for their financial assistance and support of my research. Finally, I wish to express my personal debt which I owe to my wife, to whom I dedicate this work.

McMaster University,   LOUIS J. SHEIN
Hamilton, Ontario.
September, 1965

CONTENTS

RUSSIAN TRANSLITERATION TABLE

А а – A a
Б б – B b
В в – V v
Г г – G g (in the genitive endings
        ero and oro, r = v)

Д д – D d
Е е – E e
Ё ё – Yo yo
Ж ж – Zh zh
З з – Z z
И и – I i
Й й – I i (the combinations ий = i
        and ый = y)

К к – K k
Л л – L l
М м – M m
Н н – N n
О о – O o

П п – P p
Р р – R r
С с – S s
Т т – T t
У у – U u

Ф ф – F f
Х х – Kh kh
Ц ц – Ts ts
Ч ч – Ch ch
Ш ш – Sh sh
Щ щ – Shch shch
ъ – omitted
ы – y

ь – omitted
Э э – E e
Ю ю – Yu yu
Я я – Ya ya

Section I
THE DEVELOPMENT OF PHILOSOPHICAL THOUGHT IN RUSSIA

- - - - - - - - - - - - - - - - - - -

GENERAL INTRODUCTION

STATEMENT OF THE PROBLEM

Is there a peculiarly Russian type of philosophy that may claim a unique place in the history of ideas? There is no simple answer to this important question. Before an attempt is made to find an answer to this question a distinction must be made between thinkers and philosophers. While the frontier between thinkers and philosophers is very often vague and difficult to define, nevertheless there is a distinction which is germane to our problem.

There are those who are concerned with topics of a general nature, and these topics vary from one age and one culture to another. These may be termed social thinkers. On the other hand, there are those who are professionally occupied with the topics and methods which constitute philosophy proper, namely, the disciplines of logic, epistemology, ethics and metaphysics. Russia has had an abundance of thinkers in the first sense, beginning with the fathers of the Orthodox Church to the 'philosophies of life' as dealt within the framework of the novelists like Gogol, Dostoyevsky, Tolstoy, Belinsky, Dobroliubov, Chernishevsky, Herzen, Gorky, Plekhanov, Mikhailovsky, and a host of others. If we are to speak of "Russian philosophy" in the Western sense, we must turn to the latter half of the nineteenth century, to men like Yurkevich, Chicherin, Solovyov, Karinsky, Lopatin, the Trubetskoi brothers, Lossky, Frank and others, who were primarily concerned with strictly philosophical problems.

Russian philosophical thought since its embryonic appearance in the eighteenth century experienced a very trying existence. First of all,

Russian philosophy lacked originality. Russian philosophers were merely imitators and followers of European philosophical systems. They had followed Wolff, Fichte, Schelling, Kant and Hegel as well as the French sensationalists. In the 'fifties' and 'sixties' German idealism was replaced by the materialism of Buchner and Vogt and by the French and Englisth positivists.

During the latter half of the nineteenth century the positivists were very popular in Russia. August Comte, John Stuart Mill, Herbert Spencer and Lewes, were widely acclaimed by Russian philosophers. Comte's three stages of intellectual development of mankind was considered to be the final word on the philosophy of history. Theology and metaphyhics were declared to be delusions of the human mind. The only means of attaining truth, according to this view, is to reject all efforts at penetrating the real substance of things and to limit all claims to knowledge to the ascertaining of the actual relations existing among the various phenomena of nature. Spencer's principle of cosmic evolution played the same role in Russian philosophical thought as did Hegelianism in Belinsky's time. Russian thinkers regarded Darwinianism as the last word on the processes of life.

There were however, other influences which played an important role in the moulding of Russian philosophical thought. In this connection it should be noted that the Russian mind is basically metaphysical and Russian tradition is deeply rooted in the concrete. This tradition is essentially Christian Neo-Platonism, especially in its epistemological and metaphysical ideas. These ideas found expression in Solovyov, S. N. Trubetskoi, N. O. Lossky, Berdyaev and others. Christian Neo-Platonism regards the Absolute to be distinct from the world. God or the Absolute created the world *ex nihilo* which is a peculiarly Christian idea. The very fact that God projected the world and continues to sustain it endows the world a divine value. Christian Neo-Platonism insists on the transcendence as well as on the immanence of God, whereas Hegelianism inevitably leads to pantheism. The *leitmotif* in Russian philosophy is the transcendence and immanence of God and the organic unity of the Cosmos. These ideas are basic to most Russian philosophic systems.

It may be stated that Russian thinkers made a genuine attempt to assimilate the general wealth of European philosophy in order to advance philosophical thought in their own country. Russian philosophers have endeavoured in their own unique way to find solutions to fundamental philosophical problems. Hence, philosophical thought played an important role in the development of the cultural and creative life of the Russian nation during a brief period of some fifty years. As a result of a serious soul-searching on the part of Russian intellectuals there came into being a mighty social movement known as Populism which played an important role in the life of Russia for decades. It was instrumental in producing a remarkable literature, gave rise to many progressive and radical movements which left their mark on the course of world history.

While Russia never experienced a Renaissance or a Reformation, there was a profound awakening after the 1812 war and subsequently after the 1861 emancipation of the serfs. In addition to the Populist movement which sought to bring enlightenment to the large illiterate masses, there came into being new institutions of rural and urban self-government based on democratic principles. This was, of course, on a small and limited scale. Philosophy itself embarked upon a course of self-examination. This resulted in a genuine reflection on the basic problems of philosophy, which although, not original in their solutions, were to some extent independent and unique in achieving them. It may be argued that this awakening was merely a change from Hegelianism and mystico-religious views to a scientific treatment of philosophical problems in either materialistic or positivistic dogmas. This is true to a certain extent. For in order to be of spiritual attraction to the vast masses it was necessary to present fundamental problems in a simplified and realistic interpretation of life. The role of materialism and positivism was indispensable in that respect. We may therefore say that the philosophical awakening of Russian thought may be characterised as a profound speculative concentration on the essence of things which expressed itself as the self-assertion of philosophical thought in the form of a number of genuinely metaphysical dogmas and conceptions, relying as far as possible, on philosophical criticism based on the free and creative spirit of man and not on blind and limited sense data.

THE STATE OF PHILOSOPHY IN NINETEENTH-CENTURY RUSSIA

The development of philosophical thought in Russia experienced three distinct periods. We shall endeavour to give a general account of these periods to acquaint the reader with some of the background. We shall then deal more specifically with the philosophical systems of some of the prominent philosophers of the latter half of the nineteenth century whose lives and work encompass the early part of the twentieth century.

The first period

Russia, unlike the West, had to begin with the adoption of philosophical ideas that were already deeply rooted in Western philosophy. This is quite natural. This is also true of the West. The West at first accepted Greek philosophy, and gradually developed its own systems of philosophy.

The opening of the Moscow university in 1755 marks the beginning of the appearance of philosophy in Russia. This does not mean that prior to this date philosophy was unknown in Russia. As a matter of fact, subjects under the name of philosophy were offered in the ecclesiastical seminaries in Kiev and in Moscow. It should be pointed out however, that philosophy was being taught in a very mechanical manner. Students were merely required to memorize certain views or ideas. In Moscow university for example, philosophy was taught by the text-book method in the spirit of the Wolffian school. The first professors were invited from Germany to teach philosophy and instruction was done in the Latin language. One can well imagine the effect this would have on students who had to absorb Wolffian philosophy taught by Germans in Latin. It is not surprising therefore, that philosophy could not flourish under such conditions.

The influence of French philosophy on Russian thought was much more successful during this period. French influence dates back to the period of Catherine II who was instrumental in introducing French ideas into court circles. Many translations of Voltaire, Montesquieu, Condillac, Helvetius, Rousseau and others, made their appearance in Russia. It should be pointed out however, that the dissemination of French philosophy was on a superficial level. During Catherine's reign French philosophical ideas were for the majority of Russian intellectuals merely a conversation piece. There ensued a general disillusionment with the encyclopedists and many turned to mysticism as an alternative to French materialism and sensualism. It is therefore not surprising that French influences disappeared at the beginning of the nineteenth century. However, it did help to awaken an interest in philosophical thought and prepared the ground for a more profound reception of Western philosophy.

We may therefore say that the first period which lasted some fifty years was only a preparatory period. We are not unmindful of the existence of Gregory Skovoroda (1722-94), who is generally considered to be the first Russian philosopher in the strict sense of that word. Skovoroda was a profound and original thinker and he rendered invaluable service to his native Ukraine which led to the establishment of the Kharkov university. Unfortunately, his influence was of a local nature and affected very little the dominant position held by the encyclopedists. The French encyclopedists were at least instrumental in bringing about a reconsideration of materialism and sensualism, which eventually led to a broader and more systematic consideration of philosophical problems.

The second period

In order to understand the development of Russian philosophical thought during the second period, something should be said about the historical background of this period.

The beginning of the reign of Alexander I saw a numbr of important developments which were conducive to the fostering of philosophical thought in Russia. A number of positive measures were introduced to raise the level of both theological and secular education. New universities and gymnasiums came into being, ecclesiastical academies were established along the line of higher institutions of learning and the general educational level in the seminaries was improved. The teaching of philosophy was introduced not only in universities and ecclesiastical academies, but even in the seminaries and gymnasiums. For example, obligatory instruction in logic, psychology, philosophy of law (under the title of 'natural law'), aesthetics and moral philosophy was introduced into the gymnasiums. Eighteen weekly lessons were devoted to these subjects. While instruction in these subjects was not on a high level, it did foster some interest in philosophical thought.

The teaching of secular philosophy in ecclesiastical academies and seminaries was carried out under extremely difficult conditions. This was due to the inner structure of the academies where the black clergy were in full control. The rector of the academy in St. Petersburg acted like an autocrat. Preference for teaching positions was given to those who were willing to become monks. This preference was extended to students as well. For example, a student who was considered to be unsuitable for a Master's degree was awarded the degree after he joined a monastic order. The result was disastrous for teachers and students alike.

The administration of the ecclesiastical academies regarded philosophy merely as a servant of theology. Thus, a large number of the teaching staff was made up of monks who were there for purely selfish reasons. Appointments to the teaching staff were wholly unsatisfactory from the point of view of their academic training. For example, a person who had recently completed his course was chosen to an appointment without regard to his specialization or inclination. After a while the same person was transferred to teach another subject of which he knew nothing. For instance, a person would be transferred from languages to mathematics or the natural sciences. A certain person by the name of Il'minsky was appointed to the chair of philosophy at the Kazan academy who was trained in Oriental languages who had no interest or training in philosophy.

What was the fate of secular philosophy during this period? We find that at the beginning of the nineteenth century German idealism began to supplant French materialism and sensualism. Fichte's philosophy enjoyed the least success in Russia. The only Fichtean propagator was professor Schad of Kharkov University. Kant enjoyed a great deal of popularity in academic circles. However, Schelling's influence was very considerable, and it was only toward the end of the 'thirties' that he was supplanted by Hegel.

The first person who introduced Schelling's *natur-philosophie* into Russia was D. M. Vellansky, who was professor of anatomy and physiology at the St. Petersburg academy of medical surgery. Vellansky became acquainted with Schelling's philosophy during his study in Germany while preparing himself for the Chair he was to occupy later at St. Petersburg. He was a very gifted lecturer and it is largely through his lectures that he disseminated Schelling's ideas. His two important works, "Animal Magnetism" and "Biological Investigation" were sold out as soon as they were published in spite of their difficult language. He was so popular that the Moscow Lovers of Philosophy invited him to Moscow to deliver twenty lectures on Schelling's philosophy for which they offered him the sum of twenty thousand rubles (equivalent to ten thousand american dollars).

Another person who was instrumental in spreading Schellingian ideas was A. I. Galich (1783-1848). Galich was professor at the Pedagogical Institute at St. Petersburg, and later at the University of St. Petersburg. Although he was not a Schellingian by conviction, he nevertheless succeeded in bringing to the attention of his students the basic ideas of Schelling. His "History of Philosophic Systems" published in 1819 contained an outline of Schelling's philosophic ideas. This book was received with great interest and it also helped in the spreading of Schellingian philosophy. Galich was later accused by the authorities for his 'heretical' views, because he failed to refute the philosophic systems he was expounding to his students. As a result he was deprived of his Chair at the university and one of his books was burned. This marked the beginning of a dark period in the history of Russian philosophy.

The free and unhindered dissemination of philosophical ideas was soon to experience a period of suppression and persecution. During the reign of Alexander I some of the ecclesiastical leaders, who, under the guise of piety and loyalty to the throne, managed to insinuate themselves into the Ministry of Education, and thus succeeded in combining it with the Ministry of ecclesiastical affairs. These obscurantists soon began to limit the teaching of philosophy in the Gymnasiums to elementary logic. But they did not stop there. The universities were soon to feel the brunt of ecclesiastical authoritarianism. They wanted to model the educational institutions on the French and Austrian catholic schools and insisted on a type of pietism which was completely repugnant to any enlightened person.

The attack on philosophy soon began in earnest when Professor Schad of Kharkov university, who was a Fichtean, was accused of spreading Schelling's philosophy, and in 1816 was exiled from Russia. The same fate befell the mathematician Osipovsky who was accused of propagating Kantianism while refuting the Kantian theory of space and time.

Other universities were soon to feel the heavy hand of the obscurantists. A certain Magnitsky was responsible for the dismissal of a number of the best professors at the Kazan university, among these was Solntsev, a professor of natural law. He was accused of spreading Kantianism. The teaching of philosophy under Magnitsky was limited to logic and the history of philosophy which had to be of an accusatory nature, that is, it had to prove the complete inconsistency of philosophy. Obscurantism had reached a point that even the most neutral subjects such as mathematics, had to agree with religion. This was actually the case at Kazan, when a certain professor Nikolsky went to great length to prove that there was the fullest agreement between mathematics and the Christian religion. The obscurantists succeeded in decimating the Kazan university after which Kantian philosophy ceased to be propagated and after 1820 not a single work on Kant appeared.

The same thing occurred in 1821 at the St. Petersburg university. Twelve professors lost their position in one year. The rest left on their own accord. Even Moscow University, where the persecution was not so severe, was not free from persecution. In 1823 Magnisky, in a note to the Tsar, proposed the abolition of the teaching of philosophy in all universities. He pointed out that the "Logic" by professor Davydov (1794-1863) who taught philosophy at the Moscow university, was permeated with Schellingian ideas, hence, was atheistic. As a result, Davydov was allowed to teach only Russian and Roman literature, but not philosophy.

The persecutions did not however succeed in rooting out philosophical studies in the universities. Davydov, who was appointed Inspector of the University Residences in 1815 was able to disseminate Schellingian ideas among the students. This resulted in the formation of a literary society as well as a philosophical "Circle". The latter had to give up its official name after the abortive uprising of the Decembrists in 1825. Among those who belonged to this "Circle" were the Kireyevsky brothers, Koshelev and other future Slavophiles. Some of the scientists also helped in the dissemination of Schellingian ideas, notably Pavlov, who was professor of mineralogy and agriculture. Herzen complained about this state of affairs by pointing out that any ignoramus could pass judgment on philosophy, whereas one had to be a specialist in order to pass judgment of the quality of shoes or shoe leather.

Toward the end of the 'thirties' and early 'forties' the wave of persecution abated somewhat and many "circles" emerged in Moscow where German idealism was being disseminated once again. Among those who greatly helped in the dissemination of German idealism were men like Vladimir Odoyevsky, D. V. Venevitinov, the Kiriyevsky brothers, the Aksakovs, Khomyakov, Belinsky, Herzen, Stankevich, and others. The teaching of philosophy became obligatory for students of all faculties with the exception of medical faculties.

The situation worsened after the 1848 events in Europe. Censorship became extremely rigid and members of the Ministry of Education were prohibited from going abroad. University councils were deprived of their rights to elect a rector, and it was even suggested that the universities become military institutions. Fortunately, this plan did not succeed. Uvarov, who was minister of education (1833-49) and who was responsible for reforming the universities resigned as a result of the stringent rules, and Prince Shirishkin-Shikhmatov was appointed in his place. This resulted in the abolition of the Philosophical Faculty and in the formation of two new departments in its place, namely, Historical-Philological and Physico-Mathematical departments. These departments were allowed to teach only logic and psychology under the supervision of the Holy Synod and taught by a person from the Law Faculty. The results for education in general and philosophy in particular were disastrous.

The third period

The third period of the development of philosophical thought may be said to have begun during the reign of Alexander II who encouraged the revival of philosophy in the universities after the 1863 regulations. Russian philosophical thought soon manifested a genuine search for truth which found expression in a concrete creative idealism. It recognized a creative absolute spirit as a basis for explaining the whole of reality. It was definitely a reaction against a pantheistic interpretation of reality, and it therefore refused to identify the whole of existence with the divine Absolute.

A movement known as transcendental monism was developed by F. A. Golubisnky (1797-1854) which was later systematised by V. M. Kudryavtsev-Platonov (1828-1891) and Aleksei Vvedensky (1861-1913). They tried to combine German idealism with Biblical revelation. They regarded the idea of an Absolute perfect being as the final criterion and highest meaning of existence. The self-assertion of Russian philosophical thought manifested itself in other philosophical trends. Let us now consider some of the most important trends.

Kantianism

Kantian philosophy began to exert its influence among many Russian thinkers, even among those who were its metaphysical opponents, such as Solovyov, Lopatin, and S. N. Trubetskoi. The leading protagonist of orthodox Kantianism was A. I. Vvedensky (1856-1925), who was professor of philosophy at St. Petersburg university. Vvedensky worked out his epistemology and metaphysics along orthodox Kantian lines, but he rejected Kant's 'thing-in-itself'.

Philosophy, according to Vvedensky, is primarily concerned with the problem of knowledge itself, and must lay down the conditions for authentic knowledge. In other words, philosophy must be a scientific-ally-oriented Weltanschauung. Such authentic knowledge may be found in mathematics and in the natural sciences. Philosophy should be able to establish the limits of human knowledge and should be able to discover the area where both unproven and irrefutable views are possible, i.e. where faith is possible. In this connection Hume's influence is to be seen in his doctrine of 'faith' as a specific 'source of cognition', which Vvedensky calls a 'special organ of cognition' or a 'metaphysical sense'. The first of the conditions laid down by Vvedensky is correct thinking, and epistemology must be a type of logic that evaluates the suitability of every method for ascertaining knowledge.

Vvedensky argues that since mathematics and the natural sciences make true knowledge possible, it follows that all objects studied by these sciences must be regarded as our ideas of things and being and not as THINGS-IN-THEMSELVES. We can know nothing about 'true' being' except the impossibility of having knowledge about it. According to Vvedensky, we cannot logically equate metaphysical hypotheses with non-metaphysical ones, since not a single metaphysical hypothesis can ever become knowledge. The mystic is entitled to his conviction in the objective significance of his mystical perception, but it must be regarded as faith and not knowledge. In our exploration of knowledge we are entitled to assume some hypotheses about true being, but these should only be employed as working hypotheses and not as true knowledge. Our choice of a hypothesis, should be guided by the moral principle. Here Vvedensky follows Kant's view in recommending the moral principle for a teleologically and scientifically-oriented Weltanschauung. This type of metaphysics differs from a dogmatic metaphysics in two important aspects. First, it understands that it is different from knowledge, and secondly, in knowing that it is faith it can tell us on moral grounds why it chose the one over against the other metaphysical hypotheses that are equally irrefutable.

According to Vvedensky, we cannot know the inner life of another person, since there are no objective signs for the consciousness of other beings, and our idea about the spiritual life of another being is completely subjective. Vvedensky does not wish to end up in either solipsism or scepticism (the inevitable result of his position), he therefore suggests that while our knowledge of the life of another being is theoretically impossible, 'feeling' (which is for him moral certainty), compels us to believe in the existence of other beings and in the moral foundations of the universe. To sum up, Vvedensky's epistemology contains three basic elements: (a) Indubitable knowledge, based on A PRIORI elements; (b) A POSTERIORI knowledge, and (c) faith. In the final analysis, we find in Vvedensky's system two kinds of knowledge – one which is based on critical philosophy, the other on an extra-critical basis, essential to what he calls the "cultured consciousness". He also has two kinds of being, one in the phenomenal sphere, the other grounded in "things-in-themselves".

Positivism

As a result of renewed interest in Idealism during this period, positivism was now forced to reconsider its position in regard to the genuine philosophical problems facing Russian thinkers. This could only be achieved by approaching philosophical problems on the basis of a different theory of knowledge. The man who made the transition from scientific dogmatism to critical realism is V. V. Lesevich (1837-1905). The transformation of Comtian positivism into critical realism, is, according to Lesevich, the logical development of positivism. He accepted the Kantian rejection of metaphysics by asserting that true knowledge can only be attained through 'scientific demonstrability'.

The starting point of our knowledge, according to Lesevich, is an idea. An idea however, corresponds objectively to fact, a fact, which in any given case is necessarily something concrete and individual. Hence, our knowledge is directly related to separate, concrete, individual facts. These wholly exhaust the objective material. We cannot therefore speak of any eternal immutable laws in critical philosophy. The causes of our perceptions cannot be sought exclusively in objects, since phenomena do not enter our senses as into an open door, but change their form by the very act of perception. The causes of perception are to be found just as much in objects as in the subject. Hence, the quality of perception changes not only with the changing of the object, but also with the changing of the subject.

Lesevich, under the influence of Avenarius, later formulated his Weltanschauung, which he terms empirico-criticism, as follows: (1) Everything that pertains to the realm of 'spirit' is nothing more than a reflection, a watered-down image of what is perceived. (2) All perception is sensory. (3) 'Being' and 'thinking' correspond in every respect to the thing perceived. (4) Every being and every kind of knowledge is experience. (5) Human experience is an absolutely final fact, the beginning and the end of wisdom.

Another man who played no mean role in the development of Russian philosophical thought is M. I. Karinski (1840-1917). Karinski published several important works in the field of theoretical philosophy, his most important work is *A Clasification of Inferences*, which deals with formal logic. He subjected rationalism (Kantianism) and empiricism (Mill and Spencer) to a thorough critical examination and arrived at an intermediate view of cognition. He rejected the Kantian idea of the activity of thought in the construction of a world-idea, by demonstrating the falsity of absolute associationism and by refusing to regard being as the product of thought.

Many other voices were heard during the 'seventies' and 'eighties', such as Danilevsky, K. N. Leontyev, who represented the Slavophile position. Lavrov and Mikhailovsky continued to champion the uncritical 'sociological positivism' and N. Ya. Grot, who at first espoused the cause of materialism, but later adopted a more metaphysical position. It was also during this period that the Moscow Psychological and Philosophical Society came into being and began to publish "Problems of Philosophy and Psychology". The Society and its journal became the focal point for Russian philosophical life and retained its importance until 1917.

Hegelianism

Hegelians played a very important role in the development of Russian philosophical thought, and the man who presented it in a systematic way was B. V. Chicherin (1828-1903). Chicherin's exposition of Hegelianism was almost the only systematic presentation in terms of its completeness and was, in the words of S. N. Trubetskoy, "the philosophy of absolute systematism".

Chicherin's system may be stated in the following central ideas. To understand a thing means to subject it to a higher idea. We say that we understand a thing when we perceive in its governing law a particular application of a more general law. A full understanding of a thing or object implies the subjecting of phenomena to the higher law of reason through all the intervening stages. This constitutes the supreme purpose of science, but its necessary condition consists in being conscious of the total system of logical definitions. Since the cognising mind constitutes one whole, or one active force, it follows that all its laws should be connected with each other and all its definitions should form one system. This is the task of dialectic, which constitutes the genuine foundation of philosophy.

The dialectical movement of thought contains a tetradic scheme which replaces the Hegelian triadic scheme of thesis, antithesis and synthesis. The tetradic scheme proposed by Chicherin consists of: (a) the initial unity, which contains in its fusion both the universal and the particular; (b) the opposites in abstraction, i.e., the abstract-universal and abstract-particular; (c) the higher and final unity of the two. Since however, each of these definitions is subject to the dialectical process, there results a whole series of purely intellectual categories which constitutes the task of the dialectic. Since there are only four main definitions, Chicherin comes to the conclusion that all philosophical systems can be reduced to four types. (a) Basic to the naturalistic philosophy is the productive principle; (b) for spiritualism the formal principle; (c) for materialism the material cause, and (d) for idealism the final cause. A fifth type is scepticism, which is merely a transitional stage from one system to another.

According to Chicherin, reason goes beyond the limits of experience. Reason sees in every phenomenon only a particular application of a more general law. Reason can only go as far as its own laws permit, i.e., the absolute universal principle. An absolute general form, according to Chicherin, requires also an absolute general content. This content is not attained through experience, which is always limited. But Reason, by its peculiar nature as consciousness of pure law, goes beyond the limits of all experience and presupposes a content in accordance with its form. From the relative it is inevitably raised to the absolute. The latter is cognized by applying to it those logical laws which constitute the essence of our reason and which governs all our cognition. The task of philosophy, according to Chicherin, is to develop various methods of understanding phenomena, and at the same time to develop those definitions of the Absolute which serve as a higher connection of things and which alone enable us to understand phenomena.

Chicherin identifies the Absolute with God. God is not our external feeling; he is only cognized by speculative thought and not by sense experience. It is axiomatic for him that such a Being necessarily exists, since it is the principle of all existence. For if something EXISTS, then there necessarily is a Being who exists in and by Himself. Such a Being must contain in Himself all conditions necessary for existence. There is nothing outside it which could limit it or make it dependent upon another being. Consequently, absolute being can only be a Being which contains its own reality and all existence. This absolute Being is the creative as well as the formal principle, the material as well as the final Cause. To put it differently, the Absolute is the Creative Force, supreme

Reason, infinite Matter and life-creating Spirit. The material principle constitutes the essence of the external world. The other three principles constitute the essence of the Divine. Since, however, these principles represent the development of one and the same Divine essence, it follows that all of them must be considered as the definitions of one Deity. But each one of them, which is at the same time a manifestation of the Absolute, constitutes in itself an absolute principle. Hence, the single Deity is manifested in different forms. On this basis Chicherin arrives at the Christian doctrine of the Trinity which is to be understood as Force, the Word and Spirit. This was Chicherin's peculiarly Russian way of interpreting Hegelianism.

THE SYSTEMATIZERS

Vladimir Solovyov (1853-1900). – Thus far we have endeavoured to present a general outline of the conditions under which Russian philosophical thought developed in Russia during the nineteenth century. We shall now consider more specifically some of the important philosophic systems during this period.

The man who occupies a very important place in Russian philosophy is Vladimir Sergeyevich Solovyov. Although he had written a great deal on purely philosophical subjects, his main interest lies in the realm of the religious and the metaphysical. Solovyov's earlier works are devoted to a critical examination of the various philosophical systems current in his day. He examined materialism, realism, positivism, empiricism, and rationalism and found them wholly inadequate, because they are purely abstract in character, and hence, invalid for an interpretation of reality. Truth for Solovyov, is an absolute value peculiar to the Total-Unity itself. In order to understand truth one must transcend the limits of subjective thought and enter into the realm of the Absolute. Solovyov regarded both empirical and rational knowledge to be purely relative, since its contact with the object is external. Empiricism gives us appearances without the object of which they are appearances, and without the subject to whom they appear. Rationalism on the other hand, leaves us with "thought without a thinker and without anything to think about".

Solovyov's system contains three fundamental principles: (1) The inner spirituality of all being; (2) the concept of absolute Total-Unity (vseyedinstvo); (3) the concept of God-Manhood. These main principles are a guide to an understanding of his system.

According to Solovyov, cognition of the truth cannot be attained either by abstract rationalism or abstract empiricism. Neither experience nor reason can give us the basis and criterion for truth. We must pre-suppose in cognition the unconditional existence of its object, i.e., the true being or TOTAL-UNITY, and its actual relation to the cognizing sub-ject. Solovyov insists that the principle of TOTAL-UNITY is not merely an empty form, but that it exists in its own absolute reality as true being. The principle of TOTAL-UNITY must be internally connected with the cognizing subject by virtue of which the subject is internally con-nected with everything that exists within the TOTAL-UNITY. Our experi-ence and our thinking can have genuine reality and positive universality only in relation to the absolute REAL and the absolute UNIVERSAL (Total-Unity). The real object of our cognition is not this or that being, this or that predicate PER SE (since there cannot be predicates PER SE), but the subject to which the given predicates belong. Hence, true knowledge in its universality has as its real object not being in general, but that which generally has being, i.e., absolute being, or being as the absolute principle of all existence.

The Absolute first Principle, which Solovyov identifies with God, is the creative Force of all being and the source of the different forms of reality. Since this principle is found in every being (and here he comes very close to pantheism), it follows that it is cognized in every cognition. It is true that it can never be given either empirically or logically, since it can never become a sensation or a concept or a state of our consciousness, nevertheless, this principle can be cognized even in empirical and logical cognition, because the real object is not a sen-sation or a thought, but is that which is sensed and thought, i.e., it is real being. Solovyov states paradoxically that the Absolute is both nothing and everything. It is nothing insofar as it IS NOT SOMETHING; it is everything insofar as it CANNOT BE DEVOID OF ANYTHING.

The Absolute, according to Solovyov, contains the unity of itself and its opposite. Two principles may here be distinguished. First, the principle of absolute unity and freedom from every form of external determination or limitation, i.e., from every being. Secondly, the prin-ciple or the generative force of being, i.e. plurality of forms. The first, which is the Absolute in itself, transcends existence and is therefore the POSITIVE potentiality of being; the second, is the substance of the Absolute, or the striving for existence, which is the NEGATIVE poten-tiality, or *materia prima*.

The second absolute which is the foundation of every relative exist-ence, finds for the first time in man its own inner reality, finds itself and cognizes itself. Solovyov distinguishes three basic elements in man, each one representing that reality which is characterized by the "second absolute", or the World-Soul. (1) Man is first of all an unconditional subject of all his actions and states. (2) Man not only *is*, but he *is* something; he possesses a certain absolute property or quality which distinguishes him not only as a subject distinct from his states or predicates, but as a subject distinct from all other subjects. This, in Solovyov's view, constitutes man's IDEA or his UNIQUENESS, and insofar as in his normal state man is everything, his IDEA is internally necessarily connected with all other in the TOTAL-UNITY, i.e. man's IDEA is positively fulfilled by all others in the form of absolute content. Since this IDEA which is unique, enables it to assert itself outside everything as the NOT ALL, and thus becomes the absolute limit for all others. From this it follows that since every being has its own IDEA, externally, all other beings equally limit each other. Hence, their mutual relationship, instead of being an internal positive unity, are an external negative equality, and the unique IDEA of every being in which they are related becomes undifferentiated forms of every possible content or abstract reason, thus having the possibility of relating all content to itself.

The empirical reality of man, which is the third or natural principle of his being, appears here as the contingent, the many, the particular, which can only gradually become the ONE and the ALL, and which indeed it does become insofar as man returns from his non-absolute state to the TOTAL-UNITY, thus becoming freely and consciously absolute in himself. But since the particular being can exist only in the process of becoming ALL, it follows that personal existence belongs to two inseparable absolutes which are mutually conditioned, namely, absolute being (God), and the absolute in the process of becoming (man). This finds full expression in the term "Godmanhood", for only in man does the second absolute, or the World-Soul find its actual realization in its two principles.

Solovyov defines the object in its full reality first, as the unconditional real, second, as an indivisible essence or idea, and finally, as an actual being or phenomenon. Objective knowledge is defined, first as faith in the absolute existence of the object, second, as intellectual contemplation or imagination of its reality, and finally, as creative fulfillment of this idea of empirical data of our natural sensory consciousness. The first tells us that the object EXISTS, the second informs us WHAT IT IS, and the third shows us HOW IT IS.

Truth, according to Solovyov, cannot be defined as a rational idea or as facts of experience nor as a dogma of faith. Absolute truth must manifest itself in all our relationships, i.e. it must be experienced mystically, rationally and empirically. If objective truth must express the truth of that which exists, then the true relationship between the elements of our cognition is possible only when there is a correct relationship between the elements of our reality, i.e. of that being which is the object of our cognition. The organization of reality is essential for the organization of knowledge. The whole of nature and every empirical element of our existence must be organized and must be internally subject to our spirit, just as our spirit must be internally subject to the Divine spirit. If every real object represents a certain organization of factual elements that are conditioned by a particular act of natural creation, then the organization of all reality is the task of universal creativity, the object of great artistic realization by man of the divine principle or of the divine force in the real existence of nature, namely, free theurgy. The task of art in all its fulness as free theurgy is to establish in the universal as well as in the particular an organic relationship between the divine, the human, and the natural elements.

Solovyov was deeply concerned with the role of morality in the Universe. He therefore insists that the supreme moral principle which must define the practical activity of man, is not exhausted by either the abstract empirical concepts of pleasure, happiness, utility or sympathy, nor by the abstract rational concept of duty or even the categorical imperative. All these concepts form the material of the moral principle, but do not constitute its reality. Moral action must not only possess certain qualities, but must have a definite object in view. Such an object can only be normal society characterized by free communion or practical TOTAL-UNITY. The character of such a society is defined by a religious or mystical principle in man in which all members fulfill each other in a free unity of spiritual love, which must be realized in a spiritual society or the Church.

Both political and economic interests must serve as a formal and material medium for the realization of the divine principle which finds full expression in the Church. Since the realization of the divine principle in human society must be based on the principle of TOTAL-UNITY and free communion among its members, it follows that such a society must eventually become a free theocracy. The meaning of the absolute moral principle may be stated as follows: Society in its perfect inner harmony with a higher will, and insofar as it expresses the image and likeness of God, must fully participate in the task of realizing God's kingdom in the world.

Solovyov was also deeply concerned with philosophy of history, or historiosophy. There were three historical cultures in his day, the Moslem East, Western civilization, and the Slavic world. He regarded the Moslem East as a force that is extremely exclusive in character because of its religious principle. The emphasis here is on the supremacy of God and the denial of individual freedom. Western culture on the other hand, stresses man's autonomy which results in atomism in every area of life. Solovyov regarded Western culture as a second transitional phase in the organic process of mankind; a third phase is needed to complete this process. Solvyov suggests that the third force necessary to complete this process must be found in a nation whose raison d'être is to manifest the vision of a divine world. The task of such a nation is therefore to communicate a living spirit in an effort to make humanity whole by uniting it with the perfect divine principle. It is not required of such a nation to possess special gifts or advantages. All that is required is to be free from any spirit of exclusiveness and to have a perfect faith in the positive rality of the divine world. The Slavs, and especially the Russian people, according to Solovyov, possess such qualities. Russia's vocation is of a religious nature in the highest sense of the word, for Russia alone can become the historical bearer and transmitter of the third principle. This idea is of course, basic to the Slavophile Weltanschauung.

Solovyov's cosmology is part and parcel of his philosophical system, we shall therefore present a brief summary of his cosmological views.

In trying to explain the origin of the world, Solovyov suggests that the answer is to be found in the nature of the Absolute. The fundamental property of the Absolute is his SELF-DEFINITION. The other aspect of the Absolute is His absolute freedom which is inseparably bound up with His self-definition. Since all existence is contained within the Absolute, it follows that nothing exists outside the Absolute. The World's soul, or essence, is a living image of the Absolute which is repeated in an eternal ideal creation. Hence, freedom and self-definition arc the fundamental properties of the world in the same way as they are of the Absolute or Deity. The freedom of the world implies that it can dwell in harmony with the Deity, but it can also choose to live apart from the deity. The choice is wholly voluntary. But since the world chose to live apart from God, it *ipso facto* destroyed the Divine image and made ITSELF the centre rather than the Deity.

There are three essential phases in the cosmic process. (1) There is the MECHANICAL UNITY produced by the cosmic gravitation which creates the material body of the universe. It is in this phase that the soul of the world achieves its first realization as a universal unity. (2) The second phase is manifested in the DYNAMIC UNITY. In this phase the world's soul realizes itself in the form of rarified matter or ether which envelops all the elements of the cosmic body and sets them in varying relations to each other. The fundamental characteristic of this phase is pure altruism. (3) The ORGANIC UNITY is the third phase which presents a true image of the Total-Unity in the material world by means of the ideal union.

The natural process attains its supreme goal and true purpose in the creation of man. It is through man that the world must become a single living body and an embodiment of Sophia – the Divine Wisdom.

Man is capable of the deifying nature only because he is himself inwardly deified. Solovyov therefore calls mankind the second Absolute who is in the process of becoming absolute, and who will gradually realize his ideal purpose.

Solovyov applied his general moral principles to social ideals. He regarded the law of love, human justice and the infinite worth of man as the absolute criteria of all social, political, national and international relations. He knew of no double moral standards. This made him a valiant champion of human freedom.

We may now sum up Solovyov's philosophical views. Solovyov's philosophic system is subject to various interpretations which makes it difficult to categorize it. In his views regarding the primary basis of things he is a theist, but in his cosmology he is a pantheist. His view on the inner essence of things is monistic, while his ideas regarding the fundamental powers that control the life of the world are dualistic. He is optimistic about human existence, but is pessimistic about the actual conditions of human development. He is a protagonist of pure freedom as contained in his idea of the absolute self-definition of God, but he is a determinist as regards the cosmic and historical process. He is a mystic in his doctrine of the intuitive nature of human knowledge of the Divine, and a rationalist in his approach to speculative philosophy. He is an idealist in his views on the inner essence of things, but an empiricist in as much as all cognition presupposes an actual relationship between the cognising subject and the independent object of cognition. He is also a realist inasmuch as he considers space, time, and causality to possess a certain independent reality. These apparent contradictory aspects form nevertheless an organic whole within his philosophic system. Whatever may be said about his system, and various cirticism have been offered by different critics, the fact remains that Solovyov's contribution to the history of philosophical thought in general and to Russian philosophical thought in particular is very great indeed.

L. M. Lopatin (1855-1920). – Lopatin's interest in psychology led him to develop a philosophical system which was basically concerned with the nature and meaning of man and his place in the universe. Out of this general concern he developed his anthropology that was based on the metaphysical idea of the creative power of the human spirit. His other central idea is that of 'moral upheavals', or 'moral creativity'.

The two central themes in his philosophical system are: (1) The *substantial* nature of the human spirit, and (2) the doctrine that free human creativity is 'prior in existence to all necessity'. These views are elaborated in his important work "The Theoretical Foundations of the

Conscious Moral Life". Lopatin's ethics presupposes two fundamental principles: (a) Freedom of the will, and (b) the moral rationality of the universe. We can only arrive at the idea of moral rationality of the universe by means of speculative data and not by means of empirical data, since empirical experience actually contradicts this idea. The underlying fundamental principle in man's nature is his transfiguring power which is expressed in his creative activity.

In his basic philosophical work, "The Positive Tasks of Philosophy", Lopatin discusses the various philosophical trends in Russia and finds them unsatisfactory. Materialism is wrong because of its arbitrary rejection of the spiritual life. Positivism is unsatisfactory because of its limited examination of man's psychic life by ignoring man's volitional as well as his mental activity. This limited approach neglects the non-empirical factors of reality. He also found that rationalism fails to pay attention to concrete reality because of its pre-occupation with schemes and abstractions and concentration on intellectualism with total disregard of the volitional aspect of man. This does not mean that philosophy is against reason. On the contrary, Lopatin insists that one must never identify philosophical knowledge with religious faith. Philosophy of knowledge must never become a philosophy of faith, since this would lead to all sort of confusion and even to superstition. The highest form of philosophy, according to Lopatin, is achieved only when the idea of a creative reason acting within man finds expression in clearly-defined concepts which are inwardly united with clarity. Philosophy is knowledge of truth; it is clear and rational knowledge. Philosophy strives to be a system of organically-connected concepts, hence, it necessarily has access only to the rational aspect of reality, although it must constantly be conscious of the unity of this aspect with the irrational aspects of reality and must aim to master them.

Lopatin was fully aware of the fact that while philosophy must be rational in its approach to reality, in the final analysis, philosophy can give us only an abstract knowledge of reality. Philosophy cannot make any absolute affirmation regarding the concrete sequence of events in the world; it can only speak with some certainty about individual facts and thus establish a critical criterion for a fuller construction of reality. The content of philosophy will always be comparatively poor and abstract in comparison with religion, according to Lopatin. Philosophy must however, establish its own laws within its limits.

Lopatin believed that philosophy affirms the reality of both the Absolute and the finite world. When we refute the one at the expense of the other we negate reality altogether. How are we to make the transition from one concept to the other? Any kind of metaphysical dualism is a logical contradiction based on the fundamental fact of existence, and an absolute unity is just as meaningless as an abstract plurality. We must therefore, look for the truth in a living union between the one and the many. The Absolute is primarily a self-assertion, i.e., pure activity, but self-assertion presupposes a bifurcation, a manifestation of the force of being in a series of events which is infinite since absolute self-assertion is itself infinite. Hence, true being is conceivable only as ONE living centre of an actually living plurality, as the monad of monads, as absolute organism.

God for Lopatin is conceived of as a life that is absolutely eternal containing within himself all things, but in his non-temporal ideal unity he constantly contemplates within himself all existence gathered into a single perfect image, enclosed within a single indivisible point as a world of eternal ideas. Lopatin warns us that this is not pantheism because the inseparableness of God from the world implies that God does not exist without his reason, in all other respects, however, God's transcendence over the world is affirmed by him. From this view point, the spatio-temporal world stands in opposition to the eternal realm of absolute being. The spatio-temporal world is imperfect, it belongs to the second order of things, while it is rooted in the first order, it is not commensurate with it. The mutual opposition that exists between the spatio-temporal world and the eternal world is due to the very essence of finiteness. God's power is positive in all things; in this sense everything exists in God. But the individuality of separate beings is expressed by their "selfness", by the limitation of their being, by their non-being.

Lopatin accepts the doctrine of *creatio ex nihilo* as a profound philosophical concept. Immanence and transcendence are not mutually exclusive concepts, but are merely two aspects of one and the same universal truth. The absolute principle is in itself indivisible and creative Reason. God is the monad of monads, internally one spiritual and living force. This definition excludes the possibility of identifying the absolute with a material substance. Philosophy must either reject the idea of an Absolute, or must accept theism as a basic truth. Lopatin sees no logical inconsistency in the premise that the absolute Cause, in spite of internal unity, creates a variety of individual beings. He thinks that it is quite possible to make a speculative transition from the ONE to the MANY. While it cannot be said that God creates other beings out of necessity, yet, the idea of causal relationship between the Absolute and the finite contains a very important but difficult philosophical truth. The difficulty is to be found in the fact that this idea expresses a relationship of terms for which there is no corresponding analogy in human knowledge, for it is a relationship *sui generis*. This relationship is not a relationship of substance and its accidents, because substance is something that is inseparable from its states. The Absolute is by its very nature independent of all relationships to its finite creative acts and always remains the supreme reality. Individual beings, on the other hand, are not rational abstractions of the absolute, but possess their own reality. They may be termed actions of a divine substance, with this important reservation, namely, that they are in themselves an action of a SUBSTANTIAL nature, this removes the idea that they are accidents of a single substance.

Lopatin asserts that God's creative act is not directed toward some result; He creates only that which is internally perceived by Him, and that alone is reality. It follows that the whole reason of the world was already in the mind of God before its creation. God knows the world, because prior to its coming into being He already perceived all the possible creative forces peculiar to it. That is why the relation of the Absolute to the world is that of a living creative Reason wholly endowed with will. God's relation to His creatures is not an abstractly-logical or geometrically necessary relation; it is an organic relation based on a free choice of ways and means of creating things. Hence, freedom to create is the final key to all the riddles of life. That freedom is neither blind nor meaningless, but is teleological in its creative acts. This view of creation and of God ought to, in Lopatin's view, deliver the *coup de grâce* to every type of pantheism, and should make us realize that theism is the necessary premise of philosophy. Philosophy recognizes that the idea of a living God is the necessary result of man's attempt to explain that which is in itself an individual and living Being. Hence, the world is the realization of the ideal potentials of will and reason. In the final analysis, Lopatin's monadology includes both MONISM and PLURALISM. He is not very consistent in his idea of causality. On the one hand, he refuses to attribute the idea of causality in connection with God's relation to the world, on the other hand, he tries to develop the idea of 'creative causality' in his philosophy. His main difficulty is undoubtedly due to the fact that he tries to combine philosophy with theology which involves a rationalization of the irrational.

S. N. Trubetskoi (1862-1905). – S. N. Trubetskoi's contribution to philosophical thought in Russia may be grouped around three main points: (1) His *Metaphysics in Ancient Greece* and *The History of the Doctrine of the Logos* brought to the attention of Russian thinkers the importance of Greek philosophy for the development of philosophy in Russia. (2) His very able exposition of German idealism greatly contributed to the dissemination of philosophic ideas among Russian intellectuals. (3) He provided a general outline of his scientific metaphysics which he termed "Concrete Idealism" which influenced other Russian philosophers in formulating their systems.

Trubetskoi was a typical Russian thinker rather than a philosopher in the formal and professional sense, although he did attempt to develop his own system. He was primarily concerned with truth and the kingdom of righteousness rather than with abstract ideas. In his search for truth he addressed himself to three fundamental questions: (a) Does human life have any rational meaning and purpose? (b) Does human activity and human history have any meaning? (c) Does the whole cosmic process have any rational meaning and purpose? Having convinced himself that there was meaning and purpose in history and in the cosmic process, Trubetskoi endeavoured to elucidate the answers to these questions in his writings and to apply them in a practical way.

Trubetskoi's concern for human freedom was deeply rooted in His Christian view of man. According to this view, man is a person of infinite worth and dignity who in himself reflects the very image of God. The basic attribute of man is freedom and to deny man his freedom is to deny his humanity. Trubetskoi devoted all his time and energy to the cause of human freedom. He wrote on many subjects and became the spokesman for the national mood of his day. It is to his eternal glory that in the midst of reactionary suppression of freedom he fought for freedom to the very end of his turbulent life.

Trubetskoi's reaction against Western individualism and rationalism led him to an epistemological investigation of the nature and function of human consciousness in its relation to a knowledge of reality. In his long essay "On the Nature of Human Consciousness, Trubetskoi examines the various theories of knowledge and finds them inadequate for an objective knowledge of reality. In his view, both empiricism and idealism reduce the universal and particular to personal consciousness or to pure subjectivism. Reality for empiricism is "what appears", idealism identifies thought with being, while mysticism regards reality as 'in-and-for-itself'. None of these theories provides a true basis for an objective knowledge of reality.

Trubetskoi seeks to rectify the situation by offering his own peculiar theory of knowledge. The source of human knowledge of reality in his view, is to be found in the concrete activity of human consciousness. He distinguishes PERSONALITY and PERSONAL consciousness from INDIVIDUALITY, and asserts that "human consciousness is not my personal function, but a collective function of the whole human race ... human consciousness is not an abstract term indicating separate individual consciousness, but is a living concrete universal process".[1] He regards the individual mind as a manifestation of a cosmic consciousness and a cosmic memory in which the Self and the not-Self are closely inter-

[1] S. N. Trubetskoi, "O prirode chelovecheskogo soznaniya" [On the Nature of Human Consciousness], *Voprosy*, Vol. I, Bk. 1, p. 98.

related. According to Trubetskoi, "personal consciousness presupposes universal collective consciousness (*sobornoe soznanie*) . . . and, in turn, collective consciousness presupposes absolute consciousness, cosmic reason . . . which gathers and unites by universal ties all separate minds".[2]

According to Trubetskoi, collective consciousness has its source in a cosmic principle and every individual consciousness is grounded in a cosmic consciousness. He calls this hypothesis "metaphysical socialism" whose underlying principle is the Slavophile doctrine of *'sobornost'*. In order to relate individual consciousness to cosmic consciousness, Trubetskoi introduces the physiological factor of consciousness which is based on Herbert Spencer's view according to which human consciousness is socially conditioned. According to Spencer's view, consciousness is a racial and hereditary process, and man's psychic development is socially conditioned by his nervous system as well as by his environment. There is "a conscious cosmic organization which realizes itself in nature, and contains in itself the general norm and productive principle of individual consciousness".[3] Whether we view consciousness empirically or psychologically, we are bound to arrive at the concept of ORGANIC-TOGETHERNESS (*sobornost*) of consciousness. The universal consciousness manifests itself in every living organism, whether it be an amoeba or a human being.

Two basic metaphysical assumptions underlie his philosophy. The first is that the universe is an organic and harmonious whole. The second assumption is that all living beings, including man, are part and parcel of this organic whole. This would seem to contradict his Christian position which he tries to maintain. For his "metaphysical socialism" is just another way of stating the pantheistic or at best, the panpsychic position. This is not what he had really intended to do. His theory of knowledge, which is closely bound up with his metaphysics, seeks to soften this apparent contradiction.

Let us now examine some of the salient points of his epistemology. There are three levels of reality. (1) Empirically, reality is "what appears" to our senses. (2) Reality is revealed to us as IDEA, but is not reducible to a logical idea. (3) Reality is a CONCRETE UNITY which is in agreement with logical categories, but is distinct from thought. That is, reality is distinguished from IDEA by its sensory quality, its individual concreteness and its autonomy.

Trubetskoi distinguishes three ways of knowing reality. (1) Through sense perception; (2) By means of reason, and (3) By faith, which is

---

[2]   *Ibid.*, pp. 98-99.
[3]   S. N. Trubetskoi, *Metapfizika v drevnei Gretsii* [Metaphysics in Ancient Greece], p. 36 in the Russian text.

"the condition of our self-consciousness". Faith, in his view, reveals to us the inner unity and harmony of the world of appearance with its hidden spiritual foundation. It alone enables us to apprehend reality directly and thus reveals to us the spiritual harmony of the universe. Faith is the objective condition of a true apprehension of reality in thought and in experience. The spiritual harmony revealed to us by faith is made possible through love. Love is the *sine qua non* for the attainment of the truth which is revealed to us in the Church by the whole fellowship of believers who are united in spirit by Christian love. This view, is of course, the Christian doctrine as expressed in Russian Orthodoxy.

In support of his theory of knowledge, Trubetskoi introduces the Law of Universal Correlation which enables man to know not only himself, but other beings as well, since relation is the basic condition of consciousness. He then proceeds to introduce the concept of the Absolute which "can be neither relative nor non-relative, but supra-relative". He then equates the Absolute with cosmic Reason or the concrete Logos, which is in reality the Logos of the Fourth Gospel. His CONCRETE IDEALISM and Christian dogmatics thus coincide in his Weltanschauung.

To sum up, Trubetskoi failed to effect a genuine reconciliation between science, philosophy and religion, which was his chief purpose. He never really freed himself from German Idealism in spite of his efforts to do so. His epistemology is philosophically unacceptable, since one must still make a 'leap of faith' in order to bridge the gap between subject and object. It is difficult to separate philosophy from theology in his system. Trubetskoi apparently tried to obviate that distinction by equating the two. In spite of these criticisms, Trubetskoi's contribution to Russian philosophical thought cannot be questioned.

N. O. Lossky (1870-1965). – Lossky's philosophical system cannot be explained in terms of one single idea or influence. There are many influences in his system, which he assimilated, distilled and formulated into a system of his own. Plotinus, Jacobi, Lotze, Schuppe, Leibniz Bergson, and Solovyov, all left their mark on his system. Solovyov's influence was undoubtedly very considerable. This is especially true in regard to his epistemological views. According to Solovyov, knowledge of reality cannot be achieved through experience alone or through reason alone. The REAL is a perfect unity and is not external to the subject, neither is it inherent in the subject, but is given to the subject by direct apprehension of the totality of the REAL, or by intuitive knowledge. Hence, the Absolute is "that which is experienced intuitively". Lossky embodied these ideas into his theory of knowledge.

Lossky may be said to be the first Russian philosopher who made a serious attempt to disentangle the epistemological-metaphysical problem from its ethico-religious superstructure which was so characteristic of earlier Russian philosophical thought.

Lossky's theory of knowledge can properly be understood in terms of his metaphysical system which he calls "Concrete Ideal-realism". He views the world as an organic whole composed of super-spatial and super-temporal substances, or 'substantival agents', who have their ground in the Absolute in Whom they find their final goal and activity. He was led to this view when he examined the idea of RELATEDNESS of things revealed to us in knowledge. We cannot think of any kind of perception without becoming aware of relations. Similarity, difference, causality, and a host of other relations form an integral part of the world. They are apprehended by means of sense experience, but are non-temporal and non-spatial. They are supersensuous. These considerations led Lossky to the formulation of his theory of knowledge.

Lossky's epistemological views originally appeared in the Russian journal *Voprosy filosofii i psikhologii* [Problems of philosophy and psychology] in 1904-05, and later came out in English translation under the title *The Intuitive Basis of Knowledge*. These views were further elaborated in his *Sensory, Intellectual, and Mystical Intuition*. Lossky's point of departure is his criticism of the subjective empiricists (Locke, Berkeley, Hume). The empiricists are accused of basing their theory of knowledge on certain fallacious premises that cannot be proven. These premises are: (a) that the Self is completely separated from the not-Self; (b) that the content of consciousness are subjective mental states of the knowing subject; (c) that human experience is the result of a causal action of the not-Self on the Self; (d) that the states of consciousness are merely representations or copies of reality. In Lossky's view this is their *cul-de-sac* and it inevitably leads to scepticism. This is equally true of pre-Kantian rationalism which fails to bridge the gap between the Self and the external world. In fact, Kant himself failed to bridge this gap when he asserted that empirical knowledge is the result of the action of the Self on the not-Self.

Lossky's approach to the problem of knowledge stems from a desire to understand the process of knowledge PER SE. While he regards epistemology to be the basis of science, he does not think that the results of certain sciences can be used as a basis for a theory of knowledge. At best, these results may be used as material for epistemological analysis. He insists that a distinction must be made between the subjective and objective aspects of knowledge, i.e., between the act of knowing and that which is known. The act of knowing is a mental state and takes place in time; that which is known need not be temporal. For example, the flower I see may have a certain colour and a pleasant smell, but these characteristics are not part of my act of seeing or smelling. The object which I cognize is experienced as 'given to me', whereas the cognitive activity is 'mine'. This qualitative distinction forms the criterion for distinguishing between the Self and the not-Self.

Lossky's epistemology may be characterised as a synthesis of ABSOLUTE IMMANENTISM and ABSOLUTE INTUITIVISM. The three fundamental ideas in his epistemology are: (1) the object is known as it *is*. It is neither a copy nor a representation, but is the original thing itself; (2) The peculiar relation that obtains between the Self and that of which it is conscious is a non-causal relation. He terms this IMMEDIATE APPREHENSION, or INTUITION. Intuitive apprehension is due to the attention that is directed by the subject upon some aspect of the external or internal world and is recognized by the Self as being 'given to me'. It is a non-spatial and non-temporal relation which he calls 'gnoseological co-ordination'. "This co-ordination, which is independent of time and space, is nothing other than the connection of supertemporal and superspatial agents with one another; as a result, everything which one agent experiences as its own manifestation exists not only for it, but also for all other agents in the world".[4] This does not however, in itself constitute knowledge: it is a necessary, but not sufficient, condition of knowledge. (3) The Platonic doctrine of 'beholding ideas'. Lossky calls this intellectual intuition, which is passive and purely contemplative. He identifies it with thought which reveals TRANSSUBJECTIVE RELATIONS, but does not create these relations. The Absolute is also an object of intuition, but it is mystical intuition.

All human knowledge, according to Lossky, is experienced through sensory, intellectual, and mystical intuition. These three types of intuition correspond to his three types of being: (a) IDEAL BEING, such as relations between a quality and its bearer, number, unity, plurality, etc.; (b) REAL BEING, which is spatio-temporal in character, and (c) METALOGICAL BEING, or the ABSOLUTE, which transcends the laws of identity, contradiction and the excluded middle.

In order to *know* the content of his consciousness the subject must not only attend to it, but must also compare it with other contents. In other words, the knowing process involves comparison and discrimination. This means that knowledge takes the form of a judgment. Judgment of perception consists of two elements, THAT and WHAT. Judgment of perception is basically a union of these two elements. "The object known is the real world. But since everything about which we judge is real in one sense or another, we want to know not THAT an object is,

---

[4] N. O. Lossky, *Chuvstvennaya, intellektual'naya i misticheskaya intuitsiya* [Sensory, intellectual and mystical intuition], p. 18.

but WHAT it is – *quid sit*, and not *quod sit*".[5] Every act of discrimination contains the subject, the predicate, and the relation between these two. The subject of judgment is that about which we seek information – it is the object of knowledge; the information obtained is expressed by the predicate. From this it follows that all judgments are in one respect analytic and in another respect synthetic. In relation to the still-unknown part of reality, it is analytic, but when the judgment is completed, it is synthetic. Thus, in the process of knowledge we are concerned with analysing reality in order to discover its synthetic structure. By faithfully observing that which is before us, and by being intellectually honest with ourselves, we can arrive at a true judgment. If however, we add elements that are not 'given', we get a distorted or false view of the object. Strictly speaking, a false judgment is not a judgment at all, since it does not express the relation between subject and predicate.

Judgment in knowledge is both direct and indirect. If for example, we observe the sun above the horizon we make a direct judgment "the sun is rising". Obviously such a judgment cannot be accepted in astronomy as a scientific fact. No scientific knowledge is possible without indirect or inferential judgment. Lossky seeks to solve the problem of the two kinds of judgments by making a distinction between two kinds of 'given': SENSUOUS and SUPERSENSUOUS. When we seek to know the external world as it IS, we abstract the sensuous data from the supersensuous elements of experience. He terms the process of apprehending the supersensuous, SPECULATIVE or INTELLECTUAL intuition. Universals are as real for him as are particulars.

If the idea of inferential judgment and of universals is to have any meaning, the Self must be regarded as a historical being, that is, in its *durée* together with its MEMORY. Memory condenses the aspects of perceptions for the purpose of economy of thought and leads to the formation of concepts, and these in turn enable the Self to apprehend a variety of experiences.

S. N. Trubetskoi's idea of the vicarious nature of consciousness is helpful in understanding Lossky's epistemology. According to Trubetskoi, human consciousness is a living concrete universal process, i.e. the individual mind is a manifestation of COSMIC consciousness and a cosmic memory, where the Self and the not-Self are closely interrelated. While Lossky does not actually discuss the idea of vicarious personality, he presupposes it in his view of the organic unity of the universe. He states that "it will readily be noticed that we are specially inclined to describe as rational all those activities, and generally all those aspects

---

5 N. O. Lossky, *The Intuitive Basis of Knowledge*, p. 261.

of reality which we believe to possess a higher meaning, a high super-individual significance – i.e., a significance to a greater or less degree, for the world as a whole. But significance and meaning are only possible where there is purpose; and, if so, individual things can have a super-individual significance only if there is a purpose in the universe as a whole. Consequently, the word REASON ought to denote the faculty of putting before the mind and of realizing these supreme or highest purposes." [6] Knowledge of reality is possible because the world in which the individual participates is an organic whole and has a definite purpose. Hence, knowledge is essentially teleological or practical. Lossky is certain that his intuitional theory of knowledge is the ONLY true key to reality, when he states: "In contradistinction to individualistic empiricism and in agreement with rationalism, the intuitional theory lays particular stress upon the organic living unity of the world." [7] A closer examination of his theory of knowledge shows that Lossky only succeeded in giving us an ONTOLOGY of COGNITION, i.e., a doctrine of the ideal aspect of the world, but he has not provided us with a genuine epistemology. His theory of knowledge is only of a propaedutic nature. This led him to a serious consideration of ontological problems which he discusses in his *The World as an Organic Whole.*

S. L. Frank (1877-1950). – Our account of the development of Russian philosophical thought would be incomplete without a brief exposition of Frank's philosophical system. We are fully aware that many other important philosophers have been left out of our account, but since this is merely an introduction to the subject, we were obliged to leave out many important thinkers. Frank's place in the history of Russian philosophy is of such importance that he could not be left out of this chapter.

Semyon Ludwigovich Frank was born in Moscow where he received his education. He graduated from Moscow university and did postgraduate work in Berlin and Heidelberg in philosophy and sociology. He was professor of philosophy at the university of Saratov where he taught until 1922, when he was banished from the Soviet Union for his religious views. He lived in Berlin for some seven years (1930-1937) where he lectured at the University of Berlin on the History of Russian Thought and Literature. He moved to France where he lived until 1945, and finally settled in London where he lived until his death in 1950. He wrote a number of volumes as well as articles and brochures. His chief works are: "The Object of Knowledge" (1915); "The Human Soul" (1917); "The Methodology of Social Sciences" (1922); *The Spir-*

[6]   *Ibid.*, pp. 411-12.
[7]   *Ibid.*, p. 413.

itual Foundations of Society (1930); *The Unfathomable* (1939?); *God With Us* (1946); *Reality and Man* (1949) (published posthumously in 1956).

The unique characteristic of Frank's philosophical system is the unity of its theoretical construction. His ability to expound his ideas with clarity and precision makes his books models in the field of philosophy. Frank's originality is to be found in the way he was able to lay the foundations of his system on the doctrine of TOTAL-UNITY which he borrowed from Plotinus, Solovyov and Nicholas of Cusa.

Frank's central philosophical ideas are found in his two important works, "The Object of Knowledge" and *The Unfathomable*. Both his metaphysics and epistemology are based on the doctrine of TOTAL-UNITY. According to Frank, everything that exists, including the Absolute or God, are interconnected in the TOTAL-UNITY. The TOTAL-UNITY cannot be conceived, it can only be given in metalogical form. Hence, abstract logical knowledge is only possible because of the TOTAL-UNITY. Logically, an object is subject to the laws of identity, contradiction, and the excluded middle. For example, A is only thinkable as being part of a complex (A + non -A). This type of correlation can only have its ground in some whole which transcends the determinations of A and non -A, i.e., it is a metalogical unity, or a unity that is not subject to the law of contradiction. It belongs to the realm of *coincidentia oppositorum*, i.e., the law of contradiction does not apply here. From this standpoint logical knowledge is possible only on the basis of 'integral intuition'.

The doctrine of total-unity definitely affects Frank's epistemological views. Central to his epistemology is the idea of the transcendence of the object of knowledge. In his view, the 'accessible' and the 'inaccessible' are both given in the total-unity. The system of concepts constructed by reason presupposes a basis of knowledge which is prior to its conceptual expression; it presupposes a primordial unity which Frank identifies with total-unity.

Frank differentiates between 'living knowledge' which *intuits* being in its wholeness, and conceptual or abstract knowledge which gives us knowledge of ideal being. Intuitive or 'living knowledge' is primary knowledge, i.e., it is the direct intuition of the object in its metalogical unity, whereas abstract knowledge is secondary knowledge which finds expression in judgments and concepts. There is really no logical identity between the two kinds of knowledge: there is only a 'metalogical similarity' between the two.

The idea of 'metalogical unity' is further elaborated in his book *The Unfathomable*, where the concept of 'mystical knowledge' is introduced. According to Frank, the UNFATHOMABLE consists 'in unconditionally

indivisible continuity, a primordial and initial whole'. Two other concepts are also introduced in this work, the TRANSDEFINITE, or that which
is behind everything DEFINITE, i.e., that which is a metalogical unity of
rational and irrational, and the TRANSFINITE, or that which is behind
the metalogical unity. Frank calls the latter the 'dark womb' from which
everything is born. Rational knowledge is attained by means of negation, whereas the UNFATHOMABLE lies beyond negation: it contains the
reinforced negation but is also the realm where all negation is overcome. In the final analysis, the UNFATHOMABLE is really being-for-itself,
or a reality which reveals itself to itself and to us when we participate
in it.

According to Frank, man lives in two worlds, the 'public' or objective
world, and the 'private' or subjective world. It is the experiencing self
rather than the cognitive self that is capable of intuiting inner being,
which is a unity of the experience and the experienced, and manifests
itself in the form 'I am', which is one of the modes of being. In spite
of his efforts to establish a metaphysical monism, Frank involuntarily
arrived at a monodualism. Frank insists that both objective existence
and direct being-for-itself belong to the same world. The opposition
between the external and inner world can be overcome by viewing beauty
as HARMONY, or as inner wholeness that possesses absolute value. Hence,
the unity of existence and value enables us to transcend the limits of
existence. It is a unity of opposites that combines being and justice.
This unity is the UNFATHOMABLE or Deity. Frank makes a distinction
between 'Deity' which is 'prime-reality', and God, who is 'Deity as
revealed to me and experienced by me'. Frank's chief contribution to
philosophical thought is to be found in his theory of knowledge. It is
his epistemology that probes beyond the sensory and the rational. We
are made aware of the fact that knowledge of objects does not reveal
to us all that reality contains; it is mystical or intuitive experience that
reveals to us the inexpressible in concepts. Frank tells us that the
deeper sphere, the 'unfathomable' is discovered on three levels of being:
(a) in objective existence; (b) in subjective existence; (c) the level of
reality which unifies these two worlds and provides a basis for them.
His concept of primary and secondary knowledge, and the unity of
existence and value are indeed important contributions to an analysis
of human knowledge of reality.

CONCLUSION

We may now ask, what is the significance of Russian philosophy, and
what are its particular contributions? There are some who say that
Russian philosophy is unoriginal, hence, its results are of little interest

to a western philosopher. It is further alleged that Russian philosophy is overloaded with the ecclesiastical elaboration of its Byzantine origin and is deeply affected by German romantic metaphysics that spreads more obscurity than light. These allegations are undoubtedly true of its early, formative period, when philosophy was merely a servant of theology, rather than the guiding principle.

A significant change took place during the second half of the nineteenth century when 'pure' philosophic thought made its appearance in Russia. Russian philosophers developed their own system and within a few decades they were able to take their rightful place in the history of philosophic thought. The particular contributions of Russian philosophy are in the realm of epistemology, philosophy of history and ethics. The peculiar characteristic of Russian epistemology is intuitivism which has its roots in the metaphysical doctrine of total-unity. While it does not deny the empirical and rationalistic methods of knowing reality, it insists that true reality is cognized by direct intuition. Intuitive epistemology found expression in the philosophy of concrete-realism, whose chief representatives are Solovyov, the brothers Trubetskoi, N. O. Lossky, S. L. Frank, N. A. Berdyaev, and L. P. Karsavin.

Russian philosophy has always been anthropocentric, i.e., it was concerned with the nature and destiny of man. This accounts for its preoccupation with historiosophy. Russian philosophy sought solutions to three basic problems; (a) the nature of man; (b) the nature of freedom; and (c) man's moral responsibility to society. These problems constitute the *leitmotiv* of Russian philosophy. It is in this area that Russian philosophy made its greatest contribution. For it placed great emphasis on human freedom and moral responsibility and man's infinite worth. This emphasis resulted in a concentration on ethical problems. The preoccupation with historiosophy and ethics had negative as well as positive results. On the one hand, Russian philosophers, because of their emphasis on moral and social problems, were slow in developing 'pure' philosophy. On the other hand, they developed a moral consciousness that was reflected in art and in literature, and gave rise to important social and political movements, such as the Slavophiles, the Populists, etc. These eventually changed the course of Russian as well as world history. Russian philosophy must not therefore be evaluated solely from the point of view of strict philosophic speculation, but must be judged from a cultural and social standpoint as well. In Russian philosophy these two views coalesce.

Section II

EPISTEMOLOGICAL PROBLEMS

— — — — — — — — — — — — — — — — —

BIOGRAPHICAL SKETCH

Georgi Ivanovich Chelpanov (1863-1936) was born in the city of Mariupol where he received his early education. He later entered the university of Odessa where he studied under the well-known philosopher N. Ya. Grot. He later became lecturer at Kiev University, and was soon appointed to the chair of Philosophy, after his Master's and doctoral dissertations, both written on the same subject "The Problem of the Perception of Space", later published in two volumes. He was enabled to establish a Psychological Institute which was very successful until he was relieved of his duties by the Soviet government. His scientific and philosophic training stood him in good stead in developing his philosophical position. His philosophical system may be termed transcendental realism, this view is forcefully stated in his book "On the Perception of Space" especially in the seventh chapter ('On the Origin of Geometrical Axioms'). He argues for the a priori origin of geometrical axioms. His other writings are: "Introduction to Philosophy" (1898); "Brain and Psyche" (1912); "Introduction to Experimental Psychology" (1924); and "Outlines of Psychology" (1926). He also wrote a number of articles in *Voprosy Filosofii i psikhologii*. The present selection appeared in *Voprosy Filosofii i psikhologii* (Vol. 12, Bk. 59, pp. 529-559).

G.I. Chelpanov

A PRIORI ELEMENTS OF COGNITION

THE CONCEPT OF NUMBER

Is there a priori knowledge or "a priori" elements of knowledge? Before answering this question, I shall first of all consider the concept of number, since it is easier to elucidate the philosophical importance of apriority through the concept of number. I hasten to say that I shall speak only of an integer, positive number, since all the other forms of numbers (fractions, negatives, irrationals, etc.) derive their principle from the integer, positive number. Hence, whatever will be said of the former will also apply to the latter.

How do we arrive at the idea of number? Some say that the idea of number is of "a priori" origin, that it cannot derive from sense experience. Others, on the other hand, state that this concept is of the same origin as are all other concepts, i.e. that it is derived from experience.

I propose to show in the present article that the concept of number is of "a priori" origin, that it cannot arise from ordinary sense experience. It may seem to many that my assertion that the concept of number is of "a priori" origin presupposes that for every experience there are innate ideas in our mind. I do not suggest anything of the sort, since I do not recognize such "a priori" ideas, and I do not even know of any philosophers who made any such claims. Even Plato, who is said to have held such a view when he claimed that human knowledge is only a recollection of that which his soul contemplated prior to being incarnated in a human body, in all probability did not think that there are innate ideas in the human mind. This was undoubtly for him merely a way of expressing his ideas.

It is now customary to think that it would be extremely absurd to assert that some form of knowledge may have its origin not in sense experience. The assertion that there is something in our knowledge that did not originate in sense experience appears to be very strange to many, since every science, especially natural science, developed on the basis of sense experience. Hence, the assertion that "our knowledge is derived from sense experience" has become a cliché which many accept without deeming it necessary to doubt it. This results in a confusion of the concept "experience" which is based on sense data, with experience (*ispytyvaniye*) in its simple sense. Many even detect in the phrase "origin from sense experience" the word "experiment", which played such an important role in the development of natural science.

Let us first examine how the proposition that our knowledge originates in sense experience is commonly understood.

Those who make this assertion, base it on the fact that our knowledge is a "copy" of everything that exists in the external world. It is quite natural for the defenders of empiricism to think and to express themselves in this fashion. According to the empiricists concepts in general and the concept of number in particular, are merely abstractions from sense impressions.

To clarify the distinction between what I intend to prove and that which is commonly recognized in current empiricism, I shall employ that comparison which the empiricists themselves adduce, namely, the comparison of knowledge with "copies" of the external world. While this is a crude comparison, it ought the better to serve as a means of clarifying what is being discussed here.

Let us imagine that there is a thing in the external world, or there occurs some event which could be expressed schematically in terms of ABCD. Let us suppose that there is a photographic plate in front of this thing on which we would get the image of this thing or event. If the image ABCD were to appear on the plate, then in view of the correspondence between the image and the object, we could say that this image is a copy of the given object. But supposing we were to obtain on the plate an image of such a nature that every member of the series occupying an even order is doubled so that we get the image ABBCDD. Even in this case we could say that the image is a copy of the thing in the external world, but since there is something on the image not found in the object, we ask ourselves, how do we get this addition on the image? Evidently, this is due to the fact that the plate possesses something which produces duplication of every number which is in an even order. The same thing should be said regarding the case where we get the image of the object ABCD in the form CADB. We then say that the changed order is explained by the fact, that while the plate obtains separate elements of external objects, yet has the capacity of adding its own personal "order". Finally, if we were to get the image on the plate AaBbCcDd, then the only explanation admissible in this instance, is that the plate "adds" from itself something which is not found in the object.

If we were to employ this analogy for our purpose, then the following distinction would obtain between current empiricism and the theory which I advocate. The object in front of the photographic plate – is the object and events of the external world. The photographic plate, is the mind perceiving things and events of the external world. According to the empiricist's view, our mind acts like the plate in the first instance, i.e. it expresses exactly that which is found in the external world. According to my theory, our mind, in the case of perceiving the external world, acts according to the second scheme, namely, it does not simply reflect wholly that which is found in the external world, but introduces from itself something which is not found in the external world. According to empiricism, our knowledge is merely a copy of the external world, according to my theory, it is the mind which introduces into our knowledge of the world something of itself.

Let us now examine what is "abstraction". This is necessary, since it is commonly stated that all concepts, among them the concept of number, are obtained from sense data by means of abstraction. Since I refute this view regarding the concept of number, I must prove how abstraction is commonly understood.

Let us examine, how for example, the concept of a tree is conceived? It consists of separate representations. Everyone knows the difference between what is called a concept (*ponyatie*) and a representation (*predstavlenie*). That mental construction which refers to any individual object (this table, this tree) is called a representation. That mental construction which refers to a whole class of objects (for example, a table in general, a tree in general), is called a concept (or idea). The concept occurs later in the psychic history of the individual than does a representation. At first we recognize individual objects and only later is a concept created in our mind out of the separate representations. Suppose, a child sees some tree, for example, an oak; he receives a certain "representation" of this tree. Suppose, he then sees another tree, for example, a birch. There is no doubt a difference between the oak and the birch, but they also have some points of similarity. The child examines their similarities: both have a stem, branches, colour, leaves, etc. but he ignores the differences, for example, that the trunk of a birch is thinner, that its colour is different from the colour of the oak, etc. If the child should encounter a series of other trees, then he would act in a similar manner, i.e. he would seek out that which is different.

That is common, which is found in various representatives of one and the same class, united into a single whole producing an idea, which thus consists of the separate representations.

Let us consider still another example. How is the idea of the colour "red" formed in a child? He sees the red colour of the sky, the red colour on lips, red colour of blood, and red colour of fire. In all these instances there is something common, namely, "red" colour, but with various nuances. In all these instances, he takes that which is common, and rejects that which is different in them.

This process of the formation of ideas from representations is called "abstraction", because in this process we abstract, segregate, all dissimilar elements, we reject these elements, and combine into a single whole only those elements which are similar and common, by means of a separate representation.

This process has quite often been compared recently with the development of the so-called compound photography. If we were to combine several portraits of different persons on one and the same plate instead of six portraits, we would get only "one" portrait, made up of these six portraits. This will be a compound portrait, which represents the expression not of one person, but, so to speak, of a class of persons. This is due to the fact that the separate portraits are fused together by their similarities, while at the same time their dissimilarities are cancelled out. Some think that something similar takes place in the formation of ideas from separate representations.

We shall not try to discuss what precisely is true in this comparison. We shall simply make use of what is true in this comparison, namely, that we would not have had an empirical idea that there is a series of representations which gave rise to this concept, and still more important is the fact that its content is acquired from the content of separate representations. If for example, we were to consider the idea of "fire", we would discover that it is made up from the material contained in those representations from which this idea was composed. The content of this concept is obtained from that which I directly perceived. This is true of all such concepts which are of an empirical nature, such as the concept of an animal, a tree or of any concrete event, etc.

Let us now examine the question of how we arrive at the idea of number, but let us state beforehand, that there is a great difference between the idea of number and the usual empirical ideas, which will become clear when we examine the distinction between arithmetic and all other sciences. Let us compare, arithmetic with natural science.

All premises in natural science refer to some separate group of phenomena, all have their individual application. For example, Mariotta's law refers only to gases, Keppler's law to the movement of planets, whereas the premises of arithmetic have absolute "universal" application; there is not an object or an event to which could not be ascribed some kind of numerical property.

The idea of number is applicable to anything: it may be applied to a material as well as to a spiritual thing. We can say, "four fundamental virtues", "seven deadly sins", as well as "seven cows", "seven houses", "seven miles", etc. Indeed, is there anything to which the concept of number could not be applied? Definitely not.

There is also a real distinction between natural science and arithmetic as regards certainty. Arithmetical premises are of an apodictic nature, i.e. they are absolutely true. In natural science we are concerned only with a more or less approximation to certainty. One may speak of arithmetical premises as being necessary. For example, the statement that "twice two are four" is not only true, but it is "necessarily" true. In this premise we not only ascertain the fact that obtains in general in natural science, but also its necessity.

There is still another distinction between arithmetic and science which is basic to its proof. The source of the premises of natural science lies in the proof of our senses, whereas the source of arithmetical premises has no sensual character. To prove some arithmetical premise (proposition) I do not refer to the evidence of the senses. For example, to prove that "twice two are four" I will not resort to a calculating machine to prove its truth. I would merely illustrate one or another arithmetical proposition, but would not prove its truth. Whereas in natural science whatever we wish to prove we must in the final analysis resort to the evidence of experience.

Hence, there is a tremendous distinction between arithmetic and other sciences. This distinction, according to the apriorists is due to the fact that the concept of number has a completely special origin, it does not originate from the same source from which the concepts of natural science do. The empiricists do not make this distinction and endeavour to prove that the concept of number is of the same origin as are all other concepts.

John Stuart Mill, one of the most typical representatives of modern empiricism, tries to prove that arithmetic is a science about physical phenomena, like natural science, that its laws have as their object "physical" facts, which we perceive by means of our sense organs.

Why Mill reasoned in this fashion is not difficult to understand. He deduces all our knowledge from experience. All properties of objects cognized by us are found in objects. Number is not an exception; it also is found in objects.

We wish to draw your attention to the fact that in accordance with the true idea of the empirical theory, "number must be found in objects", otherwise it would be incomprehensible how the concept of number could result from the contemplation of things. Since it ought to be an abstraction of that which exists physically. Consequently, it must exist physically. This is precisely the view defended by Mill.

In Mill's view, number is a property of things, it is found in things in the same way as other properties of things are found in them. Hence, it is easy to understand Mill's assertion that there is simply no abstract number. "All numbers must be numbers of something, there is no such thing as an abstract number. "Ten" must designate ten bodies, or ten sounds, or ten strokes of the pulse. Nevertheless, while numbers must be numbers of something, they can be numbers of anything. . . . . All things possess quantity, all consist of parts which can be enumerated, and in this sense possess all those properties which may be called numerical properties." [1] According to Mill, number always possesses a concrete character, and therefore is capable of universal applicability. Thus, the most difficult point in the theory of the origin of the idea of number, its universal applicability, is simply explained by the fact that he does not recognize the existence of an abstract number.

In order to explain how it is possible to visualize the idea that numbers are found in things, Mill brings the following example. "The expression, 'two pebbles and one pebble' and the expression 'three pebbles' are used to denote one and the same sum of objects, but in no way do they denote one and the same 'physical' fact. This is indeed the name for one and the same objects, but in two different states. Three pebbles in two separate groups and three pebbles in one (group) do not produce one and the same impression on our senses."

Here Mill wants to say that things possess something which physically produce the distinction between two objects and three objects, although he does not quite explain wherein consists that physical fact which gives birth to numerical properties.

The empirical school usually adduces facts to prove that the concept of number is obtained from sense experience, and is not found in the mind in ready form as the apriorists contend. As a matter of fact, when we see that a child gradually learns to count, or that a savage could not count at all, then it is possible to visualize such a state, where there are no concepts of number, and this, according to the empiricists is proof of the experimental origin of the idea of number. The very method of counting, according to the empiricists, is the clearest proof of the empirical origin of the idea of number.

If we recognize the empirical origin of arithmetic, then we shall also

[1] Quoted from Mill's *Logic* (people's edition, p. 167).

have to recognize the fact that it also possesses the same certainty as does every other science, i.e. it is of the same hypothetical character as is every other empirical science.

Let us now examine why Mill's theory must be considered to be unsatisfactory.

We saw that in order to form some idea we compare similar objects, and we combine into one single whole that which is similar to them. It is the combination into a single whole that gives us a concept. This process is also called abstraction. Let us now observe that separate representations in the form of elements enter into concepts. This combination (sum) of representations which we appropriated from external experience, is what we call the content of a concept.

I consider it necessary to underline the fact that there is in the content of empirical concepts that which belongs to real objects, as we shall see below, this is precisely not present in the concept of number. Every empirical concept actually contains that which it acquired by sense experience, and it thereby manifests in a most obvious manner its origin. There is no such sensual content in the concept of number, and this real difference between empirical concepts and the concept of number points to a special origin of the latter.

Let us consider the most important proposition of empiricism, namely, that there exists something "physical" whereby we ascribe to certain objects certain numerical properties, and to other objects other (properties). In order to see the inadequacy of this theory, we need only take a series of different objects and phenomena and ask, why we ascribe to them, for instance, the number "one". For example, "the sun is one", "the moon is one", etc. What, we may ask, is common to all these objects that we ascribe to them the numerical property "one"? If we call an eagle a bird and a humming-bird also a bird, then it is quite obvious that in all the differences between these objects there is something that is common to them; but what is common to the above objects that we ascribe to them the property "one"? There is only one answer to this question: "one should not look for such common factor in objects, because it is not there."

The defenders of the empirical origin of the concept of number say, that number is an abstraction from sense data. We will agree that it is an abstraction, but an abstraction from what? It is quite understandable that when we are told that red colour is an abstraction, but an abstraction from what? It is quite understandable that when we are told that red colour is an abstraction from that which is in objects, or that sound is an abstraction, but when they say that number is an abstraction, then one must ask, what is there in objects that we abstract the concept 'number'? If it is analogous to colour or sound, from what is number abstracted? According to the empiricists, objects possess properties to which we ascribe some kind of number. Upon a closer examination however, it turns out that it is impossible to discover such properties in objects.

Let us attempt to determine at least in the most general outlines, what are indeed those "physical" conditions, which in the view of the empiricists, determine the perception of number. Let us take for example, group OOO and group OO. There is no doubt that there is a physical difference between these two groups, and it is this difference, according to Mill, that enables us at one time to perceive "two" and at another time, "three". But what is this physical difference? Let us suppose that it is due to the fact that objects which belong to one group or another are "spatially" differentiated. In perceiving apples, pebbles, sheep, etc., we are concerned with spatial differentiation. Thanks to this we ascribe to objects numerical properties. Apparently, it is spatial differentiation that is that physical factor which determines the perception of number.

Let us take another case when we ascribe numerical properties. Suppose we count the strokes of a pendulum. Let us say that at one time there are two strokes, at another three. What difference is there for perception between the first instance and the second? What do they have in common by virtue of which we ascribe to them these or other numerical properties? The empiricist would say that the difference between these two cases (in apprehending the pendulum's strokes) is due to the fact that the sound impressions are separated by different intervals of time.

Here is another physical difference.

Suppose the empiricist is right; suppose that the differentiation in time is really a physical cause of that which we distinguish two strokes of the pendulum from three. Let us now compare those instances when we count pebbles and apples with those instances when we hear the strokes of the pendulum and try to find what they have in common. Surely there must be something that is common that causes numerical apprehension. But it can easily be seen that that which we recognize to be common in one instance is not common in another. If for one group of things to which we ascribe numerical property, its cause is "spatial" differentiation, and for another group of things the cause of numerical apprehension is temporal, then, since there is a great difference between spatial and temporal differentiation, we are bound to declare that there is no common factor which would give us the right to ascribe to things numerical property.

That "physical" properties are not the cause of numerical apprehension, will become more obvious when we examine further instances when ascribing to objects numerical properties. Let us take "three thoughts" and ask, how are they differentiated, what are their physical features thanks to which we apply to them the idea of number? If Mill's view is correct, then we could not apply numbers to such ideas as "relation", "sin", etc. We could not use such expressions as "Two relations", "seven sins", etc. If there is something physical that determines number, then how could we apply number to something that is completely not physical?

Furthermore, how is it possible to explain universal applicabilty of the concept of number on Mill's position? If the concept of number has its origin in sense experience as Mill supposes, it could only apply to one class of things, for example, to the class of pebbles, apples, animals, etc.

According to Mill, the proposition that "two plus one are three" is obtained as a result of having had the occasion to repeatedly observe the combination of different objects one time in the form OOo, at another time in the form OOO, and therefore concluded that 'two and one" and "three" are one and the same thing. This conclusion is of an inductive nature, since it is the result of observing many instances where the same thing is repeated again and again.

If we allow that Mill is right and that we can actually find out about numerical relations by his scheme. Could we be convinced that two and one "generally" equal three? No. We could only be convinced that two pebbles plus one pebble are three pebbles, that two lambs plus one lamb equal three lambs, since we actually observed them. If we apprehended numerical relations by Mill's scheme, we could be convinced of the fact that "two and one equal three" only in regard to certain groups of objects, this would not give us the right to transfer the generalization to all objects, which was made about a certain group of objects. We would not consider ourselves to have the right to apply to all objects, especially with "apodictic" certainty, that which we observed in one or in several groups of objects.

Arithmetic would not possess that "apodictic" certainty which it actually possesses. We could always doubt the certainty of its premises, which in reality is not the case.

Let us examine other consequences resulting from Mill's theory. According to Mill's theory, arithmetic is similar in all respects to natural sciences, consequently, its trustworthiness is also similar, i.e. it is based on the assumption that its original premises are true, for example, that one equals one. If however we assume that the axioms are not true, then arithmetic itself is as untrustworthy as is natural science. Since all fundamental premises of natural science are of inductive origin, then they possess no absolute certainty. Arithmetic as well as all the other forms of natural science, have only a conditional certainty, since we cannot actually prove that $1 = 1$. We accept it only conditionally as being certain.

In order to confirm his view that arithmetic is not a trustworthy science in an absolute sense, and that it is of empirical origin, Mill employs the following example.[2] In his view, it is quite possible to visualize a world in which every time we place two alongside two we would get not four, but five, due to the action of some divinity, which in this process would insert every time an extra object. For inhabitants of such a world twice two would not equal four but five. Since our ideas of numerical relations arise so to speak from physical circumstances, thanks to the environment, then it is quite natural, that in such an environment the very idea of number and numerical relations would have been different. But this example of Mill's is no proof: it would only be permissible to use it as an illustration, and only after the empirical theory has been proven.

If Mill were right, that in apprehending number the real role in this case must be attributed to our sensory physical apparatus, then it would be impossible to explain the following case. Before me there is a pile of ten kernels. In perceiving this object I can attribute to it two numerical predicates. I can say, "one pile", or I can say "ten kernels". Hence, objects which physically produce on me one and the same impression, I nevertheless attribute to them two numerical predicates.

It is true that the physical impression in both instances is one and the same; nevertheless, numerically, it seems to us to be different in one and in the other instance.

In the perception of physical properties of objects nothing of the sort is possible. For example, we cannot say that one and the same object can be both red and blue at the same time, that a sound can be loud and quiet, or that one and the same object is both sweet and bitter. Why? Because these perceptions are wholly defined by the physical properties of the perceived objects; in our perception we depend upon them. Why then in our example does one and the same pile appear to us both as one and as ten? Obviously because the apprehension of numbers is not determined by physical causes in the same sense as the perception of other qualities are determined.

The possibility of attributing to one and the same object in one and the same time two different predicates is explained by the fact that at one time we turn our attention on one aspect of the object, and another time on another (aspect). In this instance it is not the physical fact that is decisive, but the attention that we pay to one or the other aspect. The physical fact remains unchanged, what changes is something dif-

[2]   J. S. Mill, *Examination of Hamilton's Philosophy* (1878), p. 89.

ferent, namely, our attention. It is the change in attention, as we shall soon see, that is the source of the origin of the idea of number.

It is thus clear that we must not look for the source of the origin of the idea of number in the change of the physical facts themselves, but in some peculiarities of consciousness itself.

When I for example, apprehend two beats of a bell, then in addition to apprehending the sounds of the bell, I also apprehend something else, i.e. I notice that my consciousness stops in the perceiving of some or other object, in other words, I observe pauses of my consciousness.[3] I notice that when one beat of the bell was heard and I apprehended it, then my consciousness stopped at the apprehension of this sound sensation, and then ceased its activity. When the second beat was heard, I noticed that again my consciousness stopped at the apprehension of the sound sensation and again began to work, since the pause, was so to speak, a state of inactivity.

Consequently, I observe that in the apprehension of the beats of the bell my consciousness now works, now ceases to work, now functions, now ceases to function.

Moreover, I notice that in order to apprehend the beats of the bell, I have to do something different than when I apprehend one beat. When I have to apprehend three beats, then my action would differ from the previous two instances. It is this difference in the number of pauses of consciousness that becomes the source of the idea of number.

Rudimentary consciousness observes only that these three instances of apprehension differ from each other in character only by the fact that they produce such an excellent impression on consciousness as objects of different colour would do. The latter could produce either a red, yellow or green impression. Just as these impressions differ from each other so do the above-mentioned apprehensions differ in relation to the pauses of consciousness.

This difference between the pauses of consciousness at first do not probably go beyond a simple "qualitative" difference. Primordial consciousness does not, properly speaking, apprehend numerical relations, but only a qualitative difference between these and other apprehensions in relation to those pauses of consciousness which they produce. Just as it differentiates qualitatively the different sensations of red, yellow and green, similarly it differentiates qualitatively the different pauses of consciousness. One group of pauses differs characteristically from the other, and this difference serves as a sign to differentiate one group of objects from another.

[3] I feel that it is permissible to introduce this artificial term, which is meant to denote that consciousness ascertains, that it stops while perceiving one or another impression, that it acts in order to stop this work the next moment.

Hence, the numerical property which we attribute to things is due to the fact that we speak about things, for example, about an apple, that in addition to being an "apple" it is also a "pause" of consciousness. Consciousness, in addition to apprehending physical properties determines also its own pauses.

Enumeration is thus due to a comparison of pauses which consciousness determines while observing its own processes. One number differs from another number for primordial consciousness only by the fact that there is a certain qualitative difference between them in regards to the pauses of consciousness which they have to make.

Our memory is capable of retaining a series of such pauses and to notice the qualitative difference between some and others. This qualitative difference subsequently becomes that difference which we call quantitative.

Quality turns to quantity when the peculiar nature of these pauses is discerned as well as their common element, i.e. the repetition of one and the same event. We notice that these pauses with all their differences, have one common feature, or one common element, namely the element of "repetition". It is at this point that consciousness ceases to be satisfied with merely a general distinction of the qualitative difference of these pauses, and becomes concerned with a more detailed differentiation which assumes a quantitative character. Quality becomes quantity, and enumeration in the real sense of the word begins.

There is undoubtedly a difference between the apprehension of numerical relations "simpliciter" and the concept of an abstract number. The apprehension of numerical relations is an apprehension of those pauses which consciousness produces when objects act upon it.[4]

[4] It may be said that in the given instance there is a "petitio principii" involved here, because, instead of showing how we get the idea of number, it is simply shown here that we count the pauses or interruptions of consciousness. Consequently, we nevertheless think that we wanted at the same time to explain how the process of enumeration originated. But such a remark would ignore the distinction between psychology and the theory of knowledge. It is of little interest to us how long it took for the idea of number to develop, but we are rather concerned to determine what elements in this idea are of an objective or subjective nature. The proposition that we "count" the pauses of our consciousness clarifies the fact that there is nothing of a physical nature in objects that could be the origin of the idea of number, it also makes it clear for us the universal applicability of the idea of number as well as its formal nature. The task of epistemology is to determine what aspect of this concept belongs to the subject and what belongs to the object. In order to solve this problem, we examine the content of the given idea and seek out what it acquired from external experience and what is a product of the function of the mind itself. We have no need to investigate the origin of this or that idea; it is simply sufficient to investigate the correspondence between the content of a given idea and objective reality. We notice that the

Hence, the concept of number is an abstraction, but not an abstraction from some "physical" properties found in the external world, as empiricism assumes, but an abstraction from the "processes of consciousness" uniformly performed at the time when we attribute to objects numerical properties.

It may readily be seen that the concept of number, is of course the product of development and experience, that it does not exist in the mind in a ready form, but the manner of development is not the one stated by the empirical theory.

We may state the difference between the empiricist theory and the theory which I advocate in the following way:

Empiricism states that the idea of number is derived from an abstraction of sensual properties of objects, whereas my theory says that the idea of number is the result of our observation of the processes of consciousness. The empiricists claim that the mind is directed toward objects and qualities of objects, whereas in my view, the mind is directed toward its own activity.

It is quite easy to understand why primordial consciousness tries to denote numerical apprehensions by means of fingers, etc. Primitive man had somehow to express concretely his numerical apprehension by means of a word or some image. In order to denote that he is talking about "two" objects he raises two fingers, wishing thereby to say that those objects which he perceives, possess still another property which requires for its perception the same work of the mind as is required for the perception of the two fingers.

In fact, we count by means of the pauses of consciousness. When I say "three" and thereby think that they represent three fingers, then I think numbers by means of pauses of consciousness. Naturally, we cannot have symbolic representation of all numbers, or use symbols in thinking about them. This is why the savage can only operate with small numbers, since his memory cannot retain a large number of pauses.

When we observe the activity of our mind, then we call this process reflexion. In this process the mind is diverted from what it ordinarily apprehends, i.e. from objects of the external world and turns its attention on itself. It is from such reflexion that a special source of ideas comes into being, which we call "a priori". The idea of number is really derived from reflexion.

If such origin of the idea of number is accepted, then it will become clear whence it derives its universal applicability. When we apprehend

---

empirical position cannot explain the content of the idea of number; it can only assert that its source is reflex action.

objects in order to attribute to them numerical properties, we do not pay attention to the content of the apprehension, we do not pay attention as to whether the apprehended is really there, such as colours, definite figures, etc. What is important for us is that they provide for us the occasion for separate perceptions. The above statement makes the universal applicability of the idea of number intelligible. When we apprehend "three people" or think about "three virtues", we do not have to pay attention to what those objects are or what their content is, because we are mainly concerned with the number of pauses our consciousness must make in order to grasp the apprehended objects.

It should now also be clear why the idea of number has a formal character, and why it is always equally applicable to any content, be it apples, rocks, or virtues. In the idea of number we are not dealing with any particular content, but with the form, while its content is immaterial. This is due to the fact that in the process of counting we are not dealing with something material, but with the process of our consciousness. In numerical relations we are concerned not with the changing phenomena of the material world, but with the immutable laws of our mind.

The difference between form and content is this. The objects which we apprehend in the external world have a particular character whereas the intervals of our consciousness possess an identical character. We can thus say that all that is material possesses this or another content, while the formal character is peculiar only to the activity of consciousness.

Arithmetic is not concerned with the physical world, but with the laws of our consciousness. In ascertaining numerical relations, we actually do not define objective relations, but the laws of our mind. When we apprehend numerical properties in objects, our thinking has no reference to an objective experience, but has reference directly to our consciousness and the external serves only as an occasion of evoking an idea about some or another numerical relations.

The view that the idea of number results from our observation of the processes of consciousness enables us to understand why the proposition dealing with number seems to us "apodictically" trustworthy (certain). When we state some arithmetical propositions, we assume that every other thinking individual has a consciousness like ours capable of producing pauses or intervals in order to apprehend numerical relations. For such a consciousness "one" is nothing more than an interval of consciousness. We base our conclusion on the conviction that all these intervals in all individuals who are constituted like ourselves occur in the same manner. An integer may be defined as that instance of counting when we complete one pause of our consciousness, and this process is absolutely uniform for all instances of numerical apprehension. An integer is therefore always equal to itself. We suggest that all beings who possess the same mental organization as we do, will be able to count by one just as we do.

If arithmetical premises had reference to external experience, we could doubt their immutability, but since even such a proposition like $2 \times 2 = 4$, has really no reference to an objective world, but expresses only the laws of our consciousness, this should make it clear why our arithmetical propositions are firmly established.

It can now clearly be seen that the concept of number has its origin not in ordinary sense experience but in the observation of the processes of our mind, and this is very important for epistemology, because we would have to refute the idea that our mind is a mirror simply reflecting that which occurs in the objective world. We, on the contrary, must assert that in cognizing the external world our mind does not merely play a passive role, but acts on what it apprehends, and takes an active part in processing that which it apprehends, it recreates, so to speak, reality, and adds to it a certain form. It thus introduces into the knowledge of the external world something of itself.

According to the empirical view, consciousness is a simple "copy" of that which is in the objective world. According to the apriorists, the subject introduces something of itself not found in the objective world. The empirical view is that numerical properties somehow migrate from the objective world into consciousness, whereas the apriorists say that they are created. One must not assume however, that the concept of number is created out of nothing. External experience is necessary, but its chief significance lies in the fact that it is an "occasion" for the formation of the idea of number, but does serve the same basic purpose as in the apprehension of sense qualities. In this sense, number may be termed "the product of a free creation of the mind".

We must not thus suppose that in this case we recognize some "innate" ideas; while saying that number is the product of the mind's activity, we do not wish to say that man is born with innate ideas. The idea of number could not arise without so-called external experience. If we could imagine that a thinking being existing in such a world where there are absolutely no changes, then we may be certain, that such a being could not develop the idea of number, because this requires experience. There can be no idea of number without external experience, but we must bear in mind that external experience does not play a determining role.

If we regard those concepts to be a priori which are determinative for experience, i.e. they are the logical conditions of experience, but are themselves not the products of experience, then the concept of

number is a priori. It is not derived from experience because its content
does not contain that which objects contain, giving origin to this idea,
but at the same time we attribute to these objects numerical properties.
It follows that we introduce something of ourselves into the objects.

We therefore call the idea of number a priori not because we think
that it precedes experience "in time", but because it is its necessary
condition, a necessary logical condition, since we could not attribute
numerical properties to things, if our mind had not developed these
ideas. It is an a priori idea because it does not depend upon sense
experience, is not determined by sense experience, numerical relations
are not proven by sense experience nor are they refuted by them.

BIOGRAPHICAL SKETCH

Sergei Nikolayevich Trubetskoi (1862-1905) came from a very ancient noble family. As a student at Moscow University he came under various influences, such as Auguste Comte, Herbert Spencer, J. S. Mill, Kuno Fischer, the German Idealists, and Vladimir Solověv. His Master's dissertation "Metaphysics in Ancient Greece" established his reputation as an independent thinker, and his doctoral thesis, "A History of the Doctrine of the Logos" (1900), finally led to his appointment to the chair of philosophy in his alma mater and in 1905 he was appointed the first Rector of Moscow University. In addition to his academic interests, he also interested himself in student activities, and founded a student Society of History and Philology. He was also interested in many public activities.

While Trubetskoi never succeeded in working out in full his philosophical system, his contribution to philosophical thought in Russia is nonetheless considerable. His earlier interests were mainly in an anthropological approach to the problem of human nature, but he later became interested in metaphysical and epistemological problems. He rejected the idea of the autonomy of individual consciousness, and offered his own "metaphysical socialism", which places consciousness in "cosmic consciousness" in which every individual consciousness participates.

The following selection is an abridgement of his larger work "The Nature of Human Consciousness" which first appeared in *Voprosy Filosofii i Psikhologii* (Bk. 6, No. 2, pp. 132-156 and Bk. 7, pp. 21-56). His chief philosophical writings are: "Metaphysics of Ancient Greece", "The Doctrine of the Logos", "On the Nature of Human Consciousness", "The Foundations of Idealism", and "The Belief in Immortality".

S. N. Trubetskoi

ON THE NATURE OF HUMAN CONSCIOUSNESS

Human consciousness presupposes a sensual, corporeal organization, which together form an independent, ideal principle. It presupposes an unconscious nature which is being formed and gradually transcends it, since it is the final product of a cosmic development. At the same time it presupposes an absolute universal consciousness, just as much as the most sensual universe in space and time presupposes such a consciousness and universal sensuality.

This accounts for the inner contradiction and duality of the whole psychic life of man. Semi-animal and semi-divine, the consciousness of man alternates between sleep and wakefulness, between knowledge and ignorance, between feelings and reason. It possesses universal forms, formulates for itself universal concepts and ideals, and at the same time is always circumscribed by its own actual empirical content. It is always limited, but at the same time never permits any defined limits, constantly transcending its limits. It is partly universal, partly individual, partly real, partly only potential. There is a permanent contradiction inherent in it which is peculiar to all its concepts, representations, perceptions, while at the same time it is aware of its own personal ideal identity, its ideal unity of truth.

This accounts for the contradictions among the different philosophers regarding the nature of human consciousness, and this has its basis in consciousness itself. Some consider its physiological conditions, others, its metaphysical, ideal principle; still others regard it as sensual knowledge, wholly empirical and limited; still others disclose its logical, universal character, its "a priori" elements. Thus far, no one has succeeded in effecting a definite reconciliation between these opposing views, and one may ask whether such a reconciliation is generally achievable. If this contradiction is inherent in reality itself, then any particular theoretical solution or its refutation, would "ipso facto" be either insufficient or false.

One of the most important services rendered by modern philosophy is the fact that in repudiating a dogmatic solution of the antinomies – the metaphysical contradictions, it tries to locate their root in the very reason and consciousness of man, or in nature itself (this is the position of the sceptics and pessimists), otherwise the contradictions among the philosophers could not be accounted for.

If we were to regard the development of consciousness from an empirical view, then there is no doubt whatsoever that its development depends upon physiological conditions, such as the nerves and the brain. Nevertheless, the physiologist would forever be deprived of the possibility of bridging the gap which separates phenomena of the material physical order from the simplest phenomena of a psychic order. Supposing we assumed that both orders, the physical and the psychic, are merely two sides, two aspects of one and the same process. These aspects are so different from each other, that such an assumption either expresses nothing, or it is unfounded, since consciousness and matter (*veschestvo*) or consciousness and motion are (*velichina*) values of a different kind. In view of the unquestionable intimate causal connection that obtains between the cerebral functions and psychic phenomena, consciousness as such cannot be explained in terms of something that is material.

If, on the other hand, we viewed consciousness from the point of view of its logical functions, its spiritual nature, we would undoubtedly arrive at a premise of absolute, ideal norms, of universal principles, in a word, at an idea of a universal consciousness. Between such a finite ideal which is simultaneously a forming principle (*obrazouyuscheye*) and the highest norm of real consciousness, and the latter, there is not merely a difference, but also a contradiction about which the mind and conscience of every person attest. No matter how inadequate our representation of this ideal is, we cannot consider it realized in actuality, or attained in our present consciousness. We cannot cognize it from reality, and we cannot deduce from it this reality until it is attained and realized by us. Our highest philosophical speculations are only of relative importance and are of a purely-speculative nature, since they contain merely an anticipated solution. In a certain sense, the philosopher speculates on the basis of the future, and he is equally mistaken when he regards his treasures as actual cash, or when he treats them without understanding their real value.

Our knowledge is unconditional only in its idea, in its ideal of full, absolute truth. In actuality, it possesses a potential, formal and purely logical universality, which is always opposed by a limited, empirical content. If consciousness is to be absolute and fully universal not only in form, but in essence and in content, it must include everything, must become the consciousness of everything and everybody, it must in truth become a universal collective (*sobornyi*) consciousness. Whether this goal is attainable or not, it cannot at any rate, be a purely theoretical problem. To know itself in everything and everything in itself, to contain the full truth in a real, absolute union with everything, is the final religious ideal of life, and not merely of knowledge. The task of philosophy is to attain a "possible" (*vozmozhno*) concrete knowledge of the ideal and to point the way to its realization. We cannot expect from philosophy a final resolution of the contradictions which are rooted in the very conditions of our temporal being, and we cannot expect from it a full revelation of the truth. It is sufficient that it is aware of the contradictions of being and can perceive that inner harmony which is hidden in them and which conditions the very relative existence of the universe, its preservation, life and development. In its different concepts and opposing systems, philosophy expresses on the one hand, a diversity of contradictions of being and grasps the basic, ontological, and real significance of these contradictions. On the other hand, in its idealism, its aspiration toward final unity, it realizes that these contradictions cannot be absolute, otherwise neither relative being nor knowledge would be possible. It is aware of the universal nature of reason, and anticipates that ideal in which the contradictions are reconciled. The more profoundly philosophy recognizes the contradictions of the universe, the better it perceives the overwhelming force of the ideal. To recognize real opposites as "contradictions", means also to recognize (*priznat'*) the inner logic of being, that hidden, ideal reason of things, that Logos of Heraclitus, around which everything revolves and in which is found the riddle of the universe.

In being aware of the nature of our consciousness, we arrive at certain fundamental contradictions which do not admit an abstract solution – these are contradictions between genus and species, particular and universal, content and form, the real and the ideal. These very antinomies however, presuppose a certain reconciliation not obvious to us, without which consciousness and even knowledge, could not be attained. These (antinomies) contain a postulate which demands such reconciliation and indicate where to look for it.

It is important first of all, to explain the racial and universal elements of consciousness, without being disturbed by their contradiction with what seems to us to be individual and personal. Along with Aristotle we must recognize the existence of such a contradiction of problems with objective difficulty (*aporia*) which is contingent upon real opposition. In its ideal activity living consciousness reconciles these contradictions, universalizes the particular, individualizes the universal, realizes the ideal, idealizes the real. While such a reconciliation is merely relative, and although an analysis reveals the contradictions inherent in all our theoretical consciousness, yet, every positive progress which it makes in the realization of truth and goodness is for us a concrete realization of its ideal, a particular expression of its final "total-unity" (*vseyedinstvo*). In its positive, true activity, hence, in its true essence as well, consciousness possesses a concrete, living universality. No matter how opposite the principles of the "universal" and the "particular", the "genus" and the "species" are, in reality, one does not exist without the other. There is no consciousness without individualities, and there is no consciousness that is absolutely subjective; there are no absolutely isolated spheres of consciousness. If we considered consciousness externally in connection with the progressively developing phenomena of life, or, internally, by means of psychological analysis, we would be convinced of its organic universality, in the ideal organic-togetherness (sobornost') of consciousness.

LIFE AND CONSCIOUSNESS

Consciousness is an essential manifestation of life. In its earlier stages its other functions are undifferentiated, it then differentiates and develops together with its general organization of the physiological and social life. It differentiates and develops along with the nervous system and the progress of social relations, with the organizations of the communion among beings.

As we know, the highest organism is a society, an aggregate, consisting of innumerable elementary organisms or anatomic elements, which are grouped in tissues, organs, instruments or complex organs. The general organic cooperation, when they have fully developed their specialized functions, conditions the unity of life in its variety. There is an increasing correspondence between the individuality of the whole and the part, the unity of life and the distribution of its functions. The higher an organism ranges in the scale of living beings the greater the degree of difference, specialization of functions, and autonomy are manifested by its separate organs. The higher the organism, the more are these elements, organs, "instruments", in harmony, the more do they complement and presuppose each other in their difference, merging into the unity of the living whole. On the other hand, every organism is itself a living member of its species and is in permanent or temporary, physiological or psychological communion with the other genera of its species – a communion which is organically necessary.

Consciousness in its elementary form – i.e. in its sensuality, precedes not only the differentiation of the nervous system, but also the primitive organs – the cells. Primitive amoebae, without any organization, already manifest sensibility and certain signs of consciousness. Careful observation shows that irritability and sensibility are the basic universal, primitive and so-called spontaneous properties of living protoplasms, of the primary material of the whole organic world. With the emergence and development of organic individuality there also emerge and develop organic unions, these are at first disconnected physiological groups and out of these are formed complex organisms and plants during the course of a complete zoogenic process. Along with it and parallel to this general development, an undefined organic sensuality also develops grows, and becomes complex. There is nothing individual in its primitive basis, in its universal psychological matter. It is this elemental racial process which forms the basis for individual development as well as complex combinations, associations of individual elements. Since every organism is a continuation of another organism, every life a continuation of a preceding life, so are consciousness and sensuality of an individual being. It is not something absolutely-novel, but is also a continuation of a preceding universally-organic sensuality in that special variety which is inherent in the species of the given organism. Sensuality is not born but continues like the life of protoplasm. Consciousness as well as life are in origin a racial and hereditary process.

Hence, from the lowest levels of rudimentary consciousness to its highest social and ethical manifestation there is among them a common basis- viz., -racial forms and functions. From the lowest levels of conscious life to its highest manifestation, we observe a gradual development of this universalism of consciousness, a gradual transition from a natural, elemental undifferentiation, and immediate elemental community of psychic functions to a concrete and free, universal unity, to a connected multiformity and living "organic-togetherness" (*sobornost'*) This progress goes on along with the development of the individual principle.

The lowest organisms possess such an insignificant degree of individualization, that there are no defined limits between the species and the genus, or more correctly, between the separate genera. Individuality of the organism and its parts are also very poorly developed. Individual parts of lower animals are poorly separated, pass into one another replace or repeat each other; the life of the whole is without a firm unity. Certain polips, mollusks, worms, and helminths, may be cut into parts without killing the individual life and sensibility of these parts they live an independent life and sometimes they themselves supply the missing whole. Separate organs thus have the same kind of individuality as the whole, or more correctly, it is the whole minus its developed central individuality.

In a higher developed animal, all separate parts and organs are co-ordinated and are subject to the control of the central organs to a much higher degree. All elementary lives, elementary consciousness merge into one general life and consciousness, into one common individuality. The nervous system of a higher animal, which is a complicated aggregate of organs of consciousness, like a whole organism, presents a picture of gradual accelerated differentiation and integration, complication and centralization.[5]

Every genus reproduces, or "represents" its species in its own person. Hence, its very consciousness as well as the complex product of its organization and its psychic reflection, contains a potential vague, and general image of its species, its "psychological" representation. This representation is strictly speaking, unconscious, although it colors to a certain extent every aspect of the animal's consciousness. The animal is not aware of its innate representation or its very organization, since the animal is not self-conscious. Nevertheless, this universal representation, this organic racial idea contains a vague definition of the mind, feeling, and inclinations of the animal, and is the hidden motive of its whole life. By virtue of this instinctive idea which is aroused in the animal due to some impressions or physiological excitation, and "by virtue of this racial consciousness", the animal recognizes members of its species, both infants and adults, understands them, seeks physiological and social communion with them, feels its unity with them knows itself with others and in others.

Such a view on the nature of instincts and racial succession of consciousness throws light also on those phenomena of collective, communal consciousness which is so often observed in the sexual and social life of animals. Such are those complex actions executed in common by herd animals with an apparent division of labor and mutual cooperation and understanding. Such instances of a highly-developed altruism is found among mammals, birds, and even fish. This is also true of societies of insects, beehives and ant-hills. These point to a unity of consciousness among many genera.

The same impersonal, racial instinctive consciousness forms the basis of human consciousness, its lower level. Man, like the higher animal, is subject to the general zoological laws and is the inheritor of preceding organizations. Man possesses more ancient traditions. As a rational being, with whole eras of culture behind him, man frees him-

---

[5] See, Herbert Spencer's *Foundations of Psychology*, Part II, where he discusses the development of consciousness in connection with the development of the nervous system.

self from the inorganic control of his environment, and as much as possible from those special and complex simple instincts, which were cultivated in certain species for thousands of years, which correspond to certain special, immutable conditions of the environment. The same general animal instincts are retained in man and achieve their own peculiar development. The major part of human action and character are determined by inherent capacities, education and influence of his social environment – by hereditary and conscious suggestion.

Training is an organic continuation of heredity for man as well as for higher animals. His native capacities must be trained by other people that he may be able to master them himself. The language which he speaks, the knowledge and ideas which he learns, the laws which he obeys, the concept of God which he serves and worships – the whole content of consciousness is given to him by people or through people. The most external medium – nature, acts on him through human environment, determining his anthropological type in the hereditary transmission of the organization which is gradually being formed, his cultural type, in the succession of local traditions, customs, and ideas, formed under general and continual influence of given natural conditions.

The social environment, the social life of humanity presupposes physiological and psychological bonds, a unique real organization of social unions. Just as every tribe, nation, and government presuppose a family as an elementary cell, a social organism presupposes physiological ties among the separate individuals. By the same token, the family union, not mentioning already the more complex social formations, are strengthened by "real" psychological bonds, by the organic collectivity of consciousness, by their racial unity. All forms of social life and communion are like an organic development, which emerges as the result of hereditary instincts, racial consciousness, common impersonal acts of creation.

The word is man's organic capacity, which is determined by the special arrangement of his brain and nerves. Languages live and are developed, like species and genus, according to certain general, permanent laws, and have their organic morphology. Moral feelings and ideas are not basically the result of personal experience or utilitarian reasons, but the fruit of the development of that spontaneous altruism without which the species could not survive.

Consciousness as well as knowledge, morality and creativity, have a history in humanity. When we examine the historical process as a whole as well as its separate great epochs, we find that universal ideas which have determined its movement, have a transpersonal, positive objectivity; these are as it were, universal principles embodied in history. Great events and revolutions are not explained by private, indi-vidual actions, but are determined by general mass movements, often completely elemental universal consciousness, general instincts and needs.

We do not wish to deny the role of personality in history. On the contrary, we suggest that personality can be, and actually is, of "general" importance. In a certain sense, everything in history is achieved by personality and through personality: in it alone is an idea embodied. It is precisely on this account that the universal importance of person-ality needs explaining, because its influence is not limited by the one purely-negative capacity to exempt itself from the general cause, to retard it by virtue of its power and authority. There are personalities capable of representing common interests and ideas and guiding people in the name of universal principles, to lead, teach and educate them. These are precisely the capacities which historical personalities possess, the genuine leaders and teachers of humanity, these need explaining.

First of all, a historical personality is the product of his society. It is formed by it, and is imbued with its common interests. It represents it organically, embodies and concentrates in itself certain of its aspira-tions, and therefore can also realize them better than others and find a way of solving urgent historical problems. Quite often people of mediocre and simple ability, either because of circumstances or special high position, are called upon to play the role of a great man. These sometimes succeed due to certain intelligence and energy, reinforced by the awareness of his authority, quite often achieved by poverty of thought and absence of originality. When certain historical problems have reached maturity, when social needs, reach a certain intensity, and when the social will with a progressively increasing force pull in a certain direction, it naturally seeks a more adaptable organ for its ex-pression as well as for its realization. It strives toward an organic focal point in society, toward the representatives of its authority, to inspire them with a certain task if not with definite solution.

Personality represents its society or epoch in one form or another. Its importance is however, thereby exhausted. For if personality merely served the interests of certain social aspirations, a passive organ of collective will and consciousness, it could not effect a real influence on the course of events and on the development of its society.

In fact, personality has an independent meaning and absolute worth in society itself, apart from the society it represents in itself. If there is to be positive progress in any area of life, if society, science, art and religion are to develop, then personality can and should introduce into its society something absolute, namely, its freedom, without which there can be neither law, nor government, knowledge nor creativity.

Beside his inherited traditional principles, man must think logically in the freedom of his consciousness, know genuine truth and realize it in his actions.

While we recognize the general necessary nature of historical events and the inner rational unity of the general course of history, we also recognize that personality is capable of representing its society as well as guide it. The concept of primordial racial unity and organic collective nature of consciousness, does not negate, but explains the providential role played by personality in history. What the personality acquires becomes racial property because of its organic solidarity with it. Personality's concern, its progress and creativity are of common importance besides its external, immediate results. On the other hand, individual personality can appropriate the universal ideal, know universal truth only in universal, racial forms of human consciousness. A separate personality possesses these forms only when it is in organic solidarity with its race. Still, in its free, individual independence it transcends its innate nature, fills its potential consiousness with the ideal content. To be realized in fact, the ideal presupposes universal forms and a free act, without which it cannot be appropriated.

An examination of the universal process reveals the fact that human personality came into being through a difficult and slow process and how slowly its self-consciousness developed. Nothwithstanding human egoism, the very concept of personality, personal rights, property and freedom, – all these concepts emerge and are developing before our eyes. In the process of their development and the development of personal self-consciousness, one becomes aware of the inner contradiction of life, the contradictions of personality and race, freedom and nature. This contradiction is not responsible for the disagreements among the philosophical schools, but is a profound fundamental, discord in human life. This contradiction is not to be located in the philosophers' speculations, but is rooted in reality itself, in the very nature of things, for reality alone shows us the struggle of these principles, whereas merely reflects this struggle, gives us merely an awareness of this universal contradiction. Philosophy cannot solve this contradiction, precisely because it is a contradiction which cannot be resolved in theory, but demands a practical solution. Any rational solution is, and can only be an approximate solution, because it is merely an anticipated and probable solution.

We have already spoken about this fated contradiction, which troubled minds from ancient times, which Aristotle had already recognized as an endless task of ontology, i.e. the contradiction between species and genus. In reality one cannot exist without the other, at the same time one makes a claim for being the only reality, whereas neither one nor the other are genuinely real (Genera). People die, humanity is immortal: "there is nothing more real than humanity". Similarly, nothing is more "ideal". Humanity as a substance, as an actual organism, does not exist at all. It is not only not one body, but is not even one solid society. Only individual people are real organisms, but these "real beings" are transient and mortal, without an abiding reality.

How then can this contradiction be reconciled? Can humanity become such a real and solid organism, like one immortal person? Can separate individuals which constitute humanity, acquire immortality in it? Thus far, the contradiction is obviously irreconcilable. It is also obvious that man by himself cannot reconcile it, and if at some future date he were to seek such a reconciliation, then this could only be achieved on a practical religious basis in some Church, of a God-manhood organization.

A SUBJECTIVE ANALYSIS OF CONSCIOUSNESS

Thus far we spoke of consciousness as being contingent upon physiological and social conditions. The racial principles which bind individual consciousness together, and the universal forms in which absolute ideal consciousness is realized, may be revealed in the consciousness of individual personality by psychological analysis. A detailed study of these would require a whole system of psychology, logic, and ethics, but we shall merely limit ourselves to a few additional points to what has already been said.

1. We know that man is an inheritor of experience of preceding generations, their organizations and sensuality. All human senses, organs of perception, all instincts and appetites are inherited, just as our organs and psychophysical organization. As was seen above, sensuality is the racial basis of individual consciousness. We can therefore discover certain racial and universal elements in consciousness itself and in our sensuality.

We attribute involuntarily perfect reality to all sensual properties and cannot imagine that these properties depend exclusively upon our subjective, individual senses, such as the eyes and ears. Light, heat, solidity, sound, color, are "naively" mistaken for objective properties of things. We commonly assume that the sun shines, the sea makes a noise the flowers smell apart from personal perception.

If we now assume that everything that is sensuous presupposes something that senses (primum sensibile – primum sentiens), it is evident, that sensuality which conditions the world of things, cannot be subjective. When we admit the objective reality of the world of things, we presuppose a universal, anthropomorphic sensuality "prior to man". We thus unconsciously presuppose in our every sense perception a general, universal character of our sensuality. The universal, basic qualities, the sensual properties of things, are the elements of which the universe is made, and correspond to the basic forms of sensation, to the elements of sensuality. The sensual universe, in so far as we admit its objectivity, presupposes universal sensuality, with which our individual sensuality is bound up.

2. One of the most curious problems of psychology, which we do not undertake to solve, would be to investigate how man recognizes the elements of sensuality (i.e. individual forms of perception). The sense of sound, color, are as innate as are their organs, while at the same time we do not know them until we experience corresponding sensations. We presuppose an independent objectivity and universality of sense qualities, which however we only recognize after we sense them. We have no innate idea about them. Whatever the physiological conditions of sensuality may be, it is first of all a psychic faculty, just like the senses which correspond to separate classes of sensation, which are such psychic faculties. We may therefore assume that just as our sensual organization is predisposed to perceive given sensory properties (sound, colored rays, etc.) as in the undeveloped sensuality of man, in his very senses, are hidden, their "universal" form of representation. These ideas are completely forgotten, dormant, potential, but a series of sensations and perceptions arouse them in us. Forgetfulness precedes memory and is its original form. Thanks to an earlier recollection it sometimes requires just a single perception to recognize an object by its properties and to "recollect" it.

3. What is memory, and what is its importance in consciousness? On the one hand, memory contains potentially all the elements of our representations. On the other hand, there is "no" abstract possibility, or 'pure potentiality": there are only more or less strong or weak degrees of action and intensity. Hence, memory, as the sum of possible recollections consists of many layers of very different intensity, but always endowed to some degree by life. Furthermore, it is impossible, without qualification, to identify memory with consciousness, which constantly goes beyond the present and the past. We may therefore say that consciousness always rises above simple memory, even if it is the basis of consciousness. In any given moment we recognize only an in-significant part of what we remember, but in this recollection there is something more than simple memory. Here we have a certain psychic act, a definite, sometimes fully conscious, intentional action in which I objectify a certain series of ideas, sometimes I "think" it as a series of recollections to present or past real phenomena. Thus, a whole series

of complex processes of psychological and logical quality are added to those representations retained by memory. Here we have choice, attention, imagination, thinking, etc. Still, it is evident that memory is not a "special act or form of consciousness", different from other acts. Not only are recognition of an object, experience and knowledge unthinkable without memory, but there is no perceptible transition from one state of consciousness to another. Because consciousness transcends separate states, temporal moments and spatial relations, and it perceives them only because it contains the ideal synthesis of successive and separate moments of states and relations.

Memory is a faculty which remembers everything that has been put to memory, since it is something real and cannot be pure potentiality. No matter how deeply we would search we would not find anywhere in our memory an isolated recollection which is not connected with other recollections. We shall go further and say that we cannot point to the beginning of memory. For if we preserved a recollection which we consider to be the first in our life, a recollection about some event, or person, then it is only preserved "complex" recollection, which we could not acquire, recognize and retain, if we did not possess a multitude of antecedent, simple recollections. Finally, even the latter, as far as we can judge, we could not have formed or retained, if there was not something in our sensuous organization an inherited racial memory. Without this (element) they (the recollections) could not be recognized, known, or retained. Memory and sensuality merge, and if some explain memory in terms of sensuality, then sensuality is inexplicable without memory.

The phenomenon of memory may be reduced to physiological heredity only because recollections are retained in the constant renewal of cerebral substances and cerebral cells. Psychic properties are transmitted in an individual organism from molecule to molecule just as in a species, from generation to generation. In another sense, however, the very phenomena of organic heredity can be reduced to the "memory" of organic element, to a psychic capacity to retain definite, infinitely complex forms of motion.

If certain physiological process underlie the complex phenomena of memory, then in turn, there is a certain organic living memory underlying all living processes. Whatever explanation we may offer to explain the physical phenomenon of heredity, in psychological heredity we discern a racial memory, i.e. "a continuation of an antecedent consciousness of some individualities in the present consiousness of others".

4. Still more enigmatic than memory is imagination which permeates just as much the whole region of our consciousness, and we artificially differentiate it as much from other activities of the spirit.

Like memory, it conditions consciousness, and if imagination is unthinkable without memory which supplies it the material, then memory itself, actual recollection, is unthinkable without imagination. Along with the organic, racial totality of representations must be noted their tendency to individuation, to embodiment in definite images, expression or "imagination". This faculty is unquestionably more of an individual nature, being directly related to our will, its pleasures and sufferings. One meaningful look is embodied in a whole poem of images, one idea is developed in a whole system of ideas, one thought, one passion often dominates in man's consciousness, subordinating collateral complexes of ideas. The stronger and clearer some psychic state is developed, the wider its atmosphere, gradually encompassing the whole field of consciousness, if new impressions do not occupy the person. In exceptional unhealthy instances we note that the person is really possessed by ideas; in a weaker degree we encounter on every step analogous phenomena in normal psychic life.

An internal, psychological analysis of consciousness shows that it possesses that hidden "multiunity" to which psychophysiology attests. Imagination, like memory, which conditions all ideas of our consciousness, is not initially a personal arbitrary human activity: we are controlled by them only to an incomplete degree, and only after a prolonged, strenuous effort. It is impossible by the most careful analysis to differentiate in this region between what is personal, one's own, and which was inherited by us, the important, from that which is directly or indirectly suggested to us by rational beings. Ideas are communicated, transmitted from one mind to another, they live in a society of minds, just as they live in separate individuals; they are developed and crystallized in their social life.

5. Every so-called psychology from a simple introspection to psychophysical experiments, convinces us of the difference between personality and consciousness. When we identify them, we negate personality. Personal self-consciousness is awakened in us a long time after birth. "Personality" disappears, is forgotten in sleep, in a fainting state, catalepsy, under different diseases of the brain, when there still remains a degree of consciousness. In cases of so-called split-personality, in "psychic dissociations", we observe in one and the same body, as though there were several personalities, several disconnected memories coexisting with each other.

There are, as it were, in all of us several different potential personalities which are only waiting for a chance to make their appearance; or, more precisely, every individual image or feeling can take the place of personality. For when the central will is ejected from consciousness, a separate "role" or a potential personality may be replaced by a normal soporific personality. This role may be suggested to a person by an outside mind or will, or develop spontaneously under the pressure of elusive recollections or impressions. For every image or recollection awakens in us a recollective or mimic activity. When imagination is given free course, it seeks to recall a given image in all its possible clarity. When a hypnotized person concentrates all his consciousness on some single idea (the so-called "monoideaism") it can attain an extraordinary clear, dramatic development. When an actor is absorbed in his role, he becomes wholly subject to it, executes automatically a whole series of actions required for its complete realization without any mistakes.

Many researchers see in these phenomena as experimental proof against the real existence of personality. Bifurcation of consciousness, parallel existence of several memories, several personalities – all these phenomena which are dependent upon certain physiological changes, are proof, according to some psychologists, that personality, as the source and condition of consciousness does not exist at all, that it is a simple phenomenon of consciousness without any transcendental reality, that human personality is not something individual, because consciousness is not individual.

6. By personality we commonly have in mind three or four things, some are completely different, and some are closely connected, these give rise to many misunderstandings and confusion of difficult and complex problems.

By personality is meant, first of all, the empirical individuality of every person as it appears to us with all its peculiarities and characteristic features. Secondly, this is the same individuality as seen introspectively.[6] Thirdly, the "ego" as a necessary subject of consciousness, is always identical with itself, conditioning the unity of consciousness. In the fourth place, the psyche is that invisible, real subject of my will and thought, the bearer of all my capacities and activities which is manifested empirically in the external and moral make-up of every person, and who recognizes his "ego" as his personal pronoun.

It is evident, that this psyche which assumes in us such different forms, cannot be identical with our external appearance, or with what we think or feel about ourselves. It is also obvious that it cannot merely be the subject of consciousness: it is the "ego" which we immediately cognize within ourselves, which is something distinct from our consciousness. I think, therefore I exist; but it seems to me that it exists even when I am not thinking and when I temporarily lose consciousness.

---

[6] This involves certain dangers of moral "split personality": I appear to others differently than to myself, and I do not appear equally the same to everybody; I may even regard myself in different ways.

Does my psyche exist not merely for me, but for everyone in general? Does it have a universal, objective existence? There can be no argument about its subjective existence. I cannot imagine that my ego does not exist, or that it would at some future time be annihilated. If however, I begin to think of myself objectively in relation to other empirical phenomena, I not only admit my inevitable annihilation, but may even begin to doubt my own real existence, the ego, the psyche.

Does the psyche, the genuine personality of man, have an objective existence? Can we objectively cognize it, or prove its existence? Is a metaphysical psychology possible, and is the psyche a cognizable object? Primitive people and spiritualists of every era recognized that the psyche is an objective phenomenon, subject to perception and even experimentation. Even if we admitted the possibility of such phenomena, can we identify a ghost with a psyche, and place on the blackboard the question about the psyche along with the question about ghosts? The only objective psychic phenomena subject to scientific investigation are essentially psychophysical phenomena. The only scientific method in psychology "can be" only the method of experimental psychophysics, which is not concerned with metaphysical questions, but explains the concrete connection between organic and psychic processes. If however, psychophysics is wrongly understood, it leads to a direct negation of the psyche, since it poses as a "definitive" psychology. In reality, psychophysics studies not the psyche, but psychical phenomena connected with psychic processes in our body. For scientific psycho-physics the psyche can and must be problematic.

Where and under what conditions can spirit have an objective universal reality? The very concepts of personality and psyche give us some indications as to what the answer is. The concept of "personality" is first of all a moral-juridical concept, formed under the influence of moral-legal relations. The idea of the psyche is primarily a "religious" idea which developed under the influence of the religious life of people, like all other concepts, about immortality, resurrection, etc.[7] Hence, no matter how we may decide beforehand the question about the spiritual personality of man, we see, that the very concept about it (psyche) is acquired only in "society". Human personality is an "end in itself"; such is the fundamental premise of moral consciousness. Our neigbours must be for us not a means, but an end in themselves, in our action and in our communion with them. In recognizing our distinctive nature we also demand from others a general recognition of our legal "right" (*prava*), our inviolable personal "dignity" (*dostoinstvo*). A full recognition of the unconditional dignity of human personality acquired in the

---

[7] To a certain extent one may also say, that the idea of individuality, i.e., the living, completed whole, is first of all, an "aesthetic" idea.

moral and religious life of people, there develops the belief in its immortality in the same way as the high value of human individuality develops belief in its resurrection.

The human spirit is objective only in society and in social activity, in communion with rational beings, where it really exists not merely in itself and for itself, but also in others and for others, and where others exist in it and for it, as it itself exists. The question about the psyche thus, actually leads to the problem of the nature of consciousness. For if my selfness (*samost'*), my "ego" can be fully objective only in the consciousness of all, then it may be asked, what is the universal consciousness, and how is my personal consciousness related to it? To put it differently, is consciousness, individual and subjective, or is it collective? In the first instance, the psyche can have no real objectivity, no universal significance or existence: if consciousness is a subjective phenomenon, then the psyche is only a subjective idea which arises and is developed in the accidental co-existence of people. In the second instance, if human consciousness is essentially collective, if it is potential consciousness of all in one (being), then its subjective ego may also have universal, objective existence in this collective consciousness: its self-consciousness achieves objective universal certainty (*dostovernost'*). We thus arrive at a paradoxical result: whereas individualistic psychology and subjective idealism equally lead to the negation of an individual psyche, "metaphysical socialism", the recognition of the collective nature of consciousness validates our belief in it.

7. In our investigation of the concept of personality, we found that it is conditioned by real collective consciousness. Earlier we spoke of real sense perception, and we pointed out that it presupposes universal sensuality. By the same token, when we examine real and universal cognition, we shall see that its logicality and positivity presupposes a formal collectivity of consciousness (*sobornost'*).

We cannot enter deeply into the many complex problems of the theory of knowledge, we shall therefore limit ourselves here to two fundamental problems around which this theory turns. We understand the question of cognition and perception of external "reality" and "causality", of true perception of real objects or "beings" (*suschestv*) and real "action" which occur outside us. How can I truly know that outside me there is a universe, and that the events occuring around me arc indeed activities of real causes?

Psychologically our idea of reality is something very complex. We are not asking, however, about the composition and origin of this idea, but what is knowledge of reality, and how it is possible. First of all, the reality of things is not our representation: otherwise actual reality does not exist at all, and we arrive at an absolute illusionism. We must naturally have an idea of reality, to speak about it. The real sign of the reality of this idea is its independence from us and from our subjective representations. We perceive and represent reality in all possible forms and images, but reality itself is distinct from the "image" (*obraz*) representing things. Everything that we cognize as an idea, is a certain substitution (*zamena*) of the represented object: I may relate it to the object and may distinguish it from the object. Reality is however, something that cannot be substituted, something which can in no way be "represented" (*predstavleno*): real, genuine reality can only be "cognized" (*soznana*). No matter what ideas I may have about my personality and character, I do not represent, I truly "cognize" (*soznaiu*) my existence. If I truly and unconditionally know that there are things and beings, a universe outside myself, and I know it as well as I know that I am – I am conscious of the "very" reality of things, I know it as much as my own reality. Such knowledge, when considered by itself, would necessarily be contentless and purely formal. I am not actually self-conscious of other beings, nor do I have a perfect knowledge of their qualities and nature; I know (cognize – *soznayiu*) their existence. But such knowledge which determines all future cognition, is something other than a simple external knowledge of things. In fact, we cannot cognize "a priori" the reality of objects independent of us out of pure ideas, because we can only deduce from such ideas some cogent possibilities, but not reality. Nevertheless, such reality cannot be cognized "a posteriori" from subjective sensations, because it (reality) is not subjective, but independent from us. Since it is not an idea, the reality of things is not cognized (*posnaetsya*), but recognized (*soznaetsya*) in the same way as we recognize our own existence. I do not merely know it "ab exteriori", but I re-cognize (*soznayiu*) it together with it and behind it "ab interiori, I possess within me its personal possible consciousness".

I cannot doubt the fact, that outside myself there is something real, something other, than myself, and I recognize this reality to be universal and absolute. If this is so, then my consciousness of this reality cannot be subjective, if it is genuine. Naturally, there is a great deal of the subjective and naive anthropomorphism in my ideas about the properties and reality of things. But at the core of our knowledge, experience, perception, there is a potential recognition of universal reality, and without this recognition we could not actually and concretely cognize both individual objects as well as universal properties of things.

Reality is thus something either true or something imaginary. I either know it in itself, or I only imagine it. If we have genuine knowledge, if we know it just as much as we know our own reality, then our knowledge is collective in essence. Once I can genuinely know other beings, this knowledge is not merely mine, but is universal, i.e. it is the potential knowledge of everyone.

8. In order to elucidate more concretely the nature of our knowledge of reality, let us here examine the consciousness of causality which wholly determines it.

Causality is a universal law of reality without being cognizant of it, a knowledge of nature or any experience in general is impossible. Without being conscious of causality I cannot differentiate the ego from the non-ego, sensation from objects, just as I cannot distinguish any object, or any objective sequence of events in time, not to mention the uniformity in the order of phenomena. If we are conscious of reality, which we recognize to be real, then we are also conscious of the causal actions on us. The question of causality is therefore directly bound up with the question of reality.

What is consciousness of causality, and how is it possible? Certain changes and events occur around us which, we, by virtue of our consciousness of causality, cognize as "actions" i.e. we presuppose that behind them (actions) there are certain known or unknown agents (*deyateli*). An "action" is that which intervenes between cause and effect. The act is itself causality, hence, the concept of action is inseparably bound up with the idea of an acting cause and an objective change – consequence.

How, and by what right do we recognize that reality of some actions besides our own, and why are we conscious of changes around us, as actions of other agents or other causes? Do we base it on some direct perception, or do we, by an analogy of personal actions attribute to other beings that which is ours? Any explanation of causality or reality, as purely subjective forms of consciousness, inevitably leads to an absurdity of absolute illusionism, which is contrary to our basic conviction, our deepest consciousness of true reality. If, however, in admitting such a reality and the universal interaction of things we recognize at the same time the subjective origin of the idea of causality, we are forced to presuppose "a pre-established harmony" between consciousness and things – an hypothesis which is not scientific and does not explain anything. For if we are not conscious of real, actual causality, then we can know nothing about external objects, and consequently, about the harmony that exists between them and us.

Consciousness of causality is "fundamental" and not derivative. If by means of it (causality) we can perceive external phenomena as well as actions, by the same token we also understand both our actions, as well as external events, capable of having universal, objective consequences. If we can know logically and positively causality and reality of other beings, then we must recognize the formal collective character of human consciousness, which enables one to genuinely know this reality and action of others – namely, universal reality. Only by virtue of this property of my consciousness can I know objectively causality, i.e., truly understand external events, as well as phenomena of independent causes or agents, existing for themselves and not for me alone.

The category of causality is first of all a "form" of cognition. Without this form we cannot cognize ourselves nor others; we cannot understand, or apprehend nature, cognize the actions of other causes, or the reality of other beings and the objective consequences of our actions. This universal "form" which generally determines our actual knowledge and experience does not in itself give us any particular, empirical knowledge, or definite knowledge in general. Man is not endowed with innate real knowledge of causes and actions, but only a "potential" (vozmozhnoye) consciousness of them. All human knowledge has a potential character. Our knowledge of causes which we acquire in experience is both certain and incomplete, true and false, absolute and relative.

Our ideas of reality and causality are determined by the internal collectivity (sobornost') of human consciousness, they are therefore logical and generally trustworthy. Since however, the very collectivity of our consciousness is still something that is in the process of realization, something potential, although it must be so, then even our very knowledge of reality and causality is superficial, formal and not quite real. This gives rise to innumerable contradictions and antinomies inherent in our ideas. All these antinomies of our reason are determined by the potential nature of our consciousness, by the contradiction or non-correspondence among these forms, its ideal potentiality and its empirical content.

Let us now examine the antinomies of causality. Our universal concept of causality is obviously related to universal reality which contains the total sum of causes, and is a law of universal action or energy. In fact however, we only apprehend individual phenomena and individual causes which we connect with our universal idea. This gives rise to innumerable contradictions. Everything that takes place around us are in many instances regarded by us as accidental. Materialism, or the so-called mechanistic world-view, which recognizes the absolute nature of empirical causality, regards the universe as the product of absolute necessity as well as the product of completely blind change. Causality in this sense is deterministic in character. In regarding causality in a formal way, we naturally see in it merely an external connection, a deterministic law. Ideas about universal causality, the law of universal action, are ideal, related to absolute reality. We however, use them to fill the real gaps of our knowledge, by uniting within these universal "catholic" forms, particularity alone. A being, defined in terms of ideal plenitude and not by the action of particular causes, would be perfectly free. Predetermined necessity, felt by us as a limit and a necessity (*necessitas*), is a false dependence upon particular causes, which contradicts genuine causality, genuine action. In the moral sphere only that action is considered good and internally free which fulfils the universal law of truth (pravda).

Such are the antinomies inherent in the very concept of causality – the contradiction between necessity and freedom, between the concept of the universal connection of phenomena and inner free action – the independence of the agents. Our consciousness of causality is at the same time ideal and empirical, objective and subjective, true and false. Insofar as it is ideal, it is objective and true, and insofar as it is empirical, it is relative, subjective, illusory. As we have already pointed out earlier, in order to resolve the basic contradictions of consciousness it must be a truly universal, collective consciousness to realize its inner ideal. The question of the nature of consciousness brings us to a consideration of the ethical problem.

9. Whatever ideas we may have about the nature and origin of theoretical consciousness and empirical knowledge, it is patent, that moral consciousness arises and is developed only in communion with rational beings. A person who is morally isolated from other people, who lives by himself and for himself, can obviously not be a moral person. Inversely, perfect morality can only be attained in a perfect society.

The good will, which is the basis of morality is called love. Every morality that is founded on something other than love is not true morality and is basically immoral. Love however, presupposes one who loves and one who is loved and in its perfect realization there is a union of loving people. Love, the highest ideal of moral goodness, is perfect plenitude, a free and indivisible unity of everything that is loved. It is in this sense that we can say that perfect love is only realized in a perfect society. Love cannot and does not wish to remain alone; it is "altruism" and inwardly presupposes others, seeks others and not itself.

Love is peculiar to man. It is not formed externally and cannot be the result of man's individual efforts. It is born in man of itself and grows, if it is not stifled. It is impossible to draw a sharp line between theoretical and moral consciousness of man. If he is directly conscious of the reality and activity of other beings, with whom he is in communion, he is already at one (in solidarity) with them in this consciousness. Just as the recognition of the reality and causality of beings is due to the potential solidarity of our consciousness, similarly, love is the active realization of this solidarity.

We recognize the moral law in the same way as we recognize the law of causality, the law of universal action. We are conscious of the true reality of other beings by virtue of our potential, formal solidarity with them. The ethical problem is thus contained in the very reality of our theoretical consciousness, in its very imperfection and falsehood. "Reason" itself must arouse our "conscience" (*sovest'*), theoretical consciousness is moral (consciousness).

The law of causality is a formal law, which does not afford us any knowledge; it is merely a form of our cognition. The moral law, the law of universal solidarity of moral goals – does not presuppose this empty form, but the most ideal content, the most true essence of universal consciousness, as an absolute "ought-to-be" (*dolzhnoe*). Its sanction does not lie in the formal harmony of separate beings, but in their ideal unity (which ought to be) (*dolzenstvuyiuschem byt'*). We cannot but cognize external reality and causality, and this consciousness "presupposes" a formal bond, a formal solidarity of reality. The moral law "demands" actual realization of the full ideal solidarity: we must recognize and love our neighbour as ourselves, the whole truth "ought" to be our goal.

BIOGRAPHICAL SKETCH

Vladimir Sergeyevich Solovyov (1853-1900) was born in Moscow where his father was professor of history at the university of Moscow and whose 29 volumes of "The History of Russia", made him famous as a historian. Like many other Russian students, he experienced a period of religious doubt, but soon returned to a much deeper faith after this brief experience.

Vladimir Solovyov is perhaps the best known Russian thinker in the West. He is especially known for his "God-manhood Lectures" and "Justification of the Good" and for his interest in bringing about the reunification of all Christian churches. However, his philosophical works are hardly known in the West. His principal philosophical works are: "The Crisis of Western Philosophy" (1874); "The Philosophical Principles of Integral Knowledge" (1877); "The Critique of Abstract Principles" (1877-80); and "Theoretical Philosophy" (1897-99). His collected works consist of nine volumes and his Letters of four volumes.

In his philosophical works, Solovyov deals mainly with epistemological problems and directs his criticism against empiricism, rationalism and German Idealism. None of these, according to Solovyov, enable us to know true reality. He offers three methods of knowing reality, all of which must be properly interrelated. They are: empirical, rational and mystical knowledge. The following selection which deals with the problem of cognition is an analysis of Descartes' 'methodical doubt'. It appeared in *Voprosy Filosofii i Psikhologii* (Vol. 8, Bk. 40, pp. 667-915), and has been considerably abridged.

V. S. Solovyov

THE FIRST PRINCIPLE
OF THEORETICAL PHILOSOPHY

The value of our goals and actions depends on the conformity with that triune idea of the Good, with which Moral philosophy deals. If our life is to have real "meaning", or be worthy of the spiritual nature of man, it must be "justified by the Good".[8] Our moral being demands it and it alone will satisfy it. The person whose goal it is to fully participate in the historical performance of good in the world, utilising every external and internal beneficial help in this cause, that person is free from moral discord, is reconciled with life, and the voice of conscience speaks within him only as a necessary monitor of personal digressions and errors, and not as a dreadful accuser of his whole way of life.

In order that man's life should have this meaning, or be the justification of the Good, it is necessary, besides the natural good feelings of shame, compassion, piety, which are natural to man, to have also a moral "doctrine" which not only fortifies these feelings in the form of "commandments", but which also develops the idea of the good inherent in them leading to a rational bond of all its data and manifestations, both in nature and in history, deducing from it the fullest moral norms, for guidance, direction and correction of the entire personal and social life.

If a moral doctrine is necessary for all people in general, we have no right to exclude from this "all" the ever-growing minority, who are willing and able not only to accept but also understand the moral norms and who can give them careful consideration.

In the realm of moral ideas, philosophical thinking, in spite of its formal independence, is essentially directly subordinated to the vital

[8] See *Justification of the Good*, especially chapters I-IV, VII and XVI.

interests of pure will, which strives toward the Good. The will demands from the mind a detailed and complete explanation as to what constitutes the genuine Good as distinct from the spurious, or is considered Good, without actually being so.

First of all, we wish, because of our moral nature, to live in accordance with the genuine Good and for this reason to know its true essence and actual demands. At the same time we simply want to "know" the truth for its own sake. This second desire is unconditionally approved by our conscience, which thus confirms the fundamental unity between the Good and the truth which is obviously necessary, since without this unity the very concept of a genuine Good which is the basis of all morality, would have no meaning.

Life and knowledge are essentially one and indivisible in their higher norms; still, the distinction between the practical and the theoretical is preserved in relation to the object. The good will and true knowledge, for all their unity are two different inner states, two separate methods of existence and reality. A similar unity and difference exists between moral and theoretical philosophy.

The idea of the Good formally demands from every agent to treat the object of his activity "honestly". This demand is universal and knows no exceptions. Because of this demand the philosopher is obliged first of all to investigate the truth honestly. Even though he believed that it was either given (empirically) or revealed, it is his obligation and duty to test or to justify his belief by unbiased thinking. The philosopher differs from the non-philosopher not so much by the content of his convictions, but by the fact that he deems it improper to accept as final in theory some major premise without preliminary rational examination and verification.

Although purely philosophical interest is wholly concerned with truth, we must not restrict ourselves to this very broad, general definition. The moralist, who is expounding the genuine Good, the theologian arguing for the true divine revelation, are also concerned with the truth, they are not all however, philosophers. Similarly, interest in truth in general is not the distinctive mark of philosophy in regards to mathematics, history and other special sciences, all of which are striving toward the truth. A philosophical mind is one which does not accept an unsubstantiated conviction of the truth, but accepts only truth that has been attested and capable of satisfying all intellectual inquiries. All sciences naturally seek certainty, but there is relative and absolute or unconditional certainty; genuine philosophy can only be satisfied with the latter.

We should not conclude that philosophy is certain in a priori manner and guarantees the unconditional attainment of authentic truth. It may never find it, but it is duty-bound to pursue it to the end, disregarding any limitations, accepting nothing without verification, demanding an account for every assertion. Even if it could not give a positive answer to the question of absolute, genuine truth, it would have still been an achievement, even though a negative one. Clear knowledge, purporting to be absolute truth, has in fact no such meaning. The philosophical mind is faced with two positions; either to overcome every possible doubt in an "accepted" truth, by genuine thinking, and thereby verify its certainty, or to honestly recognize as doubtful in the final analysis everything that is known and to reject theoretical certainty; one has to make a definite choice between these two (positions).

The essential feature of philosophical speculation is its aspiration toward unconditional certainty based on unbiased and consistent thinking. The distinctive feature of philosophy from this point of view is quite clear. Exact sciences in their search for authentic truth, are based on known data accepted on faith as indisputable limits which permit no further intellectual investigation (such as for example, space for geometry). Hence, the certainty attained by exact sciences is necessarily only conditional, relative and limited. Philosophy, as a discipline of unbiased thinking cannot, by its very nature, be restricted to such limitations, and from the outset aims at unconditional or absolute certainty.

The first basis of philosophical thinking or the first criterion of philosophical truth is unconditional adherence to principle. Theoretical philosophy must have its starting point in itself, and its process of thought must start from the beginning. This does not mean that philosophical thought must create anew from itself all its content without accepting anything from outside itself. If this were so, its activity would have to start from a "tabula rasa", i.e. from a state of pure nothingness and philosophy would then be a "creatio ex nihilo". But this would constitute a contradiction and self-repudiation. If, for the sake of negating all premises, one would have to start from some arbitrary premise, viz., from the premise that human thought in itself is an omnipotent creative force existing in an absolute vacuum, which in reality is not the case. What is apparent is that on the one hand thought is an infinite force, but not a creative force; it is only a verifying or controlling force. On the other hand, everything is subject to it. The true principle of pure thinking, or theoretical philosophy is not to accept any premise as certain until it is verified by thought. This preliminary criterion for truth speaks for itself, since by negating any arbitrary or unverified premise it (the criterion) itself accepts nothing arbitrarily but expresses only the actual striving toward philosophical thinking, or the very fact of existence of "the will to philosophize" as a German would say.

If purely-philosophical activity of the mind is the verification and application of a standard of critical thought to everything, then one may ask: what constitutes this standard or criterion of truth? Obviously, any preliminary answer would have to be very general and indefinite, in order to avoid resorting to an arbitrary or unverified premise. We can only say now that the criterion for certainty lies within thought's own nature and not in something extraneous to it. Thought can accept any representation or idea of an object as verified truth after an exhaustive inquiry, and after the matter is entirely clear and the meaning arrived at is completely and definitely satisfactory.

The criterion for truth presupposes the idea of honesty (conscientiousness). Real philosophical thinking must be a conscious search for genuine truth. In demanding honesty from thinking are we not introducing a moral element into theoretical philosophy, and are we not subordinating it to ethics? But did theoretical philosophy undertake beforehand not to admit any moral element under any circumstances? Such a commitment would be a "bias", which is contrary to the very essence of theoretical philosophy. Since the moral element is required by the very logical conditions of thinking, it not only can, but must be included into the foundation of theoretical philosophy. This is the case in the present instances.

Philosophy differs from any other discipline, and the philosophical mind from any other in that it regards interest in pure truth to be the most important interest which cannot be subordinated to anything else. Thus, our demand or primary criterion for truth is really nothing more than an analytical judgment, which may be reduced to a simple identity: philosophical thinking must be true to itself, or still more simply, philosophy is philosophy, A — A. Obviously, in the demand for intellectual honesty the moral element coincides with the theoretical one.

Theoretical philosophy, like purely-intellectual interest, poses the question of truth in its relation to "knowledge", or examines its object not from its moral, or general practical aspect, but only from its intellectual value, which consists primarily in certainty. Since the object does not exist for us other than through our knowledge of it, the question of the object is really a question "of the certainty of the knowledge about it".

There are a number of different kinds of human knowledge, such as scientific, religious, whose relative certainty is quite sufficient for practical purposes. But theoretical philosophy is basically concerned with the certainty of knowledge itself in its essence. By knowledge is generally meant the coincidence (*sovpadenie*) of a given thought about an object with its real being and property. How is such a coincidence generally possible, and how is its reality verified in each case?

We undoubtedly have a certain kind of knowledge whose certainty is absolute and is not subject to honest dispute. Such knowledge must be the point of departure in the solution of the epistemological problem. But we must be careful here. We must not begin from some abstract definition of this kind of knowledge, since such a definition is inevitably coloured by preconceived ideas and views, which make our judgment at best unsatisfactory and at worst deceptive. Starting from a general definition, we unwillingly violate the basic requirement of honest thinking, viz., not to permit arbitrary or unverified premises. Every abstract formula has too extensive a frontier, and it is impossible to guard it against thought-smugglers, who are always ready to import not only legal truth, but also truth unchecked by the intellectual customs house, and even the counterfeit money of error.

Absolute certainty of real consciousness is the fundamental truth of philosophy, and every broad sphere of philosophical development begins with this premise. Pure consciousness or the knowledge of physical reality pays dearly for its narrow limits. This knowledge for all its certainty is in itself very meagre and can in no way satisfy the mind's yearning for truth. What does it matter to me that I know with absolute certainty that I have experienced something or other, or that I have imagined such and such objects, while this certain knowledge fails to tell me the real nature of what I experienced or imagined while asleep or awake, since the subjective reality for which consciousness alone vouches, is "equally" trustworthy in both instances. But as soon as we wish to extend this evidence of consciousness beyond its inner reality, it immediately loses its absolute certainty; this opens up the possibility for all sort of doubt.

If actual and absolutely-certain consciousness in no way vouches in every case for the separate and independent reality of its given facts, such as sense representations of extended bodies, spatial movements, etc., then we have of course no right to assert that the reality of the external world "per se" is given in actual consciousness. In fact, what we are given is a certain complex of facts which are sensed, represented and thought, which we call the universe, but for which we do not have any epistemological evaluation, or this fact cannot be found in primitive consciousness by its very nature. The very demand for such an evaluation, or the question of true reality of the external world in immediate consciousness – cannot be given (*dan*) as a datum, but is only given as a task (*zadan*). As soon as it is reflected by thought, it immediately becomes its first and preliminary answer. We "believe" in the reality of the external world, and philosophy's task is to give this belief a rational justification, explanation, or proof. To deviate from this task under the pretext that the reality of the external world is given in immediate consciousness, means to substitute an arbitrary and false "opinion" in place of philosophy. In spite of the fact that this opinion is widely accepted, its vagueness and baselessness may be seen from the fact that it is quite compatible with our initial assertion, i.e., that we believe in the real existence of the external world. This assertion is accepted without any objection, and in fact one cannot say anything seriously against it. However, it would be completely absurd if the reality of the world were given (*dana*) in immediate consciousness, since one cannot believe in something that is present or actually exists. I would say it is absurd, if I began to affirm that "I believe" in the fact that I am now sitting at the table and am writing this dissertation: I do not believe this, but recognize it as an actual reality which is experienced but cannot be affirmed.

Our direct consciousness of the world of appearance vouches so little for its actual reality, that such a sober thinker as Descartes regards doubt in this reality as a necessary prerequisite for a philosophical investigation of truth. Such doubt would be quite impossible, if in direct consciousness, besides subjective reality or the actual facts constituting the universe were also given their actual reality.

In order to connect certainty of the existence of the subject with the simple self-certainty (*samodostovernost'*) of consciousness which is inherent in all its states, Descartes ingeniously takes precisely the state of "doubting" consciousness. Supposing, he says, I doubt the existence of everything, but I cannot nevertheless doubt the existence of the doubter himself, since it is present in the very fact of doubting. "Dubito ergo sum", or more generally, "Cogito ergo sum".

The founder of modern philosophy began his thesis from the fact of immediate certainty of direct or pure consciousness, i.e. the knowledge of given psychic states as such. Was he right in extending this self-evidence to the belief in the actual existence of the subject?

Descartes' certainty of the existence of the subject, makes his viewpoint dubious. Furthermore, he would have to insist that it is impossible to doubt the real existence of the subject. Moreover, such doubt in reality does exist. When a cartesian encounters this doubt as a fact, he would have to deny it, i.e. deny its real appearance on the ground that it is impossible to exist, and the skeptic could, with justification adduce the reverse argument: I really doubt, therefore such is possible – "ab esse ad valet consequentia". In defence of his position, the cartesian would have to prove that the skeptic in doubting his existence, thinks incorrectly and that he has no clear and distinct ideas of the terms of the question, etc.

Do we find in Descartes himself sufficiently clear and distinct ideas regarding the terms of the question? "I see very clearly, that in order to think, I must be" (je vois très-clairement que, pour penser, il faut être). (Discours de la méthode, 4-me partie). For an objective clarity and distinctness of this position, however, it would be necessary to define more accurately the meaning of "to be" (être), which can be used in various senses. To justify his "very clear" view that thinking presupposes being, Descartes takes refuge in his basic principle, "I think, therefore I am", whose intuitive character does not apparently safeguard him against obscurity. It is therefore necessary to subject him to a painstaking investigation.

We have before us three terms: thinking (Cogito, je pense), existence (ergo sum, donc je suis), and the subject who thinks and therefore exists, to whom both terms apply. Out of the three terms, Descartes only explains the first – "thinking". By thinking he understands any inner mental state, "known as such", i.e. unrelated to its actual or supposed objects, as well as independent of any evaluation of this state from the point of view of any theoretical or practical norms. The thinking which is Descartes' starting-point is nothing more than an observable fact of psychic occurrence. Thinking in this sense is something self-evident, not subject to doubt, argument or question. The same cannot be said of the "thinker" or the subject.

There is unquestionably thinking (in Descartes' sense) as a fact of observable sensations, representations, emotions, and complex ideas, judgments, conclusions, solutions. One of the concepts appearing in thinking is the concept "Ego", or the subject, which has the property of being connected with all other facts (or given states), as an attendent secondary act. Let us suppose that we see a red circle on a green rectangular field. The initial fact of consciousness in this case consists only in that such a circle is observed in such a field: there it is! But we soon have to relate this particular fact to the whole series or group of such facts, connected by one thinking subject, and we arrive at the statement: "I see a red circle in a green rectangle". As a function of an indefinite series of psychic facts, this Ego is naturally, separated from their aggregate, stands, so to speak, outside the parenthesis, and assumes the form of something independent, that is, the idea occurs that the logical subject of a known series of phenomena, is the expression of something that is more real than these phenomena.

Let us forget metaphysics for a moment and turn to the general popular view. According to the elementary common view, the real subject of psychic life, our real ego, or self, is a corporeal organism. This natural view, while not in itself true, is bound up with many important truths, but considered out of context, could not of course, pass the most elementary philosophical scrutiny.

We have no philosophical right to regard the body as an actual substratum of thinking, as that which thinks, simply because the actual existence of the body and other sensory objects have not as yet been proven. Thus far we have the right to assert only what is self-evident, i.e. that which is given in pure consciousness, which, only points to sensations, representations, and other psychic states, without any reference to the reality of respective objects, since pure consciousness, (or thinking in the Cartesian sense) equally points to remembered psychic states, even naive realism must admit that no real objects are given (for instance in a dream or in hallicinations, etc.).

Let us now return to the Cartesian view of methodical doubt, let us bear in mind that no external world, or sensory objects and real events are given to us. We know only a series of inner phenomena which constitute the content of pure consciousness or thinking. But "pour penser il faut être", thinking presupposes the existence of a thinker. We do not however, as yet know what being or existence is (except that it is given in pure consciousness of which there is no doubt). Most important, we still do not know what the thinking subject itself is (except that it occurs in pure consciousness of thought in the idea of a thinking subject). It is obvious, that there is no sense in posing and solving the problem of the existence of something, when we do not know what it is.

When Descartes, in order to express the essence of the subject, calls it "res cogitans, substantia intellectualis, seu spiritualis", we know (from subjective experience or pure consciousness) only the content, the participle and the adjective, but the nouns remain vague. The terms "res", "substantia" which should designate the subject itself, since it is something more than the attributes of thinking – are the main terms taken over by Descartes which should first of all have been discarded, and which our philosopher treats very carelessly, without any critical verfication taken from scholasticism.

The author (Descartes) of "Discourses on Methods" makes a direct leap from the indubitable and self-evident fact of thinking, to the metaphysical subject, inherited from the scholastics, but proves in his case to be even more devoid of content than the latter (scholastics). He also paid no attention to two other different concepts of the subject, and this is the first distinction which anyone wishing to teach well, ought to make. (bene docere).

When it is said: "I think", one may understand by the term "I" either a pure subject of thinking, or an empirical subject, i.e. a given living individuality, in other words, a subject in ,,abstracto", or the subject in "concreto". Having failed from the outset to make the necessary clear distinction regarding the subject, Descartes thereby made the fatal mistake by confusing the signs of both concepts regarding the subject and producing a hybrid; on the one hand, Descartes' spiritual substance is so abstract that it coincides completely with "thinking in general", and on the other hand, it is an individual substance or a thing (res, chose) located in the centre of the brain of every individual person. I do not say that there cannot be a third concept about the subject besides the cartesian hybrid (ubliudok). But we must first distinguish between the first two. The pure subject of thinking is a "phenomenological" fact, no less but no more than all other, i.e., it is absolutely authentic, but only in the context of the actual content of consciousness or as a phenomenon in the narrowest sense of the word.

If the so-called deceptions of feelings (illusions and hallucinations) give us the right to doubt in the authenticity of sensations, as evidence of the objective reality of the physical world, then the deceptions of self-consciousness which are observable, although not so frequently, equally make it possible to doubt its proofs regarding the genuine reality of our psychic subject.

It was reported in a recent special edition that during an hypnotic experiment in France, an ordinary working-class girl under the influence of suggestion, imagined herself to be a drunken fireman and then as the archbishop of Paris. Without vouching of course for the complete authenticity of this fact, I shall simply cite it as an example of the many cases of disturbed personalities, which have been adequately proven (to exist) and which are of interest to science.

It is evident that such facts, although few in number, undermine the imaginary certainty regarding our personal self-consciousness or our general certainty of the actual and not merely formal or phenomenological identity of our Ego. The very fact of dreaming and not so much the number of dreams, which is of importance to the cartesian doubting in the reality of the external world. Speaking in philosophical terms, we cannot have an absolute and external criterion for the normalcy of our states, or a ready-made proof in a given case for the absence of hypnosis, or anything of the sort. Even in layman's language, since the sleeping person does not usually know that he is asleep, and vaguely considers himself healthy, or more correctly, does not question the difference in these states, similarly, a hypnotized person is not being aware of his condition and readily accepts outside suggestions as his own self-consciousness. It should be noted here, that the formal or phenomenological subject does not change at all in this case: "I", "me", "mine", remain as if nothing had happened. This is not surprising: nothing changes in the subject of consciousness, since it contains nothing in itself – it is only a form which can equally accommodate psychic material of any individuality, that of a seamstress, a fireman, and an archbishop.

If in the normal course of life, doubt in one's personal existence or in the identity of one's personality is of no practical consequence, then the current pseudo-rational ideas which are in contrast to this doubt, can even less be taken seriously in a philosophical sense. It is pointed out, for instance, that the hypnotic substitution of consciousness is a transient, temporary state produced by definite artificial means, while normal consciousness of one's personal identity is constant and bound up with the sum of past experience. I am not speaking of the fact that the bifurcation and disturbance of personality is sometimes of long duration; it is true only periodically and independently of external apparent hypnotization, but the above objection can only have meaning for naive realism.

I imagine of course, that is it not since yesterday that I am conscious of this and of no other subject, my self-consciousness embraces a considerable sum of past phenomena (events). What is this "sum" of the past? It exists in fact at a given moment as only a "recollection", i.e. as a state of consciousness inseparable from what I experience "now", and it is self-evident that in the case of the illusion of self-consciousness it includes also the illusion of memory. Being conscious of myself as a doctor of philosophy and not as the queen of Madagascar, I can naturally recollect, i.e. imagine as the past, the university discussions, the lectures, the published works, rather than any scenes from African life. Instead of serving as proof of my personal identity, this could be an association of illusions in time similar to an association of illusions in space, seen in a dream. Thus, when transported in a dream to Scotland, I see Scottish lochs and moors. The seamstress who imagined herself to be the archbishop of Paris, if asked to recollect, would in all probability recollect not how she was sent to train as a seamstress, but how she was ordained into holy orders.

We have not as yet succeeded in arriving at the genuine subject of the inner world. On the one hand, there is the self-evident but completely empty form of consciousness, and on the other, there is the abundant but illusive content. We have already pointed the way to a certain plausible method of breaking this vicious circle, namely, by regarding the subject as a "potential" of psychological existence, capable of experiencing all that which forms our entire empirical activity. But such a concession to the methodical doubt, the concept of the psyche as an enduring potential cannot be disregarded without a careful examination of its form in the context of theoretical philosophy.

We are not dealing here with a straight fact of consciousness, but with a product of reflection, with an abstract concept. For instance, when we observe that the oak tree does not grow from any kind of seed, but solely from an acorn, in which nevertheless are absent the definite forms and properties of the grown oak, just as they are in any other object, then one cannot help but admit that the oak as a real object is contained in the acorn, since this contradicts the obvious, or to deny that it does not exist at all, since it would have arisen out of nothing. We distinguish two states of being – the actual and the potential (the real and the possible), and say that the acorn is a potential oak tree. Nothing prevents us from organizing our thoughts in this manner, but we must remember that the oaks, the acorns, and consequently the necessary relations between them are indeed only a part of that external world whose real existence is still in doubt.

Another source of the idea of the potential, which is closer to the goal, and clearly more reliable, is found in inner experience. When we awake from a dream, we find our psychic life in the same state and condition in which it was in our recollection prior to falling asleep. In view of this, we say therefore, that this life existed during the dream as a potential or in a hidden state. In such cases, the concept of the potential is abstracted from the facts of relativity and impermanency of our waking state or real consciousness.

Perhaps the concept of the potential substance is not very far from the truth, in any case, it is the product of reflection which demands philosophical verification, and not a direct datum of consciousness. It is also apparent that the definition of the psyche, as a special potential can only have meaning on the basis of a presupposed identity of the individual subject, hence, cannot itself serve as a basis for confirming this identity. Supposing that I am today really the same as I was yesterday according to my present recollection, I then conclude that there is in me some indestructible intervening state of actual unconsciousness or "other-consciousness" (*inosoznatel'nost'*). But it is precisely the genuine identity of personality that needs to be proven. Only the given recollection vouches directly for this identity, but it can be as erroneous in time as sense perception is erroneous in space. Simply because I remember in detail what happened yesterday, does not follow that yesterday could not be today's illusion.

Hence, the concept of the psyche as a potential cannot serve as a firm support for a philosophical conviction in the authenticity or genuine existence of the psychic subject, since this idea itself, in order to serve as proof of something that exists, is still in need of support and justification. Consequently, we have to apply this preliminary doubt to both sides of the thinker, both to the objects of the external world and to the subject of personal psychic life.

There is one thing which cannot be doubted, and that is, "actual" reality, the fact "as such", or what "is given". We are conscious of the presence of certain sensations, thoughts, feelings, desires, therefore they exist as such, as cognizable or as states of consciousness. The question is usually asked at this point: "whose" consciousness? This seems to imply that this very question in a predetermined way points to the real participation in the activity of consciousness, our Ego, as a genuine subject, a potential, or as a substance, etc.

This was once my view, and from this view I argued in my Master's dissertation [9] against Hegelian panlogism and Mill's panphenomenalism. When I recently re-examined the basic concepts of theoretical philosophy, I realized that this point of view was far from being self-evident certainty as I had imagined. The fact is, that not only must every answer be carefully verified by thought, but the same applies to every question.

Normally, one may ask, without thinking, "Whose coat, or whose boots?". But by what right can we ask in philosophy, "Whose consciousness?" thereby presupposing a real presence of various "Who" (*kto*) which necessarily attributes consciousness to private or communal ownership. The question itself is a philosophically-inadmissible expression of a dogmatic certitude in the unrelated and self-identified existence of individual beings. It is precisely this certitude that demands verification and justification by irrefutable logical conclusions from self-evident data.

At this point, the question, "Whose" is this consciousness, or to whom do the given psychic facts belong (which are the point of departure of philosophical reflection), it can, and must be answered, "We do not know": perhaps to some empirical individuality, to Tom, Dick and Harry, to the Parisian seamstress, who imagined herself to be the archbishop of Paris, or to an archbishop who imagines himself to be a seamstress. Finally, perhaps it belongs to that general transcendental subject, who, for reasons completely unknown "a priori", fell into the illusion of consciousness, or was split into a multitude of imaginary persons, similar to those produced in dreams. Which of these posibilities has the advantage of certainty, can clearly be determined only by investigation, since not only Tom and Dick, or the seamstress or the archbishop, or even the transcendental subject itself, none of these represents an immediate given fact of consciousnes, but only an expression of psychologically-mediated certitude which demands its own logical justification.

The purpose of the previous reflections was not to assert some positive truth or to refute some erroneous view accepted as truth, but only to delimit the "indisputable" area of "actual" consciousness from the area of affirmative and negative views, beliefs and convictions, which may prove to be true or false, but which have already proven to be

[9] *The Crisis of Western Philosophy* (Moscow, 1874).

"disputable". The sole interest here is to safeguard the source of philosophical thinking from any extraneous influences. The founders of modern philosophy, Bacon and Descartes, especially the latter, were guided by this interest. Had he remained thoroughly true to his principle of methodical doubt, future thinkers would not have had to begin theoretical philosophy from the beginning.

The argument against cartesianism in the present discussion is not concerned with any idea of Descartes, but is directed against his rejection of doubt before a specific idea. Descartes' preliminary skepticism proved to be onesided without any serious attempt to explain and justify this onesidedness. He ably differentiated between the indisputable and the disputable, the actual and the conjectured with reference to external objects. That table and books which I see before me is something indisputable and actual in the sense of being present in consciousness as a representation with its distinguishing geometrical and sensory signs (it is indisputable, if I see a table, then neither I nor any one else would suggest that I see a camel); but then the question arises: what is this table in terms of reality, is it a dream or is it a reality wholly conditioned by the nature of the subject experiencing it, or is it a real object or thing independent of the subject, (and to what extent, and from what aspect is it independent?). Any of the answers may be true, i.e. all these answers at first (prior to investigation and proof) are essentialy merely disputable premises. If any of these were indisputable, then there would be no problem, and if it were not a hypothesis but an obvious reality, then the other hypotheses which exclude this one, would contradict the obvious, which would be unthinkable.

Moreover, a similar distinction between the actual and the conjectured, the indisputable and disputable is also found in regard to the subject, which is cognized as something distinct from other phenomena. Inasmuch as the mental distinction of the Ego from that which is not, is present in a given consciousness, the Ego must be recognized as an indisputable fact. Is the distinction between the Ego and non-Ego made on the ground of a given idea of an external object, or on the ground of feelings, desires, efforts, or does it occur purely theoretically in abstract thought or reflection? In all these cases, since the differentiation of the subject both from everything else and from its own states "is present" in these very states, the Ego must be recognized an indisputable and actual fact. This is unquestionable. No one can doubt the fact that Ego when it is cognized. The question then arises: what is the Ego? Is it exhausted by its own apparent or phenomenological existence about which there is no doubt? Is it only one of a number of psychic states, is it an idea like any other idea, a phenomenon among other phenomena (the view of the English psychological school)? Or is it something special and unique of its kind, not one of the phenomena, but a universal formal condition of everything, an "a priori" binding act of thought, coexisting (*soprisuschii*) "implicite", although imperceptibly, in every phenomenon, yet not outside this binding function (Kant's position)? Or, finally, is the Ego some supra-phenomenal essence or substance, the real centre of psychic life, having a personal existence apart from its states (a view vaguely accepted by Descartes, and with more clarity and in more detail defended by recent spiritualists, lately in Russia, by Professor Lopatin).

The interminable dispute between these three views shows quite clearly that not one of them can be considered to be indisputable; that is all I wish to state without any foregone conclusions. Clearly, it is a question of the truth or falsity of a certain premise and not of the self-evidence of an actual fact. Let us suppose, for example, that the existence of our Ego or psyche as a substance were given directly in the actual states of consciousness, then it is obvious that there could be no question or doubt about this existence, just as there can be no question or doubt about the presence in consciousness of some idea, aberration or desire, when they actually are present there. When there is a question or a dispute, it is obvious that we are dealing with the truth of a premise and not with the reality of a fact. Truth (*istina*) can be a datum (*danna*), hidden, requiring investigation and discovery; but a non-datum (*ne-dannaya*) hidden, disclosable reality is a "contradictio in adjecto", i.e. it is nonsense.

Everybody has a philosophical right to assert and prove that the psyche is a real essence or substance, that it is the truth, but no one, without violating logic, can assert and prove that this truth is an actual fact. If it was actually given in real consciousness, it would already be proven, and if it was not given (in consciousness) it would be senseless to prove that something that is not given is given.

The psychic reality which is given, or more accurately, may be given, in consciousness, or the psychic process as such, does not depend on any views. The fact of the presence or absence of something in consciousness is the same from all points of view. Hence, it is obvious that we have no preference for that view which dwells more persistently on this reality and recognizes this reality alone. Simply because actual facts exist, does not follow that nothing else exists, and because this reality is known to us in the form of pure consciousness does not follow that there is no other way of that which "is" (*est'*).

We must differentiate between that which is given subjectively – (*danny*) and that which is given externally – (*zadanny*), between actuality and hypotheses. But to differentiate between them does not mean to be limited to one of them. Only primitive minds live by one psychic reality, just as only primitive economies exist with one natural property.

On the basis of actual consciousness there is a desire to go beyond its limits. Amidst the uncertain motley of empirical phenomena there is the search for something more stable and more true. We are not yet in a position to state whither this search will lead us, but it is obvious that the search itself is something that is certain. If the actuality of consciousness does not satisfy us, or the current of psychic states and phenomena, then it is clear that we have something else besides it: A + b cannot equal A.

We have defined the area of pure consciousness or psychic reality. This area which offers self-evident data must be the point of departure for philosophy. We see that truth here is not given (internally) (*dana*) but is only given (from outside, *zadana*). If truth were a fact of actual consciousness, it would be needless and impossible to search for it, hence, there could be no philosophy. But to the displeasure of some and the comfort of others philosophy "is" (*est'*). There is actual reality and there is a demand for something other, something greater. There is "consciousness of fact", and there is a 'yearning" for a "knowledge" of the "truth". We shall see whither this will lead us.

BIOGRAPHICAL SKETCH

Sergei Alekseyevich Askol'dov (1870-1945) was the son of the wellknown philosopher, A. A. Kozlov. After graduation from the Faculty of Science at St. Petersburg University, he accepted a position with the government, as a chemist. It was not until the age of forty that he turned to academic life. His early work, "Fundamental Problems of Ontology and Theory of Knowledge" which appeared in 1900, was written under the influence of his father's 'panpsychism' to which he wholly subscribed. In 1914 his book "Thought and Reality" appeared which dealt primarily with the theory of knowledge. This book was his M.A. dissertation which he obtained from the University of Moscow. The present selection is a summary of his introductory speech he made in defending his dissertation at a public meeting before the Historical-Philological Faculty of the Imperial University of Moscow, on November 16, 1914. It appeared in *Voprosy filosofii i Psikhologii* (Bk. 125, pp. 781-796).

His epistemological views are more profound than that of Kozlov. He is strongly opposed to the anti-psychologism which was so fashionable at the time. He insists that "individual" consciousness forms the sole basis of his epistemology which is concerned with 'pure experience'. He speaks more of cognition, which is more impersonal, than of knowledge. The two basic sources of cognition are: (a) immediate consciousness, which is a primitive reality, and (b) thought. Cognition begins with reality itself. This does away with the distinction between the "real" and the conceived.

In 1921 he founded a secret religio-philosophical organization which came to be known as "The Brotherhood of St. Seraphic of Sarove". The members of this organization along with Askol'dov were arrested in 1928. He spent seven years in the Urals as an exile, in 1941 after the German invasion of Novgorod, where he was now living, he escaped to the West. There he published a number of important articles. He died in Potsdam in 1945. His chief works are: "The Fundamental Problems of the Theory of Knowledge and Ontology"; "In Defense of the Miraculous"; "On Love for God and for One's Neighbour"; "A. A. Kozlov"; "Thought and Reality"; "Consciousness as a Whole"; "Time"; "Spirit and Matter". He also wrote a number of critical articles on A. I. Vvedenski and on Lossky.

Askol'dov is his penname. His real surname is Alexeyev. For some legal reasons he could not inherit his father's name.

S. A. Askol'dov

THE INNER CRISIS OF
TRANSCENDENTAL IDEALISM

Philohophy has always been a battleground of ideas and arguments. Heraclitus, Plato, Aristotle, Bruno, Leibniz, Kant, Schelling, Schopenhauer, and many other philosophers, developed their points of view in one form or another of either a courteous discussion or a far from courteois polemic, depending on the temperament and asperity of their disagreement. Not a single science can offer us an example of such a keen and persistent disagreement as does philosophy. The reason for this is to be found in the fact that in philosophy one can argue about any subject in contrast to the indisputable facts offered by science. This is due to the fact that it is precisely in philosophy that the higher values of the human spirit are expressed and at the same time constitutes the ultimate mainspring of the human will. In this respect philosophy is similar to religion. Every philosophy in the final analysis either confirms or rejects religion. Even if it ignores religion, it becomes a substitute for it, and hence negates it. Its religious significance is inherent precisely in this dilemma, and at the same time the justification for all philosophical battles.

One can always find among the various philosophical themes and the resulting arguments some central area of philosophical interest. Prior to Kant, the centre of attention was undoubtedly the ontological problem, i.e., the problem of the essence of the world and its nature. There were periods, for example, during the Middle Ages, when this basic question assumed an explicitly religious form when philosophy became the battleground for different theological doctrines, or the struggle between theology and unbelief. With Kant, the ontological problem, while not losing its importance, was relegated to a secondary position, since its solution was entirely dependent upon the solution of the epistemological problem. By his "Copernican Act" Kant rejected the very possibility of an ontology, i.e. of a metaphysics. This negation of the ontological problem was of course, not new even prior to Kant. Kant, however, completely revolutionized this problem. As a matter of fact, all philosophers before Kant who maintained that the world was unknowable, based their arguments on such premises that they arrived at a general philosophical skepticism. By undermining the faith in metaphysics they also undermined the faith in all other knowledge, i.e. they brought about the overthrow of science. This was especially evident in Hume who even cast doubts on the validity of mathematics. It was only in the Kantian system that the reaction against metaphysics assumed such a skillful constructive form, that by rejecting metaphysics, the exact sciences not only did not suffer, but on the contrary, were more firmly established. As a result Kantian epistemology became the last stronghold for philosophical positivism, while at the same time it became the focal battleground of ideas.

It would be very wrong to think that the Kantian system solved only the question of the possibility or impossibility of metaphysics, or that Kant was an impartial judge, or at any rate a neutral authority who reconciled some enemies, or more correctly, eliminated from the philosophical arena two opposing sides, i.e. materialist and spiritualists, theologians and atheists. Perhaps Kant as a historical person, was such a reconciler, but his system by reason of its inherent ideas its results unquestionably went beyond the intentions and plans of its founder.

As a matter of fact, "criticism",[10] in its basic presuppositions is a trend full of profound tendencies, which is manifested both as a purely theoretical and religio-moral property. As pure phenomenalism in the realm of scientific theory, criticism, which constructed the known world based on the valid laws of reason, produces a completely defined theoretical or scientific picture of reality, which inevitably assumes a mechanical aspect. In rejecting materialism as a metaphysical system, criticism subjected the phenomenal world (knowable) to the same "elementary" causality peculiar to materialism. To be sure, it equally rejected causality over freedom, a causality resulting from things-in-themselves. What, however, was the role of this free causality in the theoretical construction of the world? Naturally, the word "freedom" in Kant was only a stimulus to the will and not to thought, since the concept of freedom is definitely excluded from any critical theory of the reality of the world. Theoretical reason must regard the world exclusively in a deterministic manner. At best the protagonists of criticism must have two theories of the world: one based on the "Critique of

10   By Criticism, is meant critical idealism, or transcendental idealism.

Pure Reason" and the other on "Critique of Practical Reason". Even by disregarding the difficulty of such a combination, it is quite obvious that a valid theory in the full sense of the word, is one which is based upon the "Critique of Pure Reason", since that theory which is based on the "Critique of Practical Reason" is merely the general basis for freedom. For all its moral enthusiasm it possesses no moral guidance, since its principle remains purely formal and does not tell us what precisely free will demands from man. Even if we introduced into the formal ethical law of Kant the borrowed humanistic principle, we would have nothing but a humanistic ethics, which wrongly calls itself a religion. In fact this ethics provides no support for establishing communion between man and God, since all Christian doctrines (dogmas) are only of a moral-symbolic importance. Thus, if the prospects of criticism for scientific "elementarism" are very broad, they are very narrow for religion, if one can speak of any prospects for them at all. That this is a fact is clearly proven by the history of philosophical thought after Kant. Pure criticism which remained loyal to the Kantian rejection of metaphysics, i.e. which adhered mainly to the "Critique of Pure Reason", gave rise to the so-called neo-Kantianism. In addition to the tremendous work done in the exposition of Kant and firm reha- bilitation of his "Copernican Act", we find that there is a broad devel- opment of positivism of a rationalistic nature, which reached full devel- opment in the Marburg School and which led to a purely mathematical interpretation of reality, i.e. to the culminating point of "elementa- rism".[11]

But if we consider the fullest manifestation of the trends of criticism as exemplified by the German idealists, Fichte, Schelling and Hegel (before 1809) even though these have undergone considerable change having become a full metaphysics, nevertheless, even here the fetters (okoby) imposed by Kant upon philosophical thought are still very much in evidence. Hegel's metaphysics and philosophy of religion, who is perhaps the most complete Kantian, assumes the type of humanism where Christianity as a whole is only given a symbolic meaning. In the final analysis everything is achieved by human efforts and human philosophy which is the final expression of religious truth.

[11] We now come to the term "elementarism". We justify the coining of this term because of the deficiency in the earlier highly specialized designations: "Materialism", "Positivism", "Phenomenalism", "Energism", which in various ways and nuances lead to one and the same idea of combining, at times by simple summation, a whole out of its component elements (atoms, forces, phenomena, numbers, etc.) according to the laws of blind causality or mathematical calcula- tion. One must single out this general feature of the above trends: it is precisely here that the core of the matter is to be noted, rather to be concerned how and from what elements or epistemological method are the higher unities of life formed.

Thus, criticism is essentially not a proclamation of philosophical world view and a broad synthesis, but is only one of the litigant aspects, namely, an apotheosis of human reason and human morality. Our characterization of this litigant aspect would be incomplete, if we merely dwelt on the specific imperative nature of criticism. No other philosophy was able to control the minds, and to such an extend, as did the philosophy of criticism. Kant and his followers, like no other philosophers in history, always regarded themselves to be the supreme judges of philosophical truth and they manifested this self-consciousness in divers manners. Here we have all the transitional stages beginning with Fichte's 'thunder and lightning" foisted upon the ignorant public and the "servile thinking philosophers" who were unable to understand his "clear as day" treatise, to the more civil contemporary followers of Kant, who at the same time scorned those "who still stagnate in their dogmatic slumber" and do not understand Kant's work.

This peculiarity of the critical school is far from unimportant, if we keep in mind that it creates the mood and authority. It is precisely because of this, that even in Russia, it is expected for example, for even a beginner in philosophy, to be acquainted with Rickert, Husserl, while at the same time it is quite permissible for one not to be acquainted with Teichmuler, or the works of Vladimir Solevyev and other Russian philosophers, even though these would be of far greater educational value. One could find echos of the greatest claims of transcendental idealism in another area, but this would be trespassing into another area, which I refuse to do. I only wish to emphasize the point that the controversy with criticism is the basic controversy in modern philosophy upon which depends all its future. In solving this problem one way or another, many other problems are so to speak solved.

If we now turn to an examination of the state of criticism in modern philosophy, we are forced to say that the ideas formulated by Kant have undergone substantial changes. To criticize at the present time the historical Kant would to a certain extent, be an anachronism, since his followers and successors have themselves deviated not only from the letter, but even from certain basic concepts of his teaching and only remained true to his spirit and direction. Of course, one must reckon with criticism only in its completed forms. It is necessary to note first of all, the extremely complex and variegated forms of criticism. Philosophy has never encountered such intricate and artificial construction, as we encounter in our days. The connection of these constructions with the fundamental philosophical theme is frequently completely unclear.

One cannot for example, immediately perceive why there is so much emphasis on "anti-psychologism" in modern literature; why there is an exclusive development of the "philosophy of mathematics", or why many philosophers have established a specific category of "non-being", etc. However, there are some common principles in all these varieties of modern critical epistemology, which bind the details of thought into one whole, thus one may speak in general about criticism which is the same as transcendental idealism, leaving out individual differences and details of the various schools.

Modern transcendental idealism is represented by three fundamental schools: (1) Immanental philosophy; (2) The Marburg School, and (3) The school represented by Windelband, Rickert, etc. In spite of the differences peculiar to these three schools they hold basically three theses in common, with various nuances. The first thesis may be called "the position of immanence" which asserts that every cognizable object is always something given to consciousness or thought in one way or another, or is even generated by thought, and that generally in the realm of being there is nothing beyond the limits of consciousness and thought, i.e. transcendent to them. This thesis is quite new as far as Kant is concerned, since Kant affirmed only that the transcendent was unknowable, without denying explicitly and categorically its existence.

The second thesis logically follows from the first. If knowledge is not concerned with something that is beyond its limits, then it can neither represent or reproduce anything. It follows that the above concept of knowledge as a representative function, i.e. capable of reproducing objects, cannot be maintained. An object of knowledge is constructed from the laws of human thought itself, but is not in any way thrust upon him by external experience. One may call this thesis "autonomy of thought" in contradistinction to the old concept that thought is a representation. Finally, the third thesis of criticism, namely, that of "anti-psychologism" is also quite readily connected with the first two theses. In fact, if knowledge does not represent anything, if it is developed solely by the laws of reason itself, then this knowledge which is differentiated by internal, and hence by absolute necessity, is purely logical knowledge. It does not arise in the psyche as a result of the effects of external objects, and generally, has no basis for its origin, especially in its ideal content. Consequently, psychological conditions for the origin of human knowledge by no means justify its truth. Knowledge is obligatory and is fully independent of its origin in consciousness. This in fact constitutes the essence of anti-psychologism.

These three principles, immanentism, autonomy of thought, and anti-psychologism are the three fundamental tenets of transcendental idealism. If only one of these tenets is refuted the others must also fall and along with them the entire structure of criticism. In fact, if the object of cognition is not immanent in thought or consciousness, it means that it is found outside consciousness and is like some essence whose inner nature is yet to be disclosed. Then thought is faced precisely with the same problem that metaphysicians have wrestled with throughout the ages, namely, knowledge or "things-in-themselves". Thus, by admitting the transcendentality of the object of knowledge criticism is threatened with a continuous incursion into metaphysics. This is also the case with the concept of representational knowledge. If criticism would admit that knowledge by right reproduces something external to it, and that this in fact is its true function, then it would at the same time admit the transcendentality of the object of knowledge and along with it knowledge of "things-in-themselves". Extreme anti-psychologism is equally inevitable for criticism, because criticism wishes to use anti-psychologism as a criterion for the truth of knowledge without any reference to its origin. This is necessary for criticism because it is only thus that it can avoid an absolute apriorism of knowledge in its whole structure. And transcendental idealism stands or falls with the theory of absolute apriorism. In order to maintain apriorism of knowledge it must be based on purely formal laws, i.e. on pure logic. In the final analysis critical idealism is more concerned with the assertion of the coincidence of the theory of knowledge with logic than with anything else. This is true, because only within the framework of logical deductions is it possible to maintain, with some validity, that pure thought can produce knowledge and that its object is created by thought. The fact that the deduction of such a rationalized nature leads to its expression in mathematical schemas clearly follows from what has been stated above.

There are many approaches and possibilities of criticizing the fundamental positions of transcendental idealism, depending upon the particular features of any given School. I shall not deal with them here. I shall simply restrict myself to a consideration of the inner ideological crisis which is to be found in every variety of criticism. I maintain that in each of the above-mentioned schools a determined evolution of ideas is taking place which results in the abolition of the very foundations of transcendental idealism. This so to speak, inner, unconscious self-criticism of transcendental idealism is no less decisive than criticism from "the outside". Since thus far it received very little attention, I am taking the liberty of dealing with it now.

Let us bear in mind the fundamental assertion of transcendental idealism, or in other words, the idea of Kant's "Copernican Act". This idea consists of the fact that all reality, the whole universe, the perceived as well as the cognized (world) is constructed by the knowing

subject by the laws of pure thought.[12] This assertion inevitably leads
to the question: What then is this subject that knows and at the same
time creates its own knowledge? One possible answer is, that this subject is partly individual and partly collective; each person individually
and all people together. In fact this answer is to some extent found in
Kant himself. At least, it is precisely for this concept in psychologism
that Kant is reproached even by his followers. Kant however, pointed
to another solution of the problem. The creation of the world occurs
neither in individual or collective cognition, but in the cognizing function of reason "in general" or thought "in general". This term "in
general" is quite prevalent in Kant, since he understands reason,
thought, knowledge, as being purely epistemological, i.e. "in general".
What then is this reason "in general" which at the same time presupposes also the subject "in general"? This is indeed a simple human
abstraction, a certain general concept about the uniformity of cognizable
forms in thinking beings.

This term "in general" should at least be understood in accordance
with the demands of the critics themselves, namely, to repudiate every
kind of psychology in epistemology, and indeed, to repudiate both individual and collective subjects and even humanity as a whole. However, it is absolutely impossible to seriously insist that all the creative
potentials which produce a world of thought, are attributable to this
abstraction, i.e. to the simple concept of some kind of "in general".
Hence, transcendental idealism is forced to attribute to this abstraction, some kind of objective character, since this "a priori" universal-
creative knowledge belongs to someone. And if this "some one" is man,
even though he is collective man, without saying anything about the
"sin" of psychologism, the whole universe becomes pure illusion. Obviously this "someone" is neither man, nor people, nor humanity,
however, it is not any kind of "in general" (voobsche). Undoubtedly,
this is some sort of potentiality outside man. If this truth is admitted,
then transcendental idealism becomes an objective, and by a rigorous
application of the principles of apriorism, an absolute idealism. Indeed
such a transformation already took place once in the first half of the
nineteenth century in Fichte, Schelling and Hegel. That this transformation is an inherent necessity in criticism is proven by the fact that
both Fichte and Schelling were ardent Kantians, and were deeply convinced that they remained true Kantians, if not in letter at least in
spirit. However, in Schelling and later in Hegel, this transformation was

---

[12] According to Kant, it is absolutely necessary for cognition, to have the feature
of sensual intuition. However, this feature offers us only a special type of empiricism, by postulating only sensual "material" without the slightest addition on
the part of empiricism "forms" and "structures".

a clear return to metaphysics, hence, to a direct negation of the basic principles of criticism. Hegel already subjected Kant to a radical criticism. There then remained the alternative to either admit that Kant's efforts were fundamentally unsuccessful, or to start from the beginning. History embarked upon a new cycle of criticism in the person of Liebmann; [13] Neokantianism came into being. Thus, the inexorable logic of the inner evolution of ideas leads the second cycle in our time to the same results similar to the first cycle. In spite of the historical experience and the firm intention to interpret Kant is some other way, the whole complex work of reconstruction and interpretation of transcendental idealism leads to the same gradual fusion into the objective and even absolute idealism. Windelband, who is the most orthodox and most careful Kantian, already saw the inevitability of recognizing the Kantian "transcendental unity of apperception" as being something above individual unity. Schoppe [14] arrived at the concept of a "generic consciousness" or "ego" which differs little from a metaphysical being, as for example, Fichte's "ego".[15] Rickert's School speaks of transcendent "values", which while they are not real being, nevertheless somehow controls being, giving it meaning and sanction. A similar expression of the objectification of transcendental idealism is to be found in the Marburg School, as stated by Cogan [16] that creative thinking which produces knowledge, is of course, not human thinking. Similarly, as in the case of Fichte, Schelling and Hegel the system of categories which create knowledge have little by little been again transferred from man into a reality external to him, and has already assumed something of the nature of "universal reason", carefully designated by hazy terms, such as "consciousness in general", "a system of values", "non-human thinking", and various other kinds of epistemological "generalities". But is not this universal reason some kind of "thing-in-itself"? Further-

[13]   O. Liebmann, German Philosopher born 1840, author of *Analyse der Wirklichkeit*.

[14]   Caspar Schoppe, German Philosopher, author of *Elementa Stoicae Philosophiae Morales* (Mainz, 1606).

[15]   It is quite natural, that both Schoppe and his followers refuse to regard "generic consciousness" as some kind of hypostatized being. It is true that at times Schoppe may be so understood, i.e. that outside individual concrete consciousness generic consciousness does not exist at all. However, at the same time he ascribes to it unity and ontological significance. Moreover, it is the very thing which in Schoppe's system gives objective value and ontological permanence to everything that does not enter into individual consciousness (for example, all objects that cannot be seen by anybody). All these concepts are, of course, difficult to reconcile. It is evident, that in Schoppe's system the concept of generic consciousness "operates" as a metaphysical concept, but presents itself as an epistemological one.

[16]   T. Cogan, Utilitarian author of *Philosophical Treatise on the Passions* (1802).

more, is not this "Thing-in-itself" disclosed in a cognitive sense by the very fact that something is being affirmed about it? It is not obvious that both objective and absolute idealism, whether explicit or implicit, is already a certain type of metaphysics, hence, a philosophy which repudiates the Kantian point of view, and that it differs from it basically, i.e. in the "Copernican" sense; since it would appear that there is something beyond human knowledge, which is not created by it, but on the contrary, controls it, namely, universal reason. Is it not a metaphysical idea which had its origin in the very heart of epistemology? Is it not the enemy which has penetrated into the fortress surreptitiously in a carefully disguised form? Other enemies of criticism followed. Objective idealism naturally leads to epistemological empiricism. As a matter of fact, ideas which have become crystallized in nature appear at first to man as something irrational and only empirical. These must first of all be regarded as being factual. It is only in the evolution of knowledge that these blind facts are illumined by their ideal content, enabling us to rationally connect one with the other. Schelling recognized essentially this truth during the period of the philosophy of identity; it is implicitly recognized by Rickert's school.[17] No matter how much the supra-human and universal sources of knowledge are camouflaged by epistemological terminology, it inevitably confronts the human mind as some "thing-in-itself" hence, is discovered somehow or other. Thus, that epistemological apparatus whose purpose it was to destroy metaphysics, unwillingly introduces a philosophical idea into this forbidden territory. This truth has been clearly and definitely demonstrated by history in the first cycle of German idealism from Fichte to Hegel. The same truth has been demonstrated by the second cycle in our day, only in less vivid manner, under constant obscure metaphysical concepts and hazy terminology. One can easily recognize Fichte's fundamental philosophical idea in both Schoppe's and Rickert's basic philosophical ideas. No less striking is the similarity between Hegel and Cogan. Indeed, if there was another return to Kant, the new variation on a theme which has been played twice, would be repeated for a third time. It is quite obvious that the vague term "in general" cannot be the alpha and omega of knowledge. It would seem, that if this is true, it follows that the defenders of metaphysics must fight against criticism. Would it not be better for transcendental idealism to work out its own contradictions?

We must give a negative reply to such a possible suggestion. Even if there is in transcendental idealism an inevitable evolution which would lead it to a metaphysics, this metaphysics would always be "sui

---

[17] H. Rickert, German Philosopher, author of *Grenzen der Naturwissenschaftlichen Begriffsbildung* (1896).

generis". The despotism of pure reason makes itself felt even in the ontology which in the final analysis gives rise to it. The architechtonics of categories inevitably become a system of ideas which are in themselves real, and the logic of pure knowledge becomes a panlogism of being. Metaphysical idealism is the natural outcome of Kant's work. It is rather ironic that the philosopher, who, more than anyone else was against the wrong application of rational principles, namely, the construction of "things-in-themselves" from forms of pure thought, turns out to be the father of a more rational metaphysics. In fact, how modest are the ontological proofs of Anselm and Descartes, or Leibniz's monadology and even Spinoza's ethics in comparison with Hegel's and Cogan's schemes to deduce all categories of being from nothing, by means of dialictics. Is not this the height of arrogance and pretention when they seek to construct extra-experiential knowledge from pure forms of thought. But this is not all. If only this metaphysics of pure reason were a crystal-clear system, similar to the pre-Kantian systems of Spinoza or even Descartes and Leibniz. But this is not the case. Hegel's system – the most ingenious perfection of Kant's work – is the most ambigious philosophy. This philosophy (Hegel's) in its concrete content possesses a tremendous wealth of thought, which is capable of being incorporated into very many systems of concrete spiritualism, in its general configuration, in its highest principle of a self-creating "Idea", turns out to be very vague and is subject to various interpretations. If we were to retain as the Idea the complete ontological qualifications attributed to it by Hegel's philosophy, then it becomes indistinguishable from a self-evolving God. In this case, Hegelian idealism becomes only a particular form of spiritualism and thus loses half its originality. If we were to retain for the term "idea" its specific sense as being impersonal, without passion, without will, although it may be an all-powerful thinking form, then other indeterminates arise, since thinking forms cannot be empty. They always possess some kind of concrete content with which they are mutually enriched by definite vital meaning and importance. The abstract schemas of Hegelian idealism from this viewpoint, equally favour the incorporation of the rich psychological material of history as well as the material of the natural sciences. In its changing triad, the contradictions of philosophical constructions, the impassioned tempo of state revolutions, and the development of economic forms, and generally everything that is in one way or another evolutionary, all are equally at home in it.

But again history itself has shown how one could manipulate in different ways Hegel's schemas and the different interpretations that could be given to his final concepts. It would appear that Hegel could be interpreted in the spirit of orthodox Protestantism as well as in the negative spirit of Strauss, Bauer and Feuerbach. In general, on many fundamental questions (for example, the immortality of the soul), Hegel remained elusive and vague, like the first Idealist, Plato. It is in these features of idealism that its own self-criticism is found as some present judgment of history. Herein is the revenge for ignoring cognitive experience given to man in the self-consciousness of his personal "Ego", the image and likeness of the "Living God".

Therefore, having stated the obvious features of the crisis of transcendental idealism, one is inclined to exclaim with Liebmann, "go back . . .". But not merely back to Kant or Hegel, but even still further, to Leibniz, Plato and Aristotle, more correctly, back to pre-Kantian philosophical freedom of thought which has every way and means of uniting philosophy with religion. The above possibilities constitute the "sine qua non" for the advancement of philosophical thought.

BIOGRAPHICAL SKETCH

Nicolai Onufrievich Lossky (1870-1965) was born on December 6, 1870 in the village of Kreslavka, Vitebsk Province, Russia, where he received his early education. He studied at the University of St. Petersburg and graduated from the Faculty of Arts and Natural Science. He then went to Germany for post-graduate work where he studied under Windelband, Wundt, and G. E. Müller. In 1903 he obtained his Master's degree and four years later he was awarded the Doctorate degree.

Upon his return to Russia he was appointed Lecturer and later Associate Professor at his alma mater in St. Petersburg where he taught philosophy until 1921. In 1922 he was exiled from Russia by the Soviet Government because of his religious beliefs. He went to Prague upon the invitation of Thomas Masaryk, and was appointed Professor at the Russian University in Prague. He also taught at the Charles University in Prague and at the University of Bratislava. In 1946 he emigrated to the United States and was Professor at the St. Vladimir Russian Orthodox Seminary in New York City. After a lengthy illness he died in France in January 1965. Lossky was a prolific writer and is regarded as the dean of contemporary Russian philosophers. His books have been translated into many foreign languages.

Lossky's philosophical system cannot be explained in terms of one single idea or influence. It is a synthesis of a number of influences; the most pronounced influences are Leibnizian monadology and Bergsonian intuitionism. Lossky prefers to call his system Intuitivism or Ideal-realism. His system may be considered from the three central themes inherent in his Weltanschauung, namely, epistemology, metaphysics, and ethics.

EPISTEMOLOGY

Lossky's epistemological views were first outlined in his book, *The Intuitive Basis of Knowledge,* and were further expounded in *Sensory, Intellectual, and Mystical Intuition.* His epistemology may be characterised as a synthesis of ABSOLUTE

IMMANENTISM and ABSOLUTE INTUITIVISM. It is based on his assertion that "everything is immanent in everything else".

According to Lossky, we know an object IMMEDIATELY or INTUITIVELY. The object we INTUIT is not a copy or a representation, but is the REAL original object. There is no causal relation between subject and object. The connection between subject and object is achieved by an "epistemological co-ordination" which is supertemporal and superspatial. It is this "co-ordination" which makes knowledge possible for all substantival agents in the world. All human knowledge is experienced through SENSORY, INTELLECTUAL and MYSTICAL intuition. These three types of intuition correspond to his three kinds of being. All events of a non-spatio-temporal nature are called IDEAL BEING, such as relations between a quality and its bearer, number, unity, plurality, etc. All events of a spatio-temporal character are termed REAL BEING. The third kind of being is called METALOGICAL BEING, or the ABSOLUTE, which transcends the laws of identity, contradiction and the excluded middle. Lossky identifies intellectual intuition with thought, which reveals TRANS-SUBJECTIVE RELATIONS but does not create them. While the Absolute is a Supramundane Being, it is also an object of intuition. It is cognized by the subject through mystical intuition. By substituting "epistemological co-ordination" for "causal relation", Lossky does not really succeed in explaining how this "co-ordination" operates in relating object and subject. His epistemology is simply an ontology of cognition.

METAPHYSICS

Lossky's metaphysics is essentially a variation of Leibnizian monadology. Leibniz's "windowless" monads become for Lossky SUBSTANTIVAL AGENTS who can experience mutual interaction through intuition.

Lossky developed an intricate system of beings, which he calls HIERARCHICAL PERSONALISM. He begins with the lowest and simplest form of being, such as an atom, and proceeds up the scale of being leading to a higher form of being, such as man. He then introduces a supermundane Principle, or the Absolute in order to avoid a radical plurality and to make the unity of the cosmos intelligible. The Absolute creates potential beings, called SUBSTANTIVAL AGENTS. These AGENTS are supertemporal and superspatial who possess freedom of choice, which enables them to strive for a higher form of being. Thus, a human being may, through a period of billions of years, evolve from a proton. A POTENTIAL agent becomes an ACTUAL person, when he apprehends absolute values and recognizes the duty to apply them in his moral behaviour.

The Cosmos is the result of the constant mutual conflict between SUBSTANTIVAL AGENTS, which leads to the origin of space and time. Space and time are MODES of activity for the agents. Unity or CONSUBSTANTIALITY is preserved by the Absolute, who is incommensurable with the cosmos.

ETHICS

His ethical views flow directly from his metaphysics. They are based on the idea that EXISTENCE and VALUE are mutually related. The concept of freedom is central in his ethics. Since a man as an IDEAL self possesses freedom of choice, he may choose God who is Living Reality, or he may choose the path away from God, which Lossky terms the "basic moral evil". Man's ultimate destiny is to become the *ideal* self, which is the normative principle in his moral behaviour. His is an absolutistic ethics applicable to the *ideal* self.

Lossky's chief works are: "The Fundamental Doctrines of Psychology from the point of view of Voluntarism"; *The Intuitive Basis of Knowledge*; *The World as an Organic Whole*; *The Fundamental Problems of Epistemology*; *Freedom of Will*; *Value and Existence*; "Types of World-Views"; *Sensory, Intellectual and Mystical Intuition*; "Conditions of the Absolute Good"; "God and Cosmic Evil"; "The World as the Realization of Beauty", and a number of articles.

N. O. Lossky

AN EPISTEMOLOGICAL INTRODUCTION
INTO LOGIC*

EPISTEMOLOGY AND LOGIC

Epistemology, logic and the psychology of knowledge study from different points of view one and the same subject – knowledge. In order to find this out let us analyse knowledge. Knowledge is always a fact for someone's consciousness; when a scientist discovers that the specific gravity of chemically-pure iron is 7, 8, this knowledge is something of which he is conscious. Knowledge, then, is realized in consciousness, and therefore if we are to analyze it we must also analyse consciousness.

It is characteristic of consciousness that it always has two aspects: someone who is conscious and something of which he is conscious. Let us call the first aspect the *subject of consciousness,* and the second the *content of consciousness.* Between the subject and the content of consciousness there is a certain relation, the nature of which will be considered later; meanwhile the following circumstance should be noted: a content of consciousness such as knowledge is related not only to the conscious subject but to something else as well: all knowledge is of something. That to which the knowledge refers, is called the *object* of knnowledge. Thus, knowledge stands as it were between the knowing subject and the known object. True knowledge must somehow correspond to the object, must more or less express it.

In order to grasp clearly the structure of cognitive consciousness we must analyse the relation between the subject and the object, the rela-

* This selection is taken from Lossky's Brochure of above title (published by the Russian Free University, Prague, 1939), pp. 255-292. Some passages have been omitted.

tion between knowledge and the subject, and, finally, the relation between knowledge and the object.

THE RELATION BETWEEN THE SUBJECT AND THE OBJECT

Let us take, first, the relation between the knowing subject and the known object. The nature of that relation is regarded very differently by the representatives of different philosophical schools. Let us begin by considering the way in which the unsophisticated human mind conceives of this relation, apart from any philosophical theories. It is easy enough to find instances of such primitive conceptions.

The unsophisticated mind regards the acquisition of true knowledge about the world as a very simple matter; all that is required is to perceive a thing by means of vision, hearing, touch and so on. If a birch tree is growing in the forest glade, it is enough to direct attention upon it for it to enter the field of my consciousness as it is in itself. Such a conception of knowledge, or truth, and of the relation between the subject and the object is called NAIVE REALISM. It is called REALISM because it takes the contents of sense perception to be actual reality, and not subjective experiences. It is called naive because it is instinctive, unconscious, not based upon any theoretical reflection.

With this aim in view let us consider naive realism and bring to light the conceptions peculiar to it. Consciousness of truth is, from the point of view of naive realism, attained through the subject POSSESSING the object as it is in itself. In other words, it presupposes the closest possible nearness between truth and the object: not likeness of correspondence but complete coincidence or identity.

To understand how an object can enter one's field of consciousness, it is essential to distinguish between the following ideas. An object of the external world, such as a tree, for instance, can only be observed as it IS IN ITSELF, if, while being in the subject's consciousness, it nevertheless remains external to the subject as a person. To express it by a brief formula, an object such as the observed tree is immanent in the subject's consciousness but transcends the subject of consciousness, while such an object as grief is immanent both in the subject's consciousness and in the subject himself.[1]

There are, then, two aspects in consciousness – the subject and the object. Together they form the single whole of consciousness; consequently, there is a relation between them. What is this relation? Obviously it is not a spatial relation of nearness, contiguity etc., nor a

---

[1] The word IMMANENS means 'abiding within something' and the word TRANSCENDENS 'passing on somewhere or through something'.

temporal relation of succession or coexistence. It is a purely spiritual relation, the relation of having something in consciousness, not reducible to any other. We are immediately aware of it when we say. "I have such and such an object in mind". This relation conditions a special type of union between the subject and the object, making it possible even for objects of the external world to be contemplated by the knowing person as they are in themselves. It may therefore be called the COORDINATION of the subject and the object. To emphasise the fact that this type of coordination conditions the possibilty of truth, it should be called EPISTEMOLOGICAL COORDINATION. The immediate observation of the object by the subject arising in virtue of this relation, is intuition or contemplation.

In elaborating these conceptions we leave naive realism behind and develop a new epistemological theory that may be called Intuitivism. It is realistic, just as naive realism is, but of course it is not exhausted by the statements just formulated, which merely answer the question as to the relation between the subject and the object.

The intuitive conception of the relation between the subject and the object may be schematically expressed as follows:

$$E \quad \left|\begin{array}{l} A \\ B \\ C \end{array}\right.$$

The curved line symbolises the field of consciousness; E (ego) is the subject (the self); A B C is the object; the line joining E & A B C stands for the coordination of the subject and the object.

Thus we cognise not the actual object of the external world, but the states (the sensations) which arise in our body and our mental life under the influence of the object.

According to this view the image of the object is made up of the subject's mental states caused in him by the object. It is supposed that in the observer's mind there is a psychical tree (i.e. a mental image of the tree) which must as far as possible resemble the physical tree.

The better to understand the essence of the Intuitive and of the empirical theory of the type just referred to, let us bring out some of their characteristic features by contrasting them with each other.

Suppose that several subjects (two or even twenty) are observing one and the same object of the external world, e.g., a tree.

1. For empiricism, the relation between the object of the external world and the subject is causal action of the object upon the subject,

producing new states in him; in other words, it is a case of subordination of the subject to the object. For Intuitivism, the relation between the subject and the object is one of coordination; in so far as we are concerned with knowledge, and not with any other process that precedes or follows it, the relation is not one of inter-action but one of togetherness in virtue of which the subject contemplates and the object is contemplated. It is a purely THEORETICAL relation.

2. The following point of difference is particularly important. According to the intuitive theory the contemplated object may belong to the trans-subjective world; it need not form part of the subject's individuality, but may be a physical thing, an element in another individual life or belong to the realm of the super-individual. For empiricism on the other hand, all the contents of consciousness are resolved into the individual and mental states of the subject; the external world is accessible to observation not as it is in itself, but through the medium of IMAGES, formed in our minds out of sensations which are our subjective mental states.

3. Reducing, as it does, all the contents of consciousness to mental processes, individualistic empiricism is compelled to derive the properties of truth from the laws of mental life, which are established by psychology. Such a method of approaching the problem of knowledge is called PSYCHOLOGISM. At the present day it is recognised to be erroneous, since many obvious properties of truth cannot be deduced from the laws of psychical life. Intuitivism is opposed to the psychologistic method in epistemology and derives the properties of truth from the non-mental aspect which it discovers in consciousness.

4. The difference between the two theories may also be expressed as follows: According to the intuitive theory, the content immanent in consciousness may transcend the subject of consciousness, while for individualistic empiricism all that is immanent in consciousness must also be immanent in the subject of consciousness.

5. According to the intuitive theory truth is attained when the subject has in consciousness the object as IT IS IN ITSELF. For individualistic empiricism, on the other hand, truth about an external object is attained when the subject has in consciousness an IMAGE of the object which more or less corresponds to it (the representative theory of truth). The highest degree of correspondence would be reached if the image were an exact copy of the object. Let us consider whether this is possible.

The arguments in favour of the subjectivity of colours, smells, sounds etc., are applicable to the presentations of space and movement as well. Those who consider these arguments conclusive with regard to the former, are bound to go further and admit that space and movement are also only known to us as images existing in our minds, i.e., as our presentations, and that we do not know whether outside our minds there exists anything resembling them. Individualistic empiricism is then driven to the conclusion that not a single quality of the external world is knowable.

Thus, starting with its conception of the origin of knowledge individualistic empiricism is driven to the conclusion that the subject knows only his own impressions and cannot, by means of them, discover a single property of the external world.

Moreover, it follows from this, that the very existence of the external world cannot be proved with any degree of certainty. This result of individualistic empiricism has once and for all been stated by Hume who fearlessly expressed himself in favour of solipsism: "as to those impressions which arise from the senses, their ultimate cause is in my opinion, perfectly inexplicable by human reason, and will always be impossible to decide with certainty whether they arise immediately from the object, or are produced by the creative powers of the mind, or are derived from the author of our being." [2] Indeed, according to the view of individualistic empiricism we do not observe the external world directly, so that we can only prove its existence by means of AN IN-FERENCE. But according to empirical theories the essence of every inference consists not in discovering something essentially new but merely in mentally transferring the data of past experience into new surroundings (e.g., I had observed before that when it is very cold water freezes; now, observing that it is getting cold, I expect it to freeze). But if the immediate data of experience are merely my mental states, it follows that however I might combine them, whatever I might infer from them, I could never derive from them the knowledge of an external trans-subjective world.

Solipsism is the logically inevitable, and at the same time contra-dictory, result of individualistic empiricism, showing that its initial assumptions are invalid. Indeed, if knowledge of the external world is the product of CAUSAL action upon the subject from without the subject observes only his own mental states; but if he observes only his own mental states, he cannot know, or even suppose the existence of any causes external to himself.

The impass at which we thus arrive is due to the NATURALISTIC character of the empirical theory, to the assumption, namely, that knowledge of external objects is produced by causal interaction between those objects and the subject's body. The presence of such inter-action is so indisputable (the effect of light rays upon the eye, the vibra-tion of the ear-drum through contact with air waves, etc.) and so essen-

2   *Treatise*, Part III, section V, p. 84.

tial for the orgination of knowledge that it seems as though we had no choice but to agree with the fundamental assumptions of individualistic empiricism. But once we do so, we are bound to arrive at solipsism. For over two thousand years human thought has been struggling in this trap, unable to find a satisfactory way out. To get over this difficulty, we need a new hypothesis concerning the part played by the sense organs and the physiological processes in knowledge – a hypothesis which would explain how physiological processes, though they have a share in the GENESIS of knowledge, do not create the content of knowledge and from the epistemological point of view are, therefore, of secondary importance.

If a lamp is burning in the room, the rays from it fall upon my retina; the physiological process in the optical nerve reaches my central nervous system; after a number of changes in the nervous centres, the physiological process spreads from the cortex to the periphery of the body and expresses itself in some action, e.g., in my putting out the lamp. In this series of physical and physiological causes and effects, we cannot discover any COGNITIVE processes of perceiving the lamp or of judging "within twelve feet of me a lamp is burning". The whole series of these processes consists entirely of movements and cannot CREATE that which is of interest to the epistemologist – true or false judgements. And yet before I performed the action I had in mind the perception of the burning lamp or a judgement about it. How did it arise?

The following difficulty has now to be met. It seems as though according to the intuitive theory different observers must always perceive the same object exactly alike, down to the smallest detail; moreover, it would appear that every observer was bound to apprehend an external stimulus in exactly the same way, whether it affected his eye or his skin, etc. But as a matter of fact, this is not the case. The differences in perception are very well explained by thinkers who, like the individualistic empiricists, take the content of perception to be CAUSALLY conditioned by external stimulation, affecting the subject's mind or body. What is the intuitivist explanation of the facts in question? In the first place it must be pointed out that perception is contemplation NOT OF THE WHOLE CONTENT of an object but of a small part of it, which attracts our attention in accordance with our interests. The world always contains infinitely more than we apprehend. Perception is merely a selection of certain aspects of the object which are introduced from the subconscious into the sphere of consciousness. This explains, e.g., why two different stimulations affecting the same sense-organ are perceived in the same way (a ray of light affecting the retina gives a sensation of light, but if a finger is pressed on the eyeball, a circle of light is seen also). The ray of light falling upon the retina and the pressure on the eye-ball are complex events. They differ from each other on the whole but they may contain an identical aspect. It is possible, for instance, that the ray of light consists of, events a, b, c, and pressure – of events a, m, n. When the eye is stimulated we apprehend in both cases the aspect a, i, e light. Modern physical theories warrant the supposition that phenomena of light may arise in connection with pressure upon a hard body: such pressure must be accompanied by electro-magnetic disturbances, and light is conditioned by them. The sameness of perception in the two cases by no means proves the subjectivity of light.

The problem is solved in the same way as in the story told in the preface to Paulsen's INTRODUCTION to PHILOSOPHY: "two knights were disputing about the colour of a shield; one said it was white and the other that it was black. After a heated argument they began to fight. A third knight passing by asked what it was about and said: "Why, don't you see that the shield really is white on one side and black on the other?"

STRUCTURE OF THE OBJECT AND OF THE KNOWLEDGE ABOUT IT

Having considered the question of the relation between the subject and the object we can now pass to the second important problem of epistemology, namely, the structure of the object and of our knowledge about it. The three elements that have so far been indicated – the subject and the object and the epistemological coordination between them – do not exhaust the structure of knowledge. Any concrete example will show which aspect of knowledge has so far been left out of account. Suppose, as I walk down the garden, I see something on the path. Throwing a casual glance at it, I find that it is a leaf, and walk on. – If, however, I begin to wonder what kind of leaf it is, I return to it and observing its shape, say "It is a maple leaf". If subsequently a further question arises "What colour is it, it is of the same colour throughout?" I have to perform a new act of discrimination which will enable me to say "This maple leaf is yellow, with green at the base." This example shows that the epistemological coordination of the object with the subject makes the object ACCESSIBLE TO CONSCIOUSNESS but does not as such make it KNOWN. In order to know an object, the knowing person must perform a series of acts of attending, discriminating, comparing etc.; by means of these acts the object becomes known, though not entirely, but each time in some one respect (in respect of its shape, colour etc.). An indefinite number of cognitive acts may be directed upon the same object: every object is a fragment of the world infinitely rich in content and cannot be exhausted in human knowledge. Discrimination is ANALYSIS, separating out of the complex content of the object those aspects, knowledge of which satisfies the subject's interest in the object. Each particular aspect of the object cognised through attention and discrimination may be called a CONTENT OF KNOWLEDGE.

Attention, discrimination and such like activities of the subject constitute the SUBJECTIVE aspect of knowledge, while the object and the content of knowledge constitute its OBJECTIVE aspect.

The subjective aspect of knowledge consists in the subject's activities, which are "intentive acts" (attention, discrimination and so on).

There is a profound difference between the subjective and the objective aspects of knowledge. The subjective side i.e. the intentive act of knowing is always mental, is always a process (i.e. it happens in time), and takes place in a particular individual. In other words it is an individually mental process. The objective side of knowledge, on the other hand (i.e. the object and content) may be mental or physical, form part of the knowing person's or of anyone else's individuality or be superindividual, may be real or ideal (i.e. may exist in time, or be non-temporal).

The distinction between the subjective and the objective sides of knowledge is of the utmost importance to epistemology. Many errors are due to the failure to make that distinction and to transferring the characteristics of the subjective (i.e. the individually mental) side of knowledge to its subjective side. Thus, for instance, there arises the fallacious conviction that matter is not given in experience, that there is no ideal, non-temporal reality and so on.

Let us now turn to the objective aspect of knowledge and consider it more fully. It consists of the object and of the content of knowledge, i.e., of that which we have succeeded in learning about the object by means of analysing it or its surroundings.

The object, (e.g. 'this maple leaf') and the content of knowledge ('is yellow') are inter-related in a certain definite way, so that the objective aspect of knowledge consists of three elements: the object, the content, and the relation between them. Such a threefold system is called a judgement. The first part of it is the object; the second part, called the PREDICATE, is the content cognised in the given judgement. The relation between the object and the predicate consists in the circumstance that GIVEN THE OBJECT, THE PREDICATE IS ALSO NECESSARILY GIVEN. Every truth contains this necessary relation of belonging together: in the judgement "a straight line is the shortest distance between two points", there is a necessary connection between 'the straightness of the line' and "the shortest distance"; in the judgement "a body submerged in water loses in weight as much as the weight of the water displaced", there is a necessary connection between 'a body being submerged in water' and 'the decrease in its weight', and so on.

I propose to call the relation consisting in the fact that the presence of one element, S, necessarily involves the presence of another element, P, the relation of GROUND and CONSEQUENCE.

In a judgement this relation holds between the object and the predicate. As a rule, however, it is not an object as a whole but only some part of it that provides the ground for the predicate. This kernel of the object which plays the essential part in judgement is designated by a special term: I cal it the SUBJECT of the JUDGEMENT.

The subject of judgement, then, is the ground of the predicate. The object of judgement is more complex and includes elements which have no bearing on the predicate; it may therefore be said to *contain* the ground of the predicate.

The object of knowledge is a fragment of the world infinitely rich in content. The first act of knowing, directed upon some object that is new to us, results in a judgement in which the object cannot as yet be described in any words but is merely pointed to as 'this' 'that' etc. Such is the judgement quoted above: 'this is a leaf'. Schematically it may be expressed as follows:

$$: : : : - \text{S}$$

The dots within the bracket show that the object of judgement has a complex content as yet completely uncognised.

Contents cognised in previous judgements may, in further acts of knowledge be directed upon the same object, be utilised to DESIGNATE the object, e.g., "this leaf is a maple-leaf"; 'this maple leaf is yellow' and so on.

In addition to its objective aspect a judgement has an individually mental, subjective side which consists in acts of attending, discriminating, comparing etc., directed upon the object and content of knowledge. Particularly characteristic of the subjective side of judgement is the ACT OF AFFIRMATION or ASSERTION; it is only in so far as that act is present that the knowing subject can be said to maintain the truth of something: The truth which he is affirming is to be found in the objective aspect of judgement; or more exactly, it IS that aspect. The act of affirmation is directed upon it and derives its MEANING from it.

According to the Intuitive theory the objective aspect of judgement is nothing other than the actual external object and those aspects of the world which are necessarily connected with it as their ground. It may therefore be said that truth is attained in knowledge the whole content of which consists of various aspects of the object and of consequences that follow from it. Falsity on the other hand, is due to intro-ducing into the subjective aspect of the judgement some content, foreign to the object and to the consequences following from it.

Knowing, then, is the least creative of activities: it consists merely in contemplation and discrimination (or analysis); but that which is contemplated and discriminated is supplied by the object. Therefore, the chief LOGICAL criterion of truth is the PRESENCE of the cognised object, its self-evidence. There is also a PSYCHOLOGICAL criterion of truth: it consists in the fact that the acts of knowing – attending, dis-criminating, judging, etc. are felt to be subordinated to the 'requests' or 'suggestions' proceeding from the object and its connections; to put it briefly, a correct act of knowing is accompanied by a FEELING OF OBJECTIVE CONSTRAINT.

The psychology of knowledge is concerned with the SUBJECTIVE as-pect of knowledge, i.e., with the acts of knowing – with activities of attending, discriminating, perceiving, remembering etc. and their de-pendence upon non-intellectual processes of feeling and willing.

Epistemology or theory of knowledge deals with the properties of TRUTH. Now, truth is the objective side of knowledge in so far as it enters the field of consciousness, i.e., in so far as it is related to the subjective side. Epistemology, therefore, is concerned with the objective aspect of knowledge and its relation to the subjective aspect. It clearly is not based upon psychology. Its main interest is always in the non-mental aspect of knowledge, and even when it studies the relation be-tween it and the subjective aspect, it is concerned with the analysis of consciousness, i.e., with a subject far more complex than the domain of psychical experiences which enter into it merely as one of its com-ponent parts. Epistemology may, indeed be said to provide a basis for a definition of psychology, since, in its analysis of consciousness, it discovers mental processess which are the subject-matter of psychology. It draws a distinction between its own subject-matter and that of psy-chology by laying down an important negative proposition namely, that the mental acts of knowing do not create the objective side of knowledge but merely 'discover it', 'have it in view', are 'directed' upon it.

The Intuitivist conception of truth is different. If knowledge is at-tained through the contemplation of the object as it is in itself it is clear that however the knowing subjects might change and whatever their number might be, the object they have in view remains literally the same, numerically identical. Truth, therefore, is universally binding, it has an ABSOLUTE SIGNIFICANCE.

The objective aspect of judgment is, as has been shown, a threefold system consisting of the object that contains the subject of the judgement, the predicate, and the relation between them, which lies in the fact that the subject is the ground, and the predicate is the consequence following from it. In virtue of this relation every judgement has a NECESSARY character. The explanation of this extremely valuable feature of the judgement is to be found in the nature of the sequence of the predicate from the subject. The usual interpretation of the relation of ground and consequence (especially prevalent in pre-Kantian philosophy) is that it is a relation based upon the logical law of identity, or expressing the same idea from the negative side, upon the logical law of contradiction and exluded middle. Thus, in the judgement "a square is a rectangle" there is partial identity between the subject and the predicate because the idea of 'rectangle' forms part of the content of the idea of 'square'.

Schematically, such judgements may be expressed by the formula 'S P is P'. Their predicate form part of the idea of the subject (i.e. part of the DISCRIMINATED aspect of the object) and they are called ANALYTICAL JUDGEMENTS. In analytical judgements the predicate necessarily follows from the subject in virtue of the law of identity; at the same time the necessity of sequence can be explained by the law of contradiction. If someone attempted to deny the truth of an analytical judgement and to say, for instance, that 'a square was not a rectangle', he would violate the law of contradiction and make a self-contradictory judgement 'a square, i.e., a rectangle all the sides of which are equal, is not a rectangle'.

According to the Intuitive theory the object enters the field of the observer's consciousness in all its fulness, with all the relations that connect its various aspects with one another and with the rest of the world. Therefore even in sense-perception our environment appears to us not as a chaos but as something orderly. No one will deny that spatial order, the relations of 'to the right' 'to the left', 'above', 'below' etc., constitute an inalienable part of my concrete presentations of my writing table, of the window, of the street etc. Moreover, perception includes relations far deeper than those. Our environment appears to us to consist of THINGS, and a thing is that which has qualities – colour, hardness, coldness etc. Thus, relations of belonging, of unity, plurality (the unity of many qualities) etc., form part of our idea of a thing.

I propose to call concrete spatial and temporal processes REAL being, and their non-temporal and non-spatial aspect – IDEAL being.

All that belongs to the ideal realm, e.g., the relation of unity, is an object of NON-SENSUOUS contemplation. The apple I see and touch is a unity of such qualities as yellowness, hardness, coldness etc. I may be said to see the yellowness, to touch the hardness, but it is impossible to see or touch the UNITY of yellowness and hardness, if only because these two qualities are perceived by means of two different sense-organs. Nevertheless, unity is an essential element in the perception of things. This means that even the sensuous perception of a thing is not wholly sensuous: it contains an ideal aspect cognised by means of intellectual intuition or speculation.

Real being has a systematic character only in so far as it contains an ideal aspect. In virtue of the world being a system, every fragment of reality, entering our field of consciousness may be analysed into two elements related to each other as ground and consequence. Thus, it is the systematic nature of reality that gives the character of a system to the objective aspect of a synthetic judgement. The cosmos as a system involves necessary synthetic relations between its various aspects, and, in virtue of this, synthetic JUDGEMENTS also have a necessary character.

The ideal aspect of reality conditions both the systematic character of the World and the possibility of TRUTH about it, i.e. it renders the world knowable in judgements and inferences. The systematic character of reality, entering our field of consciousness, constitutes the objective aspect of the system of judgements and inferences about the world. The ideal ONTOLOGICAL aspects of the world, in so far as we are conscious of them, are the LOGICAL grounds of knowledge (an exact definition of the term 'logical' will be given later).

The systematic character of the world conditions also the realisation of goodness and beauty. Truth, goodness and beauty give meaning to the world and make it RATIONAL. The ideal basis of the world may therefore be called the WORLD-LOGOS; this term should be understood not merely in an intellectual sense, since ideal principles are not confined to the realm of thought and knowledge: they are that aspect of being which conditions not only truth but all other values.

THE DEFINITION OF THE PSYCHOLOGY OF KNOWLEDGE, EPISTEMOLOGY AND LOGIC

We have already considered epistemological questions necessary for the definition of logic: the relation, namely, between the knowing subject and the object, the distinction between the subjective and the objective aspects of knowledge, and the structure of the objective aspect of judgement based upon the ideal forms of the World Logos; we have also established the logical and the psychological criterion of truth. The logical criterion of truth is the actual PRESENCE of the known object in the objective aspect of knowledge, and the psychological criterion is the feeling of CONSTRAINT COMPELLING the subject to abide by the 'requirements' of the object.

We must now pass to questions that bring us into the domain of logic, and inquire, in the first place, into the nature of proof.

It often happens that a judgement is accepted by one person as true, while another person, though he understands the meaning of it, does not perceive whether it is true or not. The truth of the judgement has to be PROVED to him. To prove the truth of something to a person means to place him in such conditions as will enable him to see the presence of the object judged about, so that the judgement will acquire for him an objectively binding character.

Let us take a few instances. Suppose that a friend of mine who has not been to Petrograd for some years doubts the truth of the assertion that "a mosque has been built on the other side of the Troitzky bridge".

To convince him of it, it is sufficient to take him across the Troitzky bridge and let him see for himself. Immediate perception may thus provide the proof of a judgement. The matter, however, is not always so simple: Not infrequently certain aspects of the object or the connections between them cannot be perceived immediately; in that case more complex methods than direct perception have to be used in order to prove the truth of a judgement. Suppose for instance, on coming into a classroom, we ask "how many cubic-metres of air are there per person in this room?" The school-master answers "ten". How can this judgement be proved, that is, how can it be made objectively binding for every thinking mind?

To do so, we have first of all to establish a number of other judgements, namely, to count the number of persons in the room (suppose there are 32), then measure the length, the width, and the height of the room (say, 10, 8 & 4 metres); then, on the ground of the geometrical truth that the bulk of a rectangular parallelopiped equals the product of its three dimensions, to find out that the bulk of the class-room equals 320 cubic metres; then dividing 320 by 32 we discover as a wellproven truth that in this room there are 10 cubic metres of air per person.

This method of proof is obviously based upon the following remarkable circumstance: having in mind several judgements we can so combine them that it will be obviously necessary to recognise one more new judgement as true. The knowledge we already possess provides the ground for the birth of new knowledge. Such method of proof is called INFERENCE.

Judgements on the basis of which a new judgement is proved are called PREMISSES; the judgement that follows from them, i.e., is proved by them, is called conclusion. Inference as a whole is the detection of the truth of some judgement on the ground of one or several judgements, already recognised as true.

In inference, as in judgement, we must distinguish the subjective, i.e., the individually-mental, and the objective side. In the inference "a diamond is carbon and carbon burns, therefore a diamond burns" (schematically expressed as S is M, M is P, S is P), the attention with which I utter it, the feeling of the conclusion being binding upon me, etc., form part of the subjective aspect of the judgement, while the object S (diamond) and also M & P, and the relation of S & P to M in virtue of which S and P are connected with each other as ground and consequence, form the objective aspect of judgement.

In studying the objective aspect of the inferences of such different sciences as mathematics, astronomy, physics, physiology, history etc. – in investigating, i.e., the nature of the connection between the premisses and the conclusion – it is easy to see that in spite of the multiplicity of the CONTENTS of these sciences, the FORM of the inferences, i.e., their structure or the correlation of their parts, can be reduced to a small number of types and be expressed by simple schemes such as S is M, M is P, S is P. The science which studies the forms of proof is LOGIC.

Now we can clearly differentiate and define the respective fields of the psychology of knowledge, epistemology and logic.

The psychology of knowledge studies the SUBJECTIVE (INDIVIDUALLY MENTAL) aspect of knowledge. It deals with the acts of knowing (attention, discrimination, recollection etc.) and with their dependence upon other, non-cognitive, mental processes – upon feeling and will.

Epistemology is the THEORY OF TRUTH; it investigates the objective aspect of knowledge and its relation to the subject in order to discover the properties of truth (e.g. the relation between true knowledge and the object, the universality and eternity of truth etc.) and the conditions of their possibility.

Logic is the THEORY OF THE STRUCTURE OF THE OBJECTIVE ASPECT OF PROOF.

It has already been shown that epistemology is not based upon psychology. The same is true about logic, as can be seen from the definition of it which emphasises the fact that it deals with the OBJECTIVE aspect of proof.

Section III
METAPHYSICAL PROBLEMS

- - - - - - - - - - - - - - - -

BIOGRAPHICAL SKETCH

N. V. Bugayev (1837-1902) was a professor of mathematics at Moscow University, who along with other Russian mathematicians developed the theory of 'discontinuous functions' (arithmology). Like many Russian scientists and mathematicians, he became interested in philosophy and produced a number of works in that field. Our present selection is representative of his ontological Weltanschauung and his personalism.

His monadological doctrine enables him to relate natural phenomena to social phenomena, which leads him to apply moral principles to the universe itself.

His chief philosophic works are: "Mathematics and a Scientific-Philosophic World-View"; "Basic Principles of Evolutionary Monadology"; and "On the Question of Freedom of the Will".

Bugayev's monadology could be profitably compared with Leibniz's monadology as well as with modern theories of emergent or creative evolution.

N. V. Bugayev

BASIC PRINCIPLES OF
EVOLUTIONARY MONADOLOGY*

My paper consists of propositions united by one general idea. I do not offer full grounds to explain my theses. These are given in the form of brief explanations and additions. The reason for this brevity is simply due to lack of time to state the propositions with detailed proofs. Moreover, I would have had to preface my propositions with a criticism of earlier philosophical systems to clarify my views. This I did not do as it required a great deal of work and special knowledge.

My system is in some respect similar to Leibniz's monadology, or the monadology of pre-established harmony, as well as to certain theories of modern monism. It differs from them however, in many essential details. In the interest of greater coherence, I shall present my theses in one continuous exposition.

My propositions are very abstract and therefore lack concrete form. This is their deficiency. Concreteness and imagery affect not only the mind but also the imagination and the senses; they not only prove but also convince. My propositions lack artistic colours. I regret this very much and ask at the outset to be pardoned for this deficiency.

The theory of the monad is very basic to an evolutionary monadology.

1. The monad is a living unit, a living element. It is an independent and spontaneous individual.

2. It is "alive" in the sense that it possesses a potential psychic content.

---

* This paper was read at a meeting of the Moscow Psychological Society. It was published in *Voprosy filosofii i psikhologii*, Bk, 2 (17) (March, 1893).

3. The psychic content and psychism are by their nature not subject to observation, but only by their external manifestation. They are accessible only to the monad itself.

4. The psychic content in its kinetic (active) force, may be regarded as an immediate (intuitive) deduction, a synthesis, a verdict, a conclusion or an interpretation by the monad of the internal facts of its being and of its relationship to other monads. It is the existence of the monad for itself.

5. The psychic content in its (intense) potential force is an opportunity to manifest its kinetic content in some form or another or in any situation. It sometimes denotes the sum of potentialities, capacities, habits and instincts.

Explanation:

I shall endeavour to explain what I understand by the expression, "the monad is a living unit".

In mathematics the term "measure" designates the quantity with which other quantities of the same kind are compared. By the term "concrete mathematical unit" is meant the "permanent" measure with which quantities of the same kind are compared. The choice of the unit depends on the kind of quantity.

This condition is not applicable in the case of an abstract mathematical unit. An abstract mathematical unit is characterized by its permanency and does not depend upon concrete content.

By the expression "the monad is a unit" I mean, that it is defined by the sign, "permanency". Permanency is indicative of its immutability in certain relationships. The monad is something which remains immutable in a whole series of changes. It is a whole, indivisible, single, immutable principle equal to itself in all possible relationships with other monads and with itself. It remains the same for our consciousness in certain aspects of its manifestation. The monad is an element. Moreover, it is a "living" unit.

The concept of life is associated in our consciousness with the idea of change. Life can manifest itself only in the form of actual or potential change. It is not always true that where there is change there is life. For life to take place, change must occur in a definite order, it must follow a definite law, at least for some part of its course. It is this order, law, and way, this permanency and regularity in the midst of change that characterizes life. The basis for this permanency in life is to be found in a motive or a purpose. Thus, life is first of all, an order of causal or teleological changes.

However, not every order of such changes may be called life, nor do we call life every concrete unit characterized by such changes. We make a distinction between a mechanism and an organism, between a machine and a living being. We do not notice in the living content a single manifestation of external and outside purposes. Our consciousness requires that the influence of internal motives should be manifested in the activity of a living principle.

The inner motive is that which is observed, distinguished and coordinated within the active unit. In such case we call the active unit, an "individuality" or an "organism". This unit differentiates and evaluates the inner motive. It alone observes it. An external cause or motive is fully accessible to external observation. It is wholly manifested in external activity, is exhausted by it, and is identical with it. An internal motive is not wholly accessible to single external observation, is not completely exhausted by external activity and is not equal to it. From external activity we can only deduce the inner motive by analogy, by trying to find appropriate corresponding activities in our inner life. The property to deduce by analogy the feelings and inner being of another monad is based on the capacity for mutual feelings or sympathy.

An external motive (or cause) is evaluated by means of concepts, whereas an internal motive is wholly and directly evaluated only in the inner activity of the individual. This direct evaluation is not fully accessible to external observation. An inner cause is termed a motive, a ground, an incentive, a purpose, etc. We term direct evaluations a feeling, a flair for something, a consciousness, etc.

An external cause (motive) is characterized by objectivity and relativity, an internal cause, by subjectivity and immediacy. The capacity to evaluate the content of personal changes and to observe them ourselves, we shall call psychism, and its potential and inner object of this evaluation, we shall call psychic content.

The concept of life is thus necessarily bound up with the presence of causal or teleological changes, psychism and the individual, as an independent unit. A living thing can only be some definite, concrete, active unit, endowed with inner motives and purposes for its changes and capable of evaluating these changes internally. The living unit introduces this evaluation as a basis for a further series of its changes.

6.   Formally, the life of the monad is the constant series of changes of its psychism in its kinetic and potential force. The life of a monad is a series of causal and teleological changes in its organization.

7.   The bond between the psychic content and its corresponding relations and manifestations depends on laws which are above and beyond a full understanding of the monad.

8.   The laws to which the monad is subject, are called "conditions" of the monad.

9. These laws cannot always be expressed discursively in verbal terms or in concepts. At times they are not subject to quantitative relations.

10. The monad is a "unit" in the sense that, from a certain viewpoint it is indivisible and is, as it were, the final unit (element) under given conditions of analysis and existence.

11. Monads are completely dissimilar.

12. They differ in their relation to each other and are of "different orders".

13. Monads are of a first, second, and third order, etc.

14. Monads of the second order can form a monad of the first order. In such instance, the monad of the first order forms for them that world, or that condition, or one of the conditions, whose limits they generally do not cross so long as the monad of the first order is in existence.

15. Monads of the second order, or submonads, cross the limits of the monad of the first order only in exceptional cases. In which case they either attain an independent importance, or continue to enter into the formation of other monads of a higher order.

16. The following units may serve as symbolic examples of monads of various orders: mankind, state, man, who is a social monad, a cell, which is a biological monad, a molecule – a chemical monad, an atom – a physical monad, and other monads.

If man symbolically represents a monad of the first order, a cell is then a monad of the second order (*submonad*), a molecule, the third, and an atom of the fourth order. A nation or a state will be a monad of the first higher order (supra-monad), or a monad minus the first order. These examples explain symbolically only proposition 13.

17. The order of monads extends upwards and downwards ad infinitum.

18. The external world may be regarded as a monad in relation to other monads.

19. Due to the finite nature of our human understanding, it is perhaps sufficient to limit ourselves to monads of the first order and the world (supra-monads of the first order). This is because we are not endowed with such subtle capacities of senses and organs to enable us to observe phenomena which depend on the activity of monads of the second and higher orders.

20. Monads differ also in their essence.

21. Their essence is determined by the laws to which they are subject by a subjective interpretation of the facts of their inner existence. Their essence is determined by the conditions or the laws of their being. Their essence is not subject to evaluation.

22. The psychic content of monads of the first order in relation to

the psychic content of monads of the second order can sometimes be regarded as a "synthesis" (with a qualitative transformation), sometimes as a "generalization", and sometimes as an "abstraction". This synthesis is subject to special laws and becomes the product of the independent work of the monad. This synthesis comes in the form of an idea, a feeling, an incentive and an action.

23. Work, in the subjective sense, is an activity accompanied by a feeling of effort. Where there is no effort, there is no work in a subjective sense.

24. The result of the monad's work is realized to a greater or lesser extent, subject to a greater or lesser transformation of remaking.

25. This perfection, completion and transformation depend on the perfection of the monad of the first order itself, of its submonads, and supramonads.

26. Monads enter into mutual relationship.

27. Thanks to these relations, the world of knowledge, feelings and actions is at the same time a world of mutual relations of monads, subjectively interpreted. This results in the relationships and co-relationships of all our knowledge, feelings, motives and actions.

28. The development and change of the psychic content is the result of the interrelation of monads, their submonads and supramonads.

29. Several simple monads can together form one complex monad.

30. The simplest example of a complex monad is the combination of two monads or a diad.

31. Diads are very dissimilar.

32. They differ in nature and form from the monads which constitute them.

33. The relation of a complex monad to its simple monads constituting it differs from the relation of monads to submonads and supramonads.

34. The complex monad is qualitatively homogeneous with its constituent monads. The monad may differ considerably from submonads and supramonads both qualitatively and quantitatively. For example, a person and a cell may be a monad and a submonad. A family and its members are a complex monad and monads.

NOTE: These explanations are of a symbolic nature.

35. A complex monad may be divided into simple monads without losing its quality. A monad may be divided into submonads only in cases of special assumptions and premises which are sometimes beyond the limits of our comprehension.

36. In a diad (a, b) the monads a and b, are not always of equal importance and content.

37. In the diad (a, b) one must observe (the moment of the for-

mation and disintegration) of the diad, its duration, stability and purpose of its existence, the relation of the diad to each of its monads, and vice versa, the interrelation of its monads, the mutual relations of its monads, its relation to other simple and complex monads, to the whole world and vice versa.

38. The world process, viewed externally, is regarded as a succession of formation and division of complex monads into various orders.

39. The relation of monads which have a certain stability, is called the nexus of monads.

40. The quality and details of the basic elements of the mutual nexus of monads a and b determine the diad (ab) itself.

41. That general factor which forms the basis of the mutual link of the monads in the diad, constitutes the essence of the diad.

42. The essence of the diad is subject to continuous change and transformation in the direction determined by the conditions of the diad and its monads.

43. The qualitative substance of a diad consists of the qualitative substance of its component monads. Its psyche or its inner substance is contained in the psyche of its monads and in that common nexus which unites the monads in a diad.

44. The monads of a diad are not identical and are not equal to each other. They do not equally represent the diad.

45. That monad which more fully represents the diad may be called the "central monad".

46. Sometimes another monad in a diad may temporarily become the central monad. This will occur under special conditions favourable to the activity of the second monad.

47. The life of a monad in a diad and its psychic content consists of its own psychic content (of the individual, of the person) and of the psychic content of a diad in so far as it is made the property of a given monad.

48. In a diad each force or element of psychic content of a monad can become a common monad. In this case, the monad represents, as it were, the diad.

49. One can explain the psychic unity of a diad either by the unity of its origin or by the unity of the nature of the monads.

50. The monad which completely represents the diad, is differentiated from the individual psychic content or identifies the idividual with the common (content) in its life.

51. The monad of a lower level of development moves forward from its nexus with the monad of a higher (level) of development. It advances due to its efforts to raise itself to a higher ideal which it perceives in connection with the activity of the monad of a higher

development. The efforts to raise itself is accompanied by work, which in this case may be called "work of ascent" (*podnyatie*).

52. The monad of a higher (level) of development is raised in its completion thanks to its efforts to raise another monad in the diad to a higher ideal. The effort to raise (others) (*podnyat'*) is accompanied by work, which in this instance may be called "work of elevation". (*podyom*).[1]

53. Both ascent (*podnyatie*) and elevation (*podyom*) can only be realized by independent work or activity of the monad. The passive aspect in the activity plays a secondary role. It is sometimes formed into an instinct or habit, and does not become a potential resource of the monad. The psychic content of the monad greatly increases only to the extent of its activity and active participation.

54. In the interrelationship of the monads there are two activities of "ascent" and "elevation" (*podnyati, podyom*), since each of the two monads surpasses the other in some respect.

55. The work of perfection consists in the constant independent striving toward ascent and elevation, in active learning and teaching. Ascent is clearly of a passive character, while elevation is of an active nature. But this only seems so at first. Both are fruitful when they are of an active nature. When ascent is not active, it assumes the form of apprenticeship, while passive elevation will be characterized by formalism.

56. The lower monad in a diad is for the higher monad and for the diad an element of temporary and seeming regress and suffering.

57. This apparent regress is nevertheless a necessary condition for progress, since by its resistance to realization one monad raises the active energy of the other. This resistance serves the purpose of criticism and control. Action and reaction in the activity of monads are, indeed, two necessary aspects of perfection.

58. The higher monad in the diad is for the lower elements an actual success and progress.

59. The diad is the condition of progress for both monads.

60. Complex monads or complexes may consist of three, four, or any number of monads.

61. Complexes of three monads may be called triads.

62. The composition of a complex of three monads may be wholly dissimilar.

63. Triads consisting of three monads (a, b, c) may be formed as follows: (1) from three monads (a, b, c) having separate independent existence; (2) from a diad (ab) and a monad (c), i.e. (ab, c); (3) from

---

[1] The Russian term *podnyatie* is translated here as ascent which is to be taken in the subjective sense. The term *podyom* means to raise or elevate something or someone else.

a diad (ac) and a monad (b), i.e. (ac, b); (4) from a diad (bc) and a monad (a), i.e. (bc, a). In the last three instances the triad is also a diad.

64. A diad (ab) may differ from diad (ab), depending on the conditions of the mutual nexus of monads *a* and *b*.

65. The number of complex monads far exceeds the number of simple monads.

66. For X monads to make a full cycle of their mutual relations, means to accomplish a full revolution of their development, or to attain all the possible potential content under definite conditions of their existence and their relations.

67. In the mutual relation of monads two laws may be observed: "the law of monadological inertia", and "the law of monadological solidarity".

68. The law of monadological inertia consists of the fact that a monad cannot change its entire psychic content by its own action, outside of its relation to other monads.

69. This law is based on the following considerations: The monad perfects itself partly due to its relations with other monads. If these relations did not exist it would have no source for the development of those aspects of its nature for which such relations are necessary. In such instance it can only develop by the activity of its submonads, i.e. in the direction of inner harmony and in the processing of previously-obtained material.

70. The principle or the law of monadological solidarity consists of the fact that monads are developed by certain aspects of their being, only when they enter into correlation with other monads. Its perfection, which chiefly depends on this principle, may be termed "extensive". (*ekstensivnyym*)

71. Under the influence of the principle solidarity the monad may act on another monad and change its psychic content as well as its own.

72. The law of mutual solidarity of monads may be regarded (1) either as an attribute of their essence, or (2) as a law developed by their communal life, or (3) as a higher degree of evolution.

73. We must differentiate in the psychic content of a monad potential from kinetic content.

74. We must distinguish in the potential content (1) the content capable of immediately becoming kinetic, and (2) the content which becomes kinetic under special conditions, capable of manifesting itself when in combination with monads of another order, substance or development.

75. In a complex, monads achieve the whole process of development due to their relation with other monads of their own complex.

76. The relations of monads to monads outside their own complex

are reflected by relations of monads to kindred monads of the same complex.

77. These relations increase the psychism of the complex.

78. A monad of each complex lives by its own individual life, by the life of the nearest complex, by the next higher complex, etc.

79. In its relation to the world, a monad distinguishes between what is of direct importance to its individual life, and that which it introduces into the life of its nearest and the subsequent higher complex, etc. and that which it introduces into the life of the whole complex.

80. Everything that a monad introduces into the life of a complex is transformed by it, and after it has been assimilated is reflected on the monad.

81. Complex monads disintegrate and enter into the formation of new complexes.

82. The central monad of a complex may continue the life of the complex in another complex.

83. Monads capitalize their past as well as the past of the complex in their potential content by the potential peculiarity of their psychism (habits, in its embryonic state, capacities, instincts, etc.).

84. Monads do not disappear, nor do complexes.

85. The law of conservation of time and the past, may be juxtaposed with the universal laws of the conservation of matter and energy. It can be expressed by the formula: "The past does not disappear; it is accumulated". The psychic content and potential energy are thus constantly being increased. The psychism increases. This is proven by the fact that perfection of the monads and complexes is constantly increasing.

86. The mutual struggle of complex monads is due to their striving toward ideals of a higher and more perfect development. This may be termed a struggle for abstract and concrete ideals.

87. What is peculiar to one, is potentially peculiar to all monads, and vice versa.

88. This means that the development and psychic content of other monads potentially belong to it, and vice versa. Moreover, the perfection which is peculiar to other monads, may, when entering into correlation with a given monad, reflect on the change of its psychic content, and vice versa.

89. The struggle for existence of complex monads is only one of the manifestations of the law of mutual solidarity of monads.

90. When a complex monad under certain conditions, cannot continue its existence in the interests of further development, it disintegrates. It disintegrates, when the internal or external harmony is in someway violated.

91. The disintegration of the complex monad is only an apparent disintegration. Neither monads composing it, nor the monad itself disappear.

92. Monads preserve their potential content which is developed or becomes kinetic content under favourable conditions.

93. A complex monad continues its existence in the central monad as well as in the other monads.

94. One and the same monad may be a member of several complex monads.

95. If it forms a single monad in one way and a complex monad in a different way, in such case, there can be no conflict, or it occurs in rare instances. Here the simple monad serves as an organic member of several complex monads.

96. If it is an organic member of several complex monads and becomes a member through certain common aspects of its being, a conflict may then take place.

97. The monad in the latter case may be a "temporary" member of these complex monads and serve as a nexus and vital mediator between them.

98. When a complex monad disintegrates, its component simple monads sometimes enter into the formation of other complex monads and there find the elements for their further development by means of ascent and elevation.

99. As a result of this development, it will have a greater understanding of the world, a more profound feeling and a greater amount of force for its activity in the realization of the ideals of a higher order.

100. The basis of the life and activity of the monad is ethical, viz., to perfect itself and others.

101. To be perfected means in part to increase its psychism.

102. A more perfect monad is one (a) whose parts or monads best express the idea of the whole; (b) whose internal relations best correspond to external relations (the submonads to monads) where these corresponding relations are distributed in a greater number of monads in space and time. The first perfection is called "internal harmony", the second, "external" the third, the force or "potential" of the monad. The first perfection we shall call "internal intensive", the second, "external intensive", and the third, "extensive".

103. The submonad of a monad may increase internal harmony by internal activity, and external harmony within the limits of its experience and force only to a certain extent.

104. The ultimate goal of the monad's activity is to remove the difference between the monad and the world as well as between the sum of all monads, to achieve infinite perfection and to stand above the world.

105. The life of a monad ensues from its yearning to satisfy its innate desire for independent development, and for a higher happiness.

106. The development of a monad is spontaneous, since it is a-chieved by active energy in surmounting obstacles for its development by work.

107. Life and spontaneous work of perfection, are identical activities for the monad.

108. The monad is responsible to a considerable extent for its own development. This constitutes its personal worth.

109. Since life or the work of life leads to the perfection of the monad, then life, work, and the worth of the monad and perfection are essentially concepts of the same order.

110. The immediate aim of a monad's life is another monad and the world, and by reflection it is the monad itself.

111. The distant aim of the life of the monad is its aspiration to stand outside the world or above it, having first been made by the world or through the world.

112. The basis of the monad's life is purely ethical.

113. The principle of the solidarity of monads is the fundamental principle of their interrelationship.

114. This principle for complex and homogeneous monads is called love.

115. Love for oneself and for others is expressed in the life of the monads in their spontaneous and independent striving toward the perfection of themselves and others.

116. The world and the monad, the life of the world and the monad coincide in this love.

117. Loving itself rationally, the monad necessarily loves others, and vice versa.

118. The individuality and immortality of the monad are always preserved.

119. Such world-view reconciles science and history, spirit and matter, pantheism and individualism, freedom and necessity, and another view, based on so-called suffering, is achieved.

120. The general forms of their social life are worked out by the common life of the monads.

121. These forms come to be known as laws, instincts, habits, customs and conventions.

122. The simplest monads and those that are more widely distributed develop earlier than those that are more complex and less distributed monads.

123. The most prevalent and simplest of monads come to be known as the "physical laws of nature".

124. The physical laws are essentially the primordial customs or habits of the monads, – the primordial forms of their common life.

125. They are differentiated by their permanency, since they were formed earlier and developed for a longer period.

126. Instincts and the simpler forms of organic life are governed by the so-called laws of inorganic nature.

127. The simplest social forms of life precede the social forms of more complex ones.

128. There is a constant metamorphasis of customs into habits, and habits into instincts in the process of the social life of monads.

129. The monad may interpret its relation to other monads in a dual manner: (a) in terms of external changes, i.e. by extension and motion and (b) in terms of internal changes in accordance with its innate psychic content (sensations, feelings, etc.). Under such conditions the monad is a concrete subjective-object. Before it became aware of the world of appearance, it was a potential subjective-object.

130. According to the first interpretation the other monad has the attributes of "matter".

131. According to the second interpretation, the other monad appears to have the attributes of "spirit".

132. Matter and spirit are, to be sure, deductions resulting from two forms of relations of one monad to another.

133. Matter and spirit are co-related concepts. If we disregard the inner individual life of something, it appears to us as matter, but if we pay attention to the inner subjective aspect of activity, it is for us spiritual.

134. The permanent customs and habits developed by the common life place their stamp of regularity and even necessity on the interrelations of the monads.

135. The activity which is more spontaneous than the developed habits and which depends on other higher goals, are characterized by their contingent and arbitrary nature.

136. Everything that the monad potentially receives either from without or from within through permanent and established interrelations, has the character of necessity.

137. Everything that is actively developed by the monad within kinetically, bears the character of freedom: it has the mark of internal, spontaneous work, since freedom is dependent on internal relations of the monad or a dependence of the monad on itself.

138. Suffering is a purely subjective interpretation of the fact that obstacles are surmounted and the work of life or the work of perfection is advanced. Such suffering is of a "positive" nature. It is accompanied by a feeling of satisfaction.

139. Suffering is also a subjective interpretation of the fact that the standard and harmony have been violated. When it reaches a certain limit it necessarily forces the will to change its direction. This suffering is of a negative nature. It promotes the perfection of the monad in a negative way. Such negative suffering sometimes follows the so-called death or disintegration of a complex monad. In this case, suffering serves as a catharsis. Under favourable conditions it is followed by a feeling of reconciliation.

140. The perfection of monads is both extensive and intensive. Intensive perfection is of two kinds. It is represented by external and internal harmony.

141. Inner harmony may be developed by the activity of the sub-monads, i.e., by the contemplative activity of the monad.

142. The struggle of submonads for development leads to the perfection of the monad in the form of inner harmony.

143. The life of a monad is reflected on the change of its potential energy and on the expansion of its possibilities.

144. The highest good for a monad is perfection by spontaneous work.

145. These general propositions provide an explanation for all universal phenomena and problems of life. We shall attempt to answer the questions, what is the world, and what is man, from the viewpoint of evolutionary monadology.

What is the World?

146. The world is a collection of a large number of simple and complex monads of various orders.

147. The world's life consists of the continuous process of formation and transformation of complex monads as a result of the yearning of simple and complex monads to achieve mutual perfection through the ethical laws of ascent and elevation.

148. The perfection of monads and the world has as its ultimate aim, on the one hand, to raise the psychic content of the monad to the psychic content of the whole world, and on the other hand, to make the world a monad.

149. These aims arise from the general desire of the monads to remove the difference between the world and the monad and to achieve for both infinite happiness. In this process the universe, strives, as it were, to make the monad a whole world, infinite and perfect, while the monad tries to transform the world into a monad. The world increases the monad's potential, advances its extensive perfection, while the monad strives to increase in the world intensive perfection. It attempts

to realize inner harmony in the world, to transform it into an artistic edifice where the whole equals to the parts, and the parts to the whole. Their mutual harmony and conformity are the result of their mutual extensive and intensive process of perfection.

150. The individuality of simple and complex monads does not however disappear in this process. This view of the world's life offers all the benefits of pantheism and individualism and eliminates all their deficiencies.

151. The world is not equal to itself, but is constantly improving, although all the data for its infinite development and happiness is potentially found in it and in the monad.

152. Basic to the nature of the monad is the active sensation or will and its innate primordial form of psychic life, viz., its desire for existence and happiness by means of an active. spontaneous and free development.

153. This primary desire becomes manifest and makes a transition from the potential to the kinetic state thanks to the common life of monads.

154. The forms of their communal life become manifest and complex by the spontaneous, active and joint efforts of the monads.

155. In terms of extension and motion, the monad may be regarded as an "atom", dynamically it may be viewed as the "centre" of forces or as the vortex of a fixed movement of the environment psychologically, it is viewed as "spirit" or "will", or as the potential centre of sensations, feelings, consciousness and desire for existence and happiness.

156. All these definitions of the monad are only symbolic explanations of its essence. "Per se", the monad has potentially only the possibility to understand its essence by these definitions.

157. The real essence and origin of the monads cannot be explained by any philosophical system, but by the profound doctrines of the Absolute.

158. The study of the developed and permanent forms of the communal life of the monads is the object of exact sciences about physical nature.

159. The exact sciences on nature plus their laws are thus the first chapters of social science.

160. Probability and contingency are the innate elements of the life of the world.

161. The primordial state of an imperfect world is chaos where probability and contingency prevail.

162. As the world develops and becomes perfect, these contingencies and probabilities gradually become subject to law, design and

certainty, as a result of the spontaneous active effort of monads and of their inherent yearning for happiness in the form of an inner harmony and mutual concord.

163. The diminution of contingencies and probabilities in the early relations of the monads is achieved by more complex forms of their social life.

164. Depending upon the degree of development, the contingencies and probabilities move into other still more complex and higher forms of social life.

165. Ethical laws are the result of the monad's innate desire for existence, activity, happiness and perfection, as its "summum bonum". They are the results of the laws of monadological inertia and solidarity, of action and reaction in connection with the processes of the sequence of ascent and elevation of monads.

166. Death is one of the processes of transformation of complex monads and is only of relative importance.

167. Simple monads are never born and never die.

168. Complex monads which are subject to constant change and transformation, also preserve their potential existence in new monadological forms.

169. The different forms of animation and spiritualization of monads are only different forms of their perfection.

170. A real world, from an anthropological viewpoint, is only a projection or a shadow in which the world-process appears to our consciousness at a given moment.

171. Due to our limited understanding we only notice fragments of this process.

172. By its very nature, the present of the world is bound up with its past and its future by that inner nexus which is very basic to monads.

173. From the monadological point of view, the world is not only one regular phenomenon, but a historical, ethical and social phenomenon as well.

174. We can only have a general picture of the main movement of this process, but cannot foresee its full course in detail.

175. The perfection of monads is advanced by experience and observation. The inductive method plays here a very important role.

176. As the monads develop the different forms of monadological life will become more and more apparent, but this will also create an infinite number of new insoluble problems.

177. Infinity is the only expression to really characterize this process.

178. The monadological world-view does not contradict science, but is based on science and is in full accord with the ideal tasks of

ethics, sociology and with all the profound doctrines of the Absolute.

What Is Man From The Viewpoint of Evolutionary Monadology?

179. Man is on the hand, an individual, and on the other hand, he is a social system of monads, more or less bound not only by an organic unity, but by a unity of ideal aims and ideal tasks.

180. He realizes these tasks and aims in accordance with his abilities, means and capacities.

181. He is a necessary active link in the world of beings or other social systems. He consists of living elements endowed with the tasks and aims which correspond to their appointed goal and development.

182. The importance of man and his duty to the world and other monads, are the simple results of his dignity and his great purpose in the general world system of monads.

183. His concrete and embodied form, from this point of view, is not an accidental collection of atoms, like inanimate stones, but is an artistic edifice endowed throughout with life and spirit.

184. Man, from this viewpoint, is a living shrine in which the highest aims and most important task of the world's life are actively realized. Here then are the answers of evolutionary monadology to the questions: What is the world and what is man?

BIOGRAPHICAL SKETCH

Boris Nikolayevich Chicherin (1828-1903) was educated at the University of Moscow where he was enrolled in the Faculty of Law. It was there that he came under the influence of the famous professor T. N. Granovski, but the greatest influence which determined his philosophical Weltanschauung, was Hegelianism.

Like many other Russian intellectuals, Chicherin experienced a religious crisis during his student days, which shaped many of his future philosophic ideas. One chief result of this crisis was his repudiation of Hegel's basic idea, namely, that of an "Absolute in process of becoming". Chicherin argued that since Spirit is both the initial and final form of the Absolute, it follows that it cannot be subject to the process of becoming. While he is often called a Hegelian, it is more true to say that his ideas were more close to Kant and Fichte than to Hegel. He did not merely modify Hegel's views, but in many important respects deviated from them in a radical way. In his efforts to overcome Hegel's dialectual scheme, he arived at the idea of the "transcendence." of the Absolute. Thus, Hegelian transcendentalism was replaced by transcendentism.

Chicherin's anthropology is based on the idea that there is an 'absolute principle' in man, which is reason, and which is always striving to cognize the Absolute, while his metaphysics stresses the absolute importance of man's moral principle. He developed his personalistic views within the bounds of Hegelianism, based on the ideas of the existence of an 'absolute principle' in man. He tried to reconcile science, philosophy and religion on the basis of the unity of Reason.

Chicherin's epistemology is deeply rooted in his transcendentalism. His basic assumption is that "the fundamental law of reason is also the fundamental law of the material world". While he accepts the Hegelian principle of the dialectical scheme by acknowledging the inner contradiction in the principles themselves, he modifies this scheme by introducing a tetradic scheme. (a) Initial unity; (b) relations between elements, or (c) combinations of elements; (d) higher or final unity of the two. He distinguishes between 'real' unity which underlies phenomena from 'logical' which connects the phenomena in human cognition. He is forced to admit however, that we cannot know the real essence of things by means of our senses, but this merely limits the importance of our experience rather than our knowledge. Since Reason is one and indivisible, its laws are applicable to the world of appearance as well as to the Absolute.

His chief works are: "Science and Religion"; "Positive Philosophy and the Unity of Science"; "Mysticism in Science"; "Principles of Logic and Metaphysics"; "Philosophy of Law", besides his juridical works which we do not list here.

B. N. Chicherin

IS METAPHYSICS A SCIENCE?*

The opposition between metaphysics and science is one of the popular ideas at the present time. Science may be defined as that which we know for certain, a knowledge of the truth of things. Metaphysics is nothing more than vain abstractions, creations of the imagination, which have nothing to do with the real world. At any rate, it is considered to be a collection of hypotheses about which we cannot have any "certain" (authentic) information. This is the viewpoint of those who assume that experience constitutes the only source of our knowledge of objects around us as well as of ourselves.

Is this position tenable? Is experience really the only source of our knowledge? Can science itself, which is governed by reason, dispose of metaphysical ideas, which, consciously or unconsciously, are involved in everything we think or investigate? This is the question which faces the philosopher at the present time.

The first thing that strikes us in experience is that it is extremely limited. The only thing that external and internal senses reveal to us is a series of simultaneous or consecutive phenomena. They are not connected by any internal link. As a result, the protagonists of the empirical method are forced to reduce association of ideas to a simple habit. This was Hume's position, as well as that of John Stuart Mill. Hence, the direct conclusion is, if the ordinary sequence of events can be known to us, then we cannot have the slightest notion of the causes which produce this sequence. The essence of things remains for us a permanently closed world. "Ignoramus et semper ignorabimus", say

* This selection was originally read at the International Philosophical Congress in Paris, and was published in *Voprosy*, Vol. II, Bk. 54, pp. 460-657.

the leaders of empirical sciences. Being limited to a narrow region revealed to us by the senses, we are surrounded by an infinity of "the uncognizable". Nature, life, the very essence of man, all the higher problems of the moral world remain for us an impenetrable secret.

Moreover, this world of the uncognizable is precisely what man seeks to know; he alone can find an answer to the most basic needs of his mind and heart. In his introduction to his "Course of Positive Philosophy", Auguste Comte says, by a strange contradiction, man, as soon as he begins to think, asks himself precisely those questions which he is completely incapable of solving, questions about the beginning and end of things. Similarly, it would be a strange contradiction, if a thinking being, because of his bent of mind, were destined to constantly ask certain questions which he could not possibly solve. It is pointless to tell him that a mature mind should know its limits. Actual necessity causes him to get out of this vicious circle. Reason, by its very nature, goes beyond the limits of experience, and the problem of our own destiny depends on it. All our relations with people and things are closely bound up with the solution of these higher questions precisely because they arise as soon as man becomes aware of himself. If he could never solve them, then everything is chaos for him.

In recent years people used to speak about the bankruptcy of science. If by science is meant empirical knowledge, and by bankruptcy is meant the inability to solve the higher problems of the human mind and soul, then we would agree. Empirical science itself recognizes its limitations. In such an event, the only thing left for man to do is to throw himself blindly into the arms of religion which answers his profoundest needs and offers him high hopes.

But is science really in this position? Does it not transgress those limits given to us by the senses, and is there not another source of knowledge which would reveal to us incomparably wider horizons?

If we were to analyse the data and results of the empirical sciences not in the form in which they are understood by the empiricists, but as they actually exist in reality, we would easily see that they contain something other than that given to us by the senses. Empirical science does not limit itself to the assertion of coherence and sequence of phenomena; it looks for their "causes". The concept of cause is one of those (ideas) which especially troubles philosophers, who recognize nothing but experience. One should note to what strange devices Mill resorts in order to substantiate the concept of cause and effect of events which is in his view, the only coherent theory. Reid[2] has already pointed out that according to this theory which Hume developed, day

2 Thomas Reid (1710-1796), founder of the Scottish School, author of *Inquiry into the Human Mind on the Principles of Common Sense*, etc.

is the cause of night and night is the cause of day, since they invariably follow each other. By the same token, one should admit that dawn is the cause of sunrise, and not vice versa. To avoid these consequences, Mill asserts that an event which precedes another event is called a cause when this sequence is "absolute", as if the action of all causes known to us from experience does not depend on very different conditions. According to this way of reasoning we cannot say that the plague is the cause of people's death, since not all people die from it. It should be noted that Mill is the first to insist that we know only the relative, hence, anything that is unconditional, i.e. absolute, is beyond our knowledge. This explanation proves more than anything else, the inconsistency of this theory.

This concept of cause does not issue from inner experience, as certain philosophers wanted to prove. Hume already refuted this hypothesis. We actually know from experience, that we often do what we want, but we are often unable to put our wish into action, hence, we completely fail to understand how thought can be the cause of physical motion. Much less do we have the right to transfer the facts of our consciousness to material things which are devoid of consciousness. To subsume such different phenomena under one concept, borrowed from one category and, which are completely inapplicable to the other, is an act which contradicts reason. If, in spite of this, we elevate causality to a general law, this is not because we obtain this idea from this or that particular phenomenon, but because we get it from reason itself, for which it is its sine qua non, and which therefore, by virtue of its own laws, applies it to all phenomena, although he often cannot show any rational connection between them.

According to the empirical theory, the category of causality as well as the concepts of "substance" and "force" are nothing more than vain creations of speculation, yet, they are regarded by the physical sciences as indisputable truths. Water is not only a combination of sensuous qualities. The properties of liquid are completely different from the properties of snow and vapors. Yet, this is one and the same element, i.e. one and the same substance, which takes on different forms. Moreover, science tells us that this substance consists of two other elements, which are more simple, viz., oxygen and hydrogen, which have completely different qualities than their combination. No matter into how many combinations they may enter, not a single molecule of these elements will either increase or diminish. The amount of matter determined by its weight remains always the same. There are only combinations and divisions accompanied by a complete change of sensuous qualities. Such is the firm conclusion of science. In view of the above, to affirm that the concept of substance is only vague illusion, a pure mental abstraction, is to refute the obvious. It is actually the creation of the mind, and is not given to us by the senses. But it is a creation which corresponds to the reality of things without which one cannot even think them.

This is also true of the concept of force, which empirical theorists, such as Mill, consider it to be antiphilosophical, but which nonetheless is the necessary principle of the physical sciences. The conservation of force or energy is a law established on reliable scientific foundations. It turns out that this abstract illusion is a very real object, whose quantity always remains the same, although it passes through various bodies and states, manifesting itself in the form of potential energy or possibility, now as actual energy or motion. Metaphysical concepts of potentiality and reality find here a scientific application. It is interesting to see the strange explanations offered by the empiricists in order to reconcile irrefutable facts with their theory. Mill reduces the law of energy to a subjective expectation of future events.

Moreover, among the many sciences of which the human mind is proud, there is one which is based on firm foundations and whose conclusions are unmistakeable, it is the science of mathematics. This is precisely the science which does not resort to empirical data or to any of the methods used by empirical sciences. How then are we to explain this fact, if all our notions come from the senses, and we can only deduce one fact from another, i.e. by analogy? Mill affirms that in mathematics we conduct our investigations by abstract ideas, instead of resorting to experience, because these abstractions are indeed the exact replica of real objects, which does not apply to other sensuous forms. He does not tell us how this strange coincidence arises, nor why we can better discover truth by means of images rather than by investigating real objects. At any rate, this curious explanation does not apply to the concepts of pure mathematics, to numbers, to algebraic signs or to infinitely minute quantities of mathematical analysis. No one has ever seen an infinitely small quantity or a derivative, yet, science establishes laws of celestial phenomena, the movement of stars, predicts eclipses and discovers unknown worlds by calculations based on these definitions. If time permitted, it could be shown that the infallible conclusions in geometry are based on the fact that we are dealing with intellectual notions of space and not with data of experience. Analytical geometry which reduces images into formulas and calculations are expressed in figures, serves as obvious proof.

In view of the above, it is difficult to understand how great minds and even great scientists can regard mathematics as a science that has its basis in empirical data. This shows how the human mind when it is fascinated by current trends can arrive not only at a false idea about its personal actions, but also arrive at a denial of the obvious. Mathematical science shows conclusively that our knowledge has a dual source, experience and thought, the latter originating in the data of pure reason, can arrive at completely reliable conclusions about the laws governing the world. It is precisely the combination of these two sources of knowledge which constitutes the grandeur of the physical sciences. Consequently, the devotees of the physical sciences are inclined to regard the mechanical world-view as the only truly rational view.

Actually, this world-view alone could have been recognized to be scientific, if the human mind had had clear and exact ideas only of the category of quantity which is the whole content of mathematics. But is this the case? Besides quantity there are the categories of quality, modality and relation, to use Kant's expression. These are indeed forms that are peculiar to human reason; they enable him to understand things and to connect events by a link other than by coherence and sequence. Is it possible that only part of his personal reserve can provide him with reliable conclusions, while all the rest is nothing more than vain illusions which do not correspond to anything real? This cannot be. Reason is one, and all its definitions are connected by a rational link. If it can be proven that in one of its part it can arrive "a priori" at completely reliable conclusions, this ought to be true of the rest (of reason). Science should define clearly and exactly all speculative ideas employed by the mind in understanding things and should reveal the link which binds them together. Obviously, this problem can be solved, since its object is not beyond our capacities of investigation, but are the very capacities which are given to us by our self-consciousness.

The science which should deal with this investigation is logic. Its first task should be an analysis of the human mind, to distinguish in it that which comes from without from its relation to its environment, and that which is given to it by its own structure, the laws of its activity, or the a priori element. Is this task fulfilled?

Seeing what is taking place at the present time in the world of ideas, one may ask, is logic an exact science? If by the term logic is meant the sum of truths established on firm foundations and recognized by everybody, then logic less than any other branch of human knowledge can lay claim to such an appellation. There is not a single actual situation about which the investigators of this area would agree among themselves. The logic of the empiricists, which is recognized by the majority, of which Mill's logic is the standard is nothing less than a negation of logic. The human mind is regarded as an empty box into which forms, raised to the level of independent beings, enter from without, where they become more or less permanent habits, but have no rational connection. When the premise on which the whole of mathematics is based, namely, that two quantities which are equal to a third quantity are equal to each other, when this is merely considered a matter of habit recognized by everybody solely because we have not seen another (case), then we can no longer talk about logic. Facts are present, but reason is absent. We should not therefore be astonished at the monstrous explanations offered for all rational ideas, such as, causes, forces, substances as well as mathematical conclusions.

Meanwhile, as long as logic is not established upon solid foundations, how can man have a rational understanding of the world and things? Under these circumstances there is only a place for vain theories and fantasies freed from the barriers imposed upon them by reason. This is to a certain degree the spectacle which philosophy presents at the present time.

In order to extricate ourselves from this chaos in which empiricism has involved us, it is imperative that logic become a true science, based upon firm foundations. Logic has all the ingredients for this purpose. It was not in vain that the greatest minds labored during the entire development of human thought. We must resort to them to discover the true basis of human reason and rid ourselves of vain illusions with which people are trying to confuse us.

The first problem which faces us is the definition of speculative and empirical elements of our knowledge. Is there a reliable sign which would enable us to differentiate between them? The empirical element is all that is given to us by the senses, both externally and internally, excluding from the latter category the mind's awareness of its own actions, since this is a speculative element of cognition. Reason is an activity, hence, an active force, as such, has its own laws. All concepts which are derived from the modes of the mind's action, but not from empirical data, are either speculative or a priori concepts. But the actual activity of the mind consists in the union and division of representations of images; consequently, all ideas which are contained in these two actions, are indeed speculative ideas. Such is the concept of quantity which is not more than a union and division of a homogeneous (element) from which we get the idea of the one and the many. Such also are the categories of affirmation and negation, or being and non-being and their relations; then there are the categories of action, or modality, as they are usually called, i.e. possibility, necessity and reality, finally, all other concepts of pure reason which "in toto" form a whole system issuing from one source, namely, from reason as an active force, consequently, bound internally by a rational link.

An exposition of Hegel's system is not within the scope of my paper.

I must say, however, that in my opinion, a great deal of the objections raised against his Logic, especially those of Trendelenburg,[3] are generally based on an incorrect understanding of Hegel's intellectual definitions and dialectical methods, and they therefore miss the point. I do not mean to say that Hegel's Logic is a perfect work. His language is barbaric which renders understanding incomprehensible. His ideas are often obscure, the passages are at times very artificial; his arrangement of material could have been changed to a better advantage. But this is nevertheless the only grandiose and truly scientific attempt to formulate a complete system of speculative ideas which govern the human mind in the cognition of things. Hegel laid solid foundations for this edifice; all future work ought to be related to him. This is the chief task of our present time. No philosopher can deviate from it, since it is the foundation of the whole of philosophy. Without this (system) there are only vague hypotheses, which may capture the imagination, but which are incapable of satisfying the demands of science. Meanwhile these demands must be satisfied and there is no reason why this should not be fulfilled. If mathematics offers us a completely rational and infallible system of all ideas which issue from the category of quantity, why then could this not be done with other categories of the human mind? All the elements for this purpose are present; what is lacking is work. This work demands the co-operation of all those who are occupied with philosophy; but this is not beyond human strength, since in this case the mind is only concerned with itself. What is required is a clear and exact awareness of their actions.[4]

A logical deduction of the categories is the very essence of metaphysics. Hegel understood this well; all his metaphysics is contained in his logic. One must however, make a distinction here. There is a concrete logic, which is usually designated by this term and whose function it is to define and describe all the actions of the human mind in cognizing objects beginning with sensual impressions to the most abstract ideas. Moreover, there is an abstract logic, which takes only one a priori element and seeks to deduce all rational ideas contained in the mind. The latter (abstract logic) merges with metaphysics and is its foundation. If it is now asked, is metaphysics a science? The answer is obviously indubitable. If logic is a science, so is metaphysics. Of course, it is not a perfect science, but the same may be said about logic and about many others (sciences). It does not prevent it from

---

[3] A. Trendelenburg (1802-1872), he set forth the conception of "Motion" in place of Hegel's dialectical principle, and thereby tried to combat Hegel's philosophy. He is the author of *Logische Untersuchungen* and *Naturrecht*.

[4] I tried to outline this system in my *Foundations of Logic and Metaphysics* (author's footnote).

having an exactly definite content subject to investigation. Speculative ideas of mind are a reliable fact, but so is their logical conection. It is not even necessary here to discover anything new; all that is required is to define the ideas and on this basis it is possible to arrive at completely reliable conclusions, since reason is one in all creatures endowed with it (reason).

It may be asked, how is this logical deduction of the categories related to the cognition of things? This is no more than a series of abstract ideas; the reality of things, however, is completely different, it is precisely this real essence that metaphysics wishes to disclose to us. The answer given to this objection is that the laws of reason and the laws of the universe are indeed one and the same, hence, the concept of reason are an expression of these laws and correspond to the nature of things. Mathematics is a clear proof of this truth. All mathematical calculations are based on the laws of human reason, yet, on the basis of these calculations, we determine facts completely independent of reason, such as the prediction of an eclipse of the sun, new planets are discovered, etc. Only identical laws can produce such a coincidence. This also applies to metaphysical ideas.

If abstract ideas of the mind correspond to the nature of things, then we must still determine the relation between these two spheres. It is necessary to find out how these ideas and the laws which bind them apply to the phenomenon of nature and spirit. This application must be of a dual kind. Just as there is a concrete and an abstract logic, it is possible to have a concrete and abstract application of the categories and the laws which bind them to real objects.

The concrete application consists in determining what categories and speculative laws are applicable to this or that phenomenon, given to our senses, and how this application is to be achieved scientifically. This requires three things: (1) a clear and exact definition of speculative ideas and the laws which bind them; this is the task of metaphysics; (2) a clear and a sufficiently complete knowledge of facts; this is the task of empirical sciences. If our knowledge does not correspond to the reality of things, and if all aspects of a phenomenon are not sufficiently clarified, then the application of the laws may always be incorrect; (3) one must arrange the phenomena in such a way so that the general law can be applied. This method is employed by mathematics: when all the data are present, one has to arrange them in such a way as to be able to apply the calculations. This arrangement must not be arbitrary, but must be based on empirical data, otherwise its application would again be incorrect. Nonetheless, the creation of a middle term between the pure ideas of the mind and sensual phenomena is a separate task. It is the task of philosophy whose foundation is metaphysics, but which entails the philosophy of nature and spirit as well. To achieve this task in a truly scientific manner, metaphysics must, on the one hand, elaborate clear and exact ideas, capable of forming a complete system, and on the other hand, the empirical sciences must be sufficiently developed and should permit a rational construction. If one of these conditions is absent, there is always likely to be a mistake in applying the abstract ideas. Herein is the secret of all the confusion of philosophy in the history of human thought.

Besides the concrete application to this or that category of real phenomena, there may also be an abstract application, which serves as a rule for the first one. We must not have in mind a particular phenomenon, but a phenomenon in general, as a relation between object and subject, and then find out what categories are specifically applicable to these relations. This again is the prerogative of metaphysics, since we are not here dealing with empirical data, but with the very essence of those relations and those laws which direct the mind in its objective activity. How does it define its object?

It is obvious, that the most general categories of human reason, such as the categories of quantity, quality, modality, are equally applicable to both objects of the senses and to pure concepts of reason. Here we have actually nothing objective. I may reason in mathematics without having in mind any real object. But there is a group of categories which are specifically applicable to real objects. They are those which Kant called the categories of relation, but which could more accurately be termed the categories of reality. Kant enumerated three (categories), viz., (a) substantiality, or the relation of substance to signs; (b) causality, or the relation of cause and effect; (c) reciprocity, or the relation of reciprocal action to the law that governs it. Kant omitted a fourth category which however exists, and fits in with the rest, namely, finiteness, or the relation of end to means. It is the opposite of the category of causality, since the latter, the beginning determines the end, whereas in the first (case) it is the reverse, where the end determines the beginning. If we were to examine a phenomenon "per se" as a relation of object to subject in general, we would find in it precisely these four categories. We have here necessarily a substance, as a substratum of a phenomenon, or a unity which is at the basis of plurality. There is an active force which is the cause of the phenomenon. Then there is a law governing reciprocal action with the subject, finally, as a reaction of the subject, there is the aim which it sets before itself in investigating phenomena and the benefit derived from it. All the empirical sciences do not offer us anything more. It cannot be otherwise, since man thinks only in accordance with the laws of his reason.

It follows from the above that these categories are "a fortiori" applicable to the subject, as a thinking being endowed with self-consciousness. As such, it is first of all an active force. This force has its laws by which it is governed, the aim it sets for itself. Finally, the subject has also its material side which is exposed to external actions and by means of which it can act on the latter.

These four categories are identical with Aristotle's four principles: The productive cause, the formal cause, material cause, and teleological or final cause. There are no others in the history of philosophy. The difference in the philosophical systems depends on the emphasis placed on one of these principles. All the rest is either a corollary or an addition.

If these categories are applicable to every reality, to subject as well as to object, then they are necessarily applicable also to absolute reality which transcends both subject and objects and binds them by a higher link. The subject and object stand in opposition to each other, therefore they form a universe of the relative. But everything that is relative presupposes something absolute, because everything which depends for its existence on something else, presuppose something which depends only on itself and which exists by itself. This is indeed absolute Being, whose existence is the necessary condition of reason, and out of which issues everything that is relative. Cognition of this Being is not given to us by the senses; hence, the empiricists admit its uncognizability, if indeed they do not deny it altogether. But those for whom reason is not an empty box where shadows of phenomena encounter and interlace, i.e. shadows of shadows, but for whom it is a living force whose laws provide true knowledge of things, can no more doubt the existence of the absolute Being than they can doubt their own existence. This is a necessary idea of reason without which it cannot understand anything. It is only necessary to define what this Being is, and it is here that difficulties and disagreements begin. Since the senses give us no idea about it, then the idea about it must be determined "a priori", by the laws of reason. Hence, the question is, are the categories of reason applicable to this infinite Being in the same way as they can be applied to finite things and to the world of relativity?

Why would they not be applicable to it? Does the concept of the infinite leave the narrow sphere of our thought and do the categories of reason lose their meaning when they cross the limits of the relative? Kant wanted to prove that we fall into insoluble contradictions when we wish to define absolute being by the categories, but his successors showed how baseless his skepticism was. He himself laid the foundations of the ideal understanding of the relation of the infinite to the finite, and this resulted in the emergence of the greatest philosophical systems of our times. Leaving aside these debatable questions about which there may be the most diverse views, we have obvious proof that the categories of reason are applicable to both the infinite and the finite. The deductions of geometry and mechanics, which are based on the ideas of infinite space and time, serve as illustrations of this truth, and precisely on this ground that they have their value. The concept of absolute Being is however, something incomparably higher than the notions of space and time. This is the essential idea of reason without which it cannot comprehend the very existence of the relative. Is it possible that the laws of reason are inapplicable to this Being whose existence constitutes its sine qua non, logically issuing from these very laws? This would be a patent contradiction.

The application of intellectual categories to absolute Being had always been precisely the task of philosophical and religious systems. The highest Being was always defined as an infinite Power, as Supreme Reason and as the End of all things. The fourth principle – the material principle, is inapplicable to the Absolute as such, since it is the principle of all that is contingent and relative. The relation of the Godhood to the world constitute the material aspect of its existence.

The application of the intellectual categories to absolute Being is metaphysics' higher tasks. It is not its foundations, but its tasks is its completion. It is for this reason that all philosophical systems are preoccupied with this theme. In this respect they differ only in their preference for one or the other of these categories which leads to different results. The same situation obtains in religious systems. The highest religion which appeared to mankind, the one which was the turning point in history, and which even at the present time all educated nations profess, namely, Christianity, worship God in three persons, as Power, as the Word and as Spirit, i.e. as the Source, the Law and the End of all things. Philosophy recognizes in this its own ideas, and this constitutes a link which unites it with religion. Religion remains a completely closed world, if not a hostile one, for empirical science which is merely the formless material of true science. Those however, who go back to metaphysical principles, these two great areas of the human spirit, philosophy and religion, are called upon not to be hostile to each other, but rather to unite for the purpose of raising mankind anew to those summits, where whole horizons will be revealed and from whence mankind will be able to survey that spacious road which lies ahead, and that goal which it must strive to achieve. The Light which is called upon to lead it in this journey is Reason and no one can deny it (Reason) this right, and in spite of its errors it is a reflection of the eternal Light given to man for the knowledge of things.

BIOGRAPHICAL SKETCH

Lev Mikhailovich Lopatin (1855-1920) was professor at the Moscow University and was an outstanding psychologist. He succeeded Professor N. Ya. Grot as President of the Moscow Psychological Society and as editor of *Voprosy filosofii i psikhologii* (Problems of Philosophy and Psychology). Lopatin was a prolific writer, and most of his articles and books were in the field of psychology and philosophy. His master's and doctoral dissertations were published into two volumes under the title *The Positive Tasks of Philosophy* (1886, 1891). This is his most important philosophic work and deserves careful and serious reading.

As a close friend of Vladimir Solovyov, he was undoubtedly greatly influenced by him. His greatest influence came, however, from Leibniz and Lotze. His anthropological views are reflected in both his metaphysics and his ethics. He contributed nothing new to epistemology.

In his long article "Theoretical Foundations of the Conscious Moral Life" (published in *Voprosy filosofii i psikhologii*, No. 5, 1890) he discusses the nature of man and the nature of the moral principle, which in his view, 'extends throughout the universe'. Man is a supratemporal being, a creative spirit, who is nonetheless mortal and dependant upon the Absolute. Lopatin regards 'spirituality and creativity' as two inseparable concepts which characterize man. From this premise he deduces freedom of the will and the moral rationality of universal life. Man's ultimate goal is to overcome evil by striving toward the Good, which is a 'quality and law of nature'. Man, thus plays an important role in the transfiguration of the cosmos through his rational and moral creativity, and thereby achieves his destiny.

Lopatin believes that the same universal laws are applicable to the world of nature and to the moral world. His system may be characterized as rationalistic theism and personalism. His monadology seeks to reconcile monism and pluralism by recognizing that there is 'multiplicity in unity' and 'unity in multiplicity'. Most of his philosophic articles were published in a volume entitled "Philosophic Characterizations and Addresses" (1911). His articles on psychological subjects appeared in *Voprosy filosofii i psikhologii*.

L. M. Lopatin

MONISM AND PLURALISM*

I

In my previous article I did not manage to deal with one matter which is nevertheless very important in the general discussion concerning the valid place of monism in philosophy. The point is that the word "monism" has two different meanings in philosophy which, while they are similar, are by no means identical.

We understand by "monism" not only the recognition of the inner uniformity of the world (i.e. qualitative – in the sense of fundamental properties of being), we also understand that term to mean the unity of the origin of the world principle, or the unity (Cause, Source, Creative Force) of universal reality. These two meanings of the word "monism" must be distinguished, otherwise there will be considerable misunderstanding. History shows that in different philosophical theories, monism in the first sense and monism in the second sense do not often coincide. For example, the systems of medieval scholasticism were all monistic in the second sense, because they deduce the being of the universe from the creative acts of a single God. We cannot however, label them monists in the first sense, because they all held – to a greater or lesser extent – sharply-defined dualistic views regarding the interrelationship between spirit and matter. The same may be said even more emphatically regarding Descartes' philosophy and his school and even of Spinoza's world-view. Spinoza is the classical representative of absolute monism in his theory of the origin of things and their relationship to the one divine substance, but at the same time he was not only a dualist but the most decided "pluralist" in his theory of an infinite

* This selection is taken from *Voprosy*, Vol. 6, No. 116, pp. 68-92 (1913).

number of divine attributes each of which denotes an entire separate universe, very unlike the universes of the other attributes.[5] As a rule, wherever we encounter theistic, deistic or pantheistic presuppositions in modern Europe, we have a monistic theory in the second sense, but which usually accommodates itself quite successfully to a dualistic view on the inner nature of things. In this connection, modern dualism in contradistinction to ancient dualism, is very rarely argued in a conclusive manner, unless one should recognize two absolutely independent and equally valid sources of being. On the other hand, we find in both ancient and modern times a number of philosophical theories which are monistic in the first sense but are clearly pluralistic in their hypotheses regarding the origin of the existence of things.[6] First of all we have the materialistic theories of the atomistic type. Atoms are regarded here as the final elements or roots of every reality which do not presuppose any higher principles above them, but this in no way prevents them from attributing to them a completely uniform essence. The same may be said of Herbart's realities with their unattainable simplicity and their uniform quality.[7]

What kind of normal relation could there be between these two types of monism in a philosophical system which would meet all the requirements of logical thought? It is quite obvious that such a system must contain both types of monism. One must refer again to the property of the human mind which strives towards a single concept, namely, the logical necessity of recognizing some single origin of things, is based on the fact that one cannot think of a contrary hypothesis if it is driven to its logical conclusion.

There is no doubt that the universe as we experience it is a multiplicity of thing, objects and beings. Equally indubitable, however, is the inner co-relativity of the elements of this multiplicity, their mutual conditionality and connection, their evident mutual dependence, their comprehensive unity in some whole which defines them. One cannot logically refute the innate properties of the objects known to us. Everything in the world around us is a part of some single system and is from the very beginning of its existence adaptable to it, and in its very being and properties is related to other parts. They do not have a single feature or property which would not imply the existence of certain other parts of the system. I am not speaking here about any ingeneous

[5] See L. M. Lopatin, "Positive Tasks of Philosophy", Ch. 1, 2nd ed., pp. 302-308.
[6] By pluralism I understand a recognition of the primordial plurality of centres and origins of being.
[7] Johann Friedrich Herbard, b. 1776, died in 1841. Was Profesor in Königsberg and at Göttingen. His complete works consist of 12 volumes. Mostly on philosophy.

hypothetical premises, not, for example, that the smallest particle around us must reflect in itself all the changes even though it were at a considerable distance from us, but about facts that are much simpler and indisputable, e.g., that physical bodies occupy some space which will not admit any other bodies into it if they cannot move into a space that is not as yet occupied, that they interchange places, that they do not move freely like abstract geometrical bodies move in an abstract geometrical space, but that in their movement they must overcome obstacles in their way, etc. Why is it that bodies can interfere with each other and do not permit any collision to take place among themselves? This leads to a question that is irresistibly simple: What was it that united and bound the bodies in a single real space and placed them in it, as it were, face to face? Did the bodies themselves do it? But so long as there was no location in space, no impenetrability or mobility, there were no bodies there. Can we say that there is no real basis or cause for all things to be in one space or to be an interaction in it? One can, of course, say anything. But would such an answer make sense?

There is still another problem of specifically philosophical significance about which I have already said a great deal. It is one that gives the metaphysical problem about being which is transcendent to our consciousness (it is metaphysical because it does not permit a strictly empirical solution) its unshakeable vitality, its urgency, its firm practical significance. I have in mind the matter of "someone else's consciousness" or "someone else's animation". Why does someone else's consciousness exist for me, and how am I linked to it? This problem involves a large number of other questions which direct our thoughts further into the transcendent-metaphysical sphere. Why do living creatures know about each other and perceive the same medium through which they can give each other signs of their existence? Someone else's consciousness is revealed to us only through someone else's actions and expressions; in its inner subjective content it is completely closed to us. It is wholly beyond the limits of the experience of everyone of us, and by admitting it, we acknowledge the presence of real beings that are completely independent of the directly experienced content of our individual psychic life. Judging from the manifestations of someone else's consciousness, we become firmly convinced that the living creatures around us, for all the differences in impressions received in point of view and in breadth of scope, they perceive the same universe as we do. What in this case, unites and binds us? Why do we sense the same things, and why can we bear witness of to each other? This question cannot be eliminated, irrespective of our philosophical views, provided we do not lapse into absolute solipsism by trying to be honest and consistent.

Let us take the point of view of idealistic-immanentism or subjective idealism, and let us agree that every object is given directly in the subject, and there is, therefore, nothing in the world except the cognising selves and that which appears to them. We inevitably encounter the question of a single higher Self which is at the basis of all individual selves, and forces them to live in the same dream-world, or the question of a single divine spirit who is the immutable source of compulsory pictures flashing before the consciousness of finite spirits.

Let us, on the other hand, adopt a more realistic view and regard the visible world as being independent of our spiritual perception and as independent medium, we will then ask what unifies this medium with our consciousness and what permits it to be a "single" medium. The problem of the mutual bond which obtains between many cognising centres shows quite clearly that the source of its real unity is not to be found in the individual member of the general system of being.

How could we persuade ourselves to perceive the world if we did not receive any reaction or impressions from it? How could we force other consciousness to perceive the same thing as we do? And finally, how could we make the medicine to be the same for all? It is abundantly clear that there must be a unity independent of us which is prior to the multiplicity of conscious living beings of which we are so firmly convinced.

I wish to dwell on still another question – a question that is closely related to the one just considered, one that is very simple and quite real and inevitable: Where is the unity of the laws of nature of the world that is accessible to us, and the constancy of the forces acting on it? I am not talking here about the purely formal laws of logic and mathematics which can be discussed to a certain degree without any premises concerning some real basis for them. I have in mind laws that have a completely real content which unfirmly determine the manifestation of the same forces in the boundless space of the universe. Why does physical impenetrability exist and why is it the property of all bodies and why does it act equally in all of them? Why do all bodies conform to the law of inertia? Why is the law of gravity universal? Can we assume that the unity of the visible world created the ultimate units of a body, viz., the absolute atoms?

Let us even assume that there is in each atom an inner force of individual creativity which enables them to assume spontaneously the properties that belong to them. It would seem, nevertheless, that they would be able to obtain only such properties that pertain to each one of them individually. But why do they create for themselves properties which belong to all other atoms? What causes this coincidence? Why, moreover, do they attribute to themselves general laws of action which not only concern them but which control all atoms of the whole world? Does it not follow from these very simple conundrums that one cannot understand the uniformity of nature, without presupposing some inner unifying principle in it? [8]

At this point the opponents of the monistic world-view would probably object that there is no basis for assuming that each atom in nature is some miniature absolute, nor is there basis for denying that certain general laws universal in character and mode of action are acting in the world. In order to refute monism, it is sufficient to assume that there is not one but several such forces, and that they possess from the very outset independent existences and do not originate from a single primordial source.

One can hardly be happy with such an unprincipled amendment. One need only think seriously about this transposition of concepts to be convinced that there is really no change in the substance of the problem, and that the advantage consists entirely in the fact that the problem is transferred to a more abstract sphere in which the logical inconsistencies are not so glaringly obvious. I cannot at all understand why, if absolutely primordial and original atoms cannot combine themselves into a uniform and internally-connected world, then universal forces which are just as independent of each other and of everything outside them should be able to do the same as the atoms? In fact, the universal forces of nature, by their very concept, are interwoven at every point of the world in a common action; what has woven these forces together? Did they do it themselves? How is this possible when all other forces are completely independent of every given force? In fact, according to the premise under consideration, they were from the very beginning completely independent, hence, nothing could bind them together or induce them to act together. Will someone object that their independence is not absolute but only conditional, and that they are independent in some respects, but on the other hand are from the outset dependent and interrelated? If however, this statement has any definite meaning, can it be an objection to monism? Can it not rather "imply monism"? However independent individual forces of nature may be, the presence in them of some initial dependence must imply that this dependence was introduced into them by something, and not

[8] I must make a reservation here. It is not very important in this case which laws of nature possess an absolute, universal character and which do not, and which of them extend to the entire universe of space and time, and indeed whether such laws exist? The important question is that if a unified universe exists and if in parts of it one can find at least some universality, correlativity and connection, one cannot understand it without presupposing some real internally united basis for it.

of course, by themselves, if it is peculiar to them and only through it that they possess their particular mode of action. It is quite clear that this is something which points to the mutual bond and dependence of the different forces of the world and which must logically precede their difference and be their basis. It must be the unique and effective source of their diversity. Or is there nothing which introduces mutual dependence into the real forces of nature, neither in themselves nor above them? How can we speak of such dependence as a "given fact" and not as a simple illusion of our consciousness?

I have limited myself to general, simple and popular arguments in defending the monistic world-view, but it seems to me, that they are adequate to draw the following firm conclusions: absolute pluralism does not express the philosophical truth, because when driven to its logical conclusion, the pluralistic view concerning reality would result in clear and irrevocable logical contradictions. Since reality does not contain any obvious contradictions, it necessarily implies monism in a dual sense: (1) in the sense of a general unity of its inner nature and (2) in the sense of the real unity of the fundamental bases or forces which presuppose and bind the living diversity of the "real".

II

A few years ago there would have been no reason to discuss this in such detail. Until quite recently it seemed indisputable to the vast majority of thinkers of all schools, that monism contains the highest philosophical truth. In fact, it became necessary to fight against extreme monistic tendencies in general philosophic constructions and to prove that the general uniformity of the inner essence of things does not exclude a completely real qualitative heterogeneity of their individual manifestations, and that the unity of the absolute basis which creates and binds the world in no way prevents it from consisting of a real multiplicity of relatively independent separate beings and forces. The intellectual mood of the broad philosophical circles has now changed radically. A considerable number of brave and original minds have declared themselves definitely in favour of "pluralism" and against the traditional preference for monistic hypotheses in philosophy.[9]

The striving towards monism at any price was being regarded as the

---

[9] V. M. Khvostov is the thoughtful and chief representative of pluralism in Russia, his views are stated in his book, "The Ethics of Human Dignity". In it the reader will find a very clear and vivid exposition of the main arguments in favour of the pluralistic view, both in his basic theoretical premises and the moral conclusions which issue from them.

real source of the artificiality and lifelessness in the current solutions of the more vital philosophic problems. Monism is attacked for various motives, such as epistemological, metaphysical, moral and even religious. The brilliant inspirer and leader of this whole movement, as he was in many other cases, who gave rise to completely new trends in modern thought, was William James. James and his younger contemporary, Bergson, whom he later acknowledged as his teacher, were the strongest and most typical exponents of the intellectual ferment and the philosophical searchings and turmoil which has begun with such unexpected force to shake the pillars of the ruling European philosophical school which was steeped in tradition.

In the course of his many fruitful years of literary activity, James was always searching for new paths in every area encountered by his mind. He was an extraordinarily sincere and fearless seeker, who was ready to defend the most unpopular truths, once he was convinced of them. I do not know whether one could point to many propositions in his philosophy which he himself would have considered to be the final solution to any fundamental philosophical problem. His skeptical frame of mind and his sceptically-tinted method of investigation, naturally added to the lack of understanding of the general results of his strikingly brilliant philosophical works. Both James' method and his intellectual frame of mind were clearly, however, only the result of the inner duality which never left him. Where did it come from? Was it an inherent property of his insatiably inquisitive mind, or was it a random result of the interlacing contradictory influences among which he had to live and where his opinions were formed, and finally, did it depend on the conditions of his initial development and on the mental habits of a physician and physiologist? I do not know how to answer this biographical question, the fact is that sharp contradictions coexisted in James' mind, and they were never harmoniously reconciled to the end of his life.

The future historian of philosophy will have a difficult task in classifying James, this will not be due merely to the conditionality of general philosophical classifications. What, in fact, was James? He was one of the most inspired idealists in human history and an ardent advocate of pure empiricism, who considered himself a successor to John Stuart Mill, who indiscriminately censured not only contemporary forms of Anglo-American and German idealism, but also all idealistic theories of the past including Plato. He was a thinker who was fully conscious of the tremendous and vital importance of the highest truths of philosophy and one of the creators of modern pragmatism, for all its similarity to the crudely utilitarian evaluation of cognising processes, and, who, under the influence of Bergson, later arrived at a complete denial of logical laws and logical concepts as means and criteria of real knowledge. He was a deeply convinced spiritualist and mystic, who boldly advocated a more plausible proposition, viz., the idea that the divine and spiritual world was open directly to human experience. As a realist-psychologist, who, without any discussion, haughtily rejected the hypothesis of the "soul", preferring every other explanation which were not only very tenuous but were hardly comprehensible. He was one of the greatest opponents of materialism and an advocate of materialistic premises in every instance even though they had the slightest justification. He often discussed the most crucial and basic problem like a real materialist.

With such an abundance of intellectual tendencies and views, it would be difficult to arrive at any complete and perfect world-view. Indeed, in reading James' works, one is unwillingly amazed at the blatant contrast between the elegant simplicity of presentation, the subtlety and convincing clarity of argumentation and the various brilliant intuitions which at once open up new and very clear perspectives, on the one hand, and the vascillating uncertainty of the final conclusions which were often augmented by considerable concessions to the very world-view against which he indefatigably argued, on the other. It is true that James' concessions to his opponent was a unique method, sometimes very convincing to the reader. James frequently succeeds in justifying his views by first rejecting all the arguments he generally used in earlier defences of similar ideas. James' method may in this respect be characterized as the method of "maximum concessions and the minimum of assumptions". One cannot deny the unquestionable purposiveness and practical suitability of such an approach, especially in view of the circumstances under which he laboured. The juxtaposition in James' ideas of logically incompatible tendencies was something more substantial: it expresses the characteristic "indefiniteness" of James' position.

It seems to me that it is precisely this indefiniteness which is the main cause for the common and amazing lack of understanding of James' conclusions, because this is the last thing one would expect from such a powerful, clear, and remarkably sincere mind. As I understand it, it is in this indefiniteness of his ideas that we find the inner motive of his ardent and clever propagation of "pluralism" or what he called "pluralism" – I would even say that this propagation is the best illustration of the general indefiniteness of James' world-view. What in fact, is James' pluralism, if not an attempt to mechanically combine and contain within the framework of a single world concept, both a supranaturalistic theism and the crudest naturalism, as well as a comforting faith in the power of a moral world-order and a conviction in the elemental senselessness of life? Indefiniteness is never a positive achievement for any philosophical theory. Yet, one cannot but think that in the present philosophical mood, James' views are sure to meet with success among readers. This is very noticeable in several of James' successors. What, apparently attracts them most to his pluralism is, that having mastered him, they can happily retain their former realistic and naturalistic world-views, and still speak of the sanctity of ideals of the inner greatness of human personality, and of man's possibilty, with his abundance of culture and virtues, to direct the entire infinite universe onto the path of the final triumph of goodness and beauty.

III

The objections of the adherents of pluralism against the monistic philosophy are partly speculative and partly of a moral-religious nature. The purely speculative reasons are not forceful. If they produce a favourable impression it is due more to their incompleteness than to their wholly developed arguments. Thus, James dismisses as a useless verbal game his opponents' entire argument about the logical senselessness of existence which is absolutely independent and at the same time dependent and conditional.[10] One can refute any philosophical conclusion by this method, but is such a refutation of any great value? In support of his verdict he refers to the fact that it is conceivable to have a being which is independent in some respects and dependent in others. From the foregoing, we can already partially show by how much such considerations miss the mark. The point is that the absolute principles of the "real", although we may regard them as plural in number, are only conceivable as being independent and are completely inconceivable as being dependent.

To show the logical equality of monism and pluralism, James insists that it is equally permissible to regard the world from the point of view of the whole as from the point of view of the parts, that in the first case it results in monism and in the second in pluralism. But he forgets that it is still more correct logically to regard the world "both" from the point of view of the whole "and" from the point of view of the parts, and that we shall then have a real and vital monism which recognizes unity in multiplicity and multiplicity in unity. One cannot at all think about the whole, as this would be a consciously one-sided point of view. Much more convincing and irrefutable are the objections which James directs particularly against the contemporary leaders of Anglo-

10   See especially James' first two lectures in his "A Pluralistic Universe".

American Hegelianism, but because of their purpose they are of little general philosophic interest.

In my view the strongest speculative argument used by the defenders of pluralism in support of their position is their insistence on the "inverse non-deducibility of the multiplicity of reality from a presupposed unity of its absolute basis". They frequently argue thus: Monism deduces with apparent rigidity, the unity of the first principle of things from the connectedness of the elements of the cosmic life, and then stops helplessly before the problem of inversely constructing this cosmic life from its presupposed source. It is relatively easy to intellectually construct a single principle of the real, but, on the other hand, it is extremely difficult to return from it to the ever-moving multiplicity of the actual world, and monism destroys itself by its inability to explain the multiplicity of things from the primeval unity, which is however, only invented to explain the real multiplicity of the observable universe.

I repeat, that I consider this argument more forceful than the others, but this is no reason for exaggerating its importance. The argument would be quite valid if it had been previously shown that the concept of the single principle which appears in many forms and shapes of being contains a logical contradiction. But as far as I know no one has ever really proven such a contradiction despite the many attempts to do so, which dates back to the Eleatic philosophers. If this is so, then the logical step for us is to recognize that the basic unity of observable reality is not in the least eliminated by our inability to inversely construct the visible world from the internal creative processes in its first cause. This inability may be due simply to the fact that we do not have adequate knowledge of the intimate nature of this primordial unity, or, that we are simply not in the position to imagine it concretely. It should not be forgotten that in a vast number of our most basic and verified premises about reality we cannot inversely deduce an inner necessity for our presupposed agents and forces to have the nature and actions which we attribute to them.

The existence of a weightles cosmic medium is a highly probable premise of physics, since it offers a graphic explanation of the widening field of observable facts. Do we know why such a medium exists and why it possesses the properties which we are forced to attribute to it? We are certain of the existence of the force of gravity, because without it we could not understand anything. But do we really know what this force of gravity is and why its manifestations always correspond to our astronomical formulae about it? We are not disturbed by the fact that we cannot answer these questions. Why, then, must we reject the concept of a single principle in favour of any mutiplicity – although without it any real multiplicity is completely inconceivable, simply because we have no concrete knowledge of the manner and methods whereby the "one" presupposes the "many"?

The concept of "unity in multiplicity and multiplicity in unity", in fact, not only does not contain any logical contradiction, as has been shown but much more must be said about it. This is the only concept of real being which does not lead to its own negation and does not resolve itself into insoluble contradictions. "An absolutely single being" which possesses no multiplicity in any sense, – neither in its properties nor relationships nor in its manifestations and moments of self-disclosure is simply a combination of pure negatives which conceals as an excuse for thought, a complete vacuum, contentlessness, a complete absence of anything positive, it is something to which the very word "is" or "exists" loses any definite meaning and cannot be distinguished from "is not". Similarly, "an absolute multiplicity" of wholly independent elements, forces, or any other kinds of elements which are not bound by anything, ultimately results in the same sort of contentless and empty unity, only counted in a multiple number: there is nothing in hem to think about and they do not correspond to the reality that we know. Pure "monism" is an abstraction and just as dead and mute as s pure "pluralism". We perceive in ourselves a living unity in a living multiplicity, and we divine with compulsive clarity other beings around us in general.

Unity and multiplicity are interrelated concepts and cannot be separated for a clear and serious analysis. Plato recognized the great importance of the truth about the interrelatedness of the "one" and the "many", and tried, in his "Parmenides" to give it a conclusive basis through the immanent critique of the Eleatic philosophy. It has since become a necessary prerequisite of the more profound philosophical systems and the more developed theological theories. It was developed with extraordinary subtlety in German idealism, albeit in a rather one-sided interpretation, particularly in parts of Hegel's "Logic".

In my book "The Positive Tasks of Philosophy" [11] I tried to show that the logically inevitable correlationship of the "one" and the "many" is rooted in the very nature of being, and which is already assumed in the most abstract concept about it, and that this concept is of such a nature without which the very word "to be" would be meaningless. By "being" of any kind we understand its fixedness (*polozhennost'*) or its realization as a given, without this "to be" would signify nothing. But because of this, it is logically necessary to differentiate in everything

L. M. Lopatin, "The Positive Tasks of Philosophy", Part II, chapters III and IV.

that exists that which "supposes" it and that which is "supposed", that which substantiates in it its properties and relationships and its definite real "givenness", as an accomplished result, or, speaking more concretely, that which realises itself in it as a "force" or as a "realised expression" of a force. Where these relationships do not exist, there is no being. As I tried to point out in the above work, we can only attribute being to that which has some relationship to activity and somehow reveals and reflects itself in it (in whatever or however the activity is realized – in us, outside us, by thought, by an unconscious external force or by anything else).

Our entire life as we perceive and understand it, is a continuous and varied interaction of our subject and object, of the ego and non-ego, of our spirit and external forces opposed to it, and in "activity in general". We therefore have a limited concept which characterises any reality for us, and without which we cannot conceive of any positive content. According to Leibniz's formula "that which does not act, does not exist". In any activity, in whatever general sense we take it, we must inevitably differentiate between the force which produces the action and the action itself insofar as it is produced. This internal duality of any being contains a "dialectical", or if you prefer, an "irrational" element in our concept of being which prevents us from seeing in this concept any rigid definition which is isolated from any other content, but, on the contrary, compels our thought to search for a multiciplity of relationships in everything that exists. Every real being implies a duality, and this applies to it not only in the totality of the moments of its disclosure, but to every such moment individually, i only we recognize them as "existing" moments. In other words, however the unity of being may be "per se", it must contain a multiplicity once it is in fact a "being".

Such is the inner logic of any being; this must apply even more to absolute being, i.e. being that is independent of anything outside of i and which has the principle of its activity within itself. This being, b its very concept, is conceivable only as a "self-assertion", because it entire reality is rooted in its independence. Self-assertion, moreover clearly presupposes a bifurcation which directs itself toward the reali sation of power and its given realisation. It is this bifurcation that th absolute force reveals itself in all its infinity. It cannot be exhauste either in any individual action or in some limited form. On the cor trary, it realises itself in every form of its action precisely as the infinit force of life, which from time immemorial has revealed itself in a infinite multiplicity of particular moments of its realisation. This a means that the absolute principle of things is only conceivable as single living centre of a living multiplicity, and, on the other hand, tha a concrete and connected multiplicity is only possible as the creation of an internally unified creative power.[12]

The following objection will probably be made: granted that these conclusions about the logical sense of our concept of being are correct, they nevertheless express a purely human, relative point of view. But even if this is the only concept of being that we can form, does it follow that reality must be subordinated to the relative and limited forms of our thinking? We cannot understand unity without multiplicity, or multiplicity without unity – let us agree on this: this still does not prevent the real world from being without a general, single basis, and does not prevent the multiplicity of forces that establishes the life of the universe, from being mutually dependent and at the same time not be bound by anything. This is for us a logical contradiction – what does it matter? Our human logic is not a law for things.

This matter of argument is quite unvulnerable. How can one argue with premises whose illogicality has been admitted by their authors, who have previously claimed them to be beyond the competence of logical judgment? The opponents can only comfort themselves with the knowledge that they are dealing with logically meaningless propositions. This in itself puts it beyond dispute. One can hardly hope to go beyond the conditions and possibilities of human comprehension in any kind of argument. It is not, in any case, philosophy's task to do so, so long as it does not renounce its basic task of being a rational knowledge founded on logic. Rational thought is defined by the laws of the only logic we understand. I have not yet mentioned the fact that the recognition of the complete relativity of human thinking, even when it concerns the most general signs and properties of the "real" – those that are most free from subjective empirical aspects, and the most obvious relationships between them, results in illusionism that itself needs logical justification and cannot possibly be taken as the universally-obligatory truth.

The advocates of pluralism, incidentally, seldom embark on such bold attacks against general human logic, and still more rarely do they argue the matter out. They are more willing to manage without principled arguments of an ontological nature, either by simply ignoring them, or by trying to treat them purely as a verbal game, or, finally, by unexpectedly attributing to their assertions a conditional or solely empirical meaning. They often give the impression that in preferring pluralism to monism they have in mind only the world of our experience and have no desire to get involved in a discussion about the absolute essence of things. They forget that the question of monism and

[12] See, "Positive Tasks of Philosophy", Part I, second ed., pp. 347, 349, 404, Part II, pp. 252-270.

pluralism is essentially a metaphysical question, since it concerns the most transcendental bases of everything cognisable, and that in regard to the empirical world it has no meaning. Is the sensually observed world monistic or pluralistic? We undoubtedly observe many things and many forces acting in them, but they are very dependent on each other and are closely bound together. What, then does this mean? Do they originate from one general root, or are all the elements of empirical reality and all the forces in them the original roots of being? Experience is completely mute on this matter for the obvious reason that it only began when the multiplicity of the world was already given. And, finally, what kind of empirical world do we have in mind here? Is it the pure experience of our immediate consciousness? Both the "unity" of consciousness itself and the "multiplicity" of its separate experiences are unquestionably given in it. But we do not attribute original absoluteness to either of them, because we are convinced from the very structure of our life that we are not absolute beings. Or must the empirical world be understood in the popular sense of this concept, i.e. as the aggregate of things and processes are transcendent to our immediate consciousness by which we explain and logically supplement the subjective evidence of our sensory perception? For reasons just given, experience has nothing to say about the monistic or pluralistic origins of these transcendent things and processes. If, therefore, we still wish to discuss this matter we must inevitably relegate it to the realm of specifically speculative matters.

Much more convincing are the objections by the advocates of pluralism which stem from moral-religious motives. In this respect the pluralists try to use all the doubts which they had previously used against the belief in the unity of the moral meaning of life and in the goodness of an omnipotent creator of the universe, and add on their own certain important new reasons. Incidentally, they pose once again before philosophical consciousness the great problem of evil in the world, and this is in itself rendering a very important service to modern philosophy. Unfortuantely, I cannot deal with this matter now and must postpone doing so to a future occasion. The question of evil is not one that can be dealt with in passing – at least, not for the system of spiritualistic monism which I deeply am convinced, alone contains philosophical truth.[13] For a world-view which sees the final root of things in the free creation of an absolute spirit, which in all reality fulfills its eternal ideal and its eternal norms – the presence of evil in the universe must be explained and morally justified, otherwise the very world-view will be turned into an illusion of the mind. Such a

[13] See, L. M. Lopatin, "Spiritualism as a monistic system of philosophy" in *Voprosy*, 1912, bk. 5.

justification is the urgent task of spiritualism, collosal in its difficulty, but which nonetheless persistently demands a solution, even if in the form of an indication of the general possibility and inner probability of evil being given spiritualistic premises.

One should never forget, however, that the problem of evil has such a deterministic meaning only for spiritualistic monism. The advocates of pluralism are unwilling to reckon with this, as a result, all their views on religious and moral matters seem to be biased. They take as a kind of axiom the idea that monism in philosophy is only permissible when we recognise the absolute rule of the moral law over all phenomena of life. And this in turn presupposes another axiom, viz., that the moral law is fully the real mover and motivating norm of cosmic evolution. There is no argument that in accepting such views we are predetermining a great deal. But it is obvious that axioms of this sort require a speculative basis, particularly from the point of view of those who express persistent doubt in the omnipotence of a moral law over real life. It is strange how the defenders of pluralism avoid the historical fact that monism (meaning the recognition of the unity of the origin of things) is far from always coinciding with moral optimism and that, on the contrary, there are different forms of an unquestionable monistic world-view for which all moral demands are purely human inventions dictated by human interests and needs, but there is absolutely no objective moral law as a norm of being independent of man. One need only mention the naturalistic monism of contemporary realists, such as Spinoza's system and Schopenhauer's views, etc. The pluralists' criticism would only be valid if they had previously proven that a monistic philosophy is only possible in the form of "theism". We find nothing of the sort in their criticism, and one cannot expect it from them with their simplified view on all speculative arguments of an ontological nature, when they regard as a verbal game, and because of their unwavering conviction in the relativity and conditionally of all forms and laws of human thought. James simply rejects monistic hypotheses of a materialistic type without even discussing them, although he gains somewhat by this arbitrary limitation in the firmness of his results. Nor do we find in the work of the pluralists the idea which would seem to be even more necessary for their belief in an objective moral meaning of the world struggle, or actual proof of the view that the moral law is a cosmic quantity and not a human invention. In this instance, they are sometimes ready to limit themselves to the fact that the denial of a moral meaning in life is detrimental to human pride. One can hardly argue that pride is a rather dubious criterion for philosophical and religious truth and that we would go a long way if we used it as the sole criterion for the suitability and reliability of our moral beliefs.

Hence, the pluralists' basic conviction that the benevolent force in the world is generally limited and that it is in direct conflict with opposing force which strives toward evil and destruction (or many similar forces), is not adequately substantiated, because before one can make such assertions one must show that the world-controlling forces in general have some definite tendency toward what we call good and evil. The pluralists not only fail to prove this, but because of their mode of thinking, they cannot prove it, since they have no data and no material. A similar observation may be made with reference to their assertion about the limitations of God and the possible number of gods as well as the frequently expressed assurance that it is only in the pluralistic world-view that man may be regarded as the ultimate controller of the fate of the universe. It should be noted that the vast majority of contemporary supporters of monistic ideas are not affected by these conclusions; their entire world-view is based on a conscious denial of the preconceived prejudice of pluralism concerning the meaning of good and evil.

As we have already seen, spiritualistic monism cannot be indifferent to the religious and moral views of the pluralists: many of these views are of great negative importance for monism. One cannot logically insist on the inner spirituality and basic unity of the world without analysing the questions of the nature of evil, the enigmatic duality of the basic movers of life and the cosmic significance of moral freedom. I will attempt to examine these questions in my next article.[14]

---

[14] Lopatin continues his argument in a subsequent article which appeared in *Voprosy*, but which we do not include in this selection.

BIOGRAPHICAL SKETCH

Prince Dimitry Nikolaeyvich Tsertelev was born in Moscow in 1852. He received his early education in the Moscow Gymnasium number 5, and later graduated from the Law faculty of the University of Moscow. He then went to Leipzig to do graduate work where he received his doctor of philosophy degree. His dissertation which was written in German entitled: *Schopenhauers Erkenntnisstheorie* dealt with Schopenhauer's epistemology. His books written in Russian also dealt mainly with Schopenhauer's general Weltanschauung, these are: "The Philosophy of Schopenhauer". Part I dealt with the theory of knowledge and metaphysics (1880, St. Petersburg); "Contemporary pessimism in Germany; an outline of the moral philosophy of Schopenhauer and Hartmann" (Moscow, 1885); "Schopenhauer's Aesthetics" (St. Petersburg, 1888).

Prince Tsertelev was a contemporary of Vladimir Solovyov with whom he became very friendly, even though they differed in their political views. Also among his contemporaries were N. Kareyev, A. Isayev, and the young Pissemsky.

Like many other Russian intellectuals of his period, Tsertelev was very versatile. Two volumes of his poetry apeared in 1883 and 1892. His poetry is representative of his philosophy which is very close to that of Schopenhauer and von Hartmann, although he recognizes the uncognizability of the higher principles of cognition and existence. A quotation of his may indicate what we have in mind. "What is the inner essence of the cognizing, thinking, desiring subject apart from our consciousness? We cannot say, just as we cannot say what is the essence of the cognized material world, apart from our consciousness? After we will have discussed these questions we will see that these are in themselves absurd, since they lead to the question of the nature of the uncognizable; but if we had an answer to this question then it would no longer be uncognizable."

From 1887 to 1890 he was President of Justices of the Peace of Spasky and Tambov provinces. He was founder and editor of the journal "Russian Review". Prior to that he was the editor of "The Russian Herald". He also contributed a great deal to the "Journal of the Ministry of Public Education", "The Moscow Gazette" and others. Politically he was an ardent patriot and conservative, but not a super-patriot. In this man we have another example of the type of people who contributed to the development of Russian philosophical thought.

D. Tsertelev

SPACE AND TIME AS FORMS
OF PHENOMENA*

Millions of people live and dream of the future with memories of the past, but they never ask themselves what is that fatal force that continuously draws them onward. For the majority of people, this question is not only insoluble, but even uninteresting. For them reality is limited to what they can see and hear, and the rest is more or less an idle dream.

It is true that even for them a wall sometimes appears beyond which this reality suddenly disappears, and they are faced involuntarily with the problem of distinguishing between objects and appearances. This problem is however, so alarming and unusual that they try to rid themselves of it as soon as possible, having decided A PRIORI that this problem is insoluble, or at least beyond their capacity. One can not look for a solution of metaphysical problems in everyday life; one must assume that they are either solved or are incapable of a solution, otherwise there would be no time left for action.

In science, on the other hand, exactness and a rigorous method of investigation are the *sine qua non,* since without them one may arrive at some brilliant hypotheses, which nevertheless may lack a firm foundation.

A strict distinction between the necessary and the particular and incidental is the basic requirement of every scientific investigation. Whatever phenomena one considers and from whatever viewpoint they are examined, we will always visualize them in TIME; and if we were to examine phenomena of the external world they would appear to us in space.

* This selection is taken from *Voprosy,* Vol. 5, Bk. 23, pp. 235-247.

Each phenomenon necessarily presupposes two terms: the perceiver and the perceived. This applies equally to internal and external phenomena – to psychic perception and to impressions of the external world. For naive realism, which includes the majority of people, there is practically no difference between the concepts themselves and the objects which evoke these concepts. However, not only philosophers, but scientists as well, know that they have virtually nothing in common; there can only be a certain parallelism, so that certain changes in external objects may correspond to certain changes in our consciousness, but the phenomena in external world can in no way be identified with phenomena of inner consciousness, but can only be considered as their cause and only in a certain sense. Phenomena in the external world are never perceived directly by our consciousness which perceives only certain changes within our organism and objectifies them in space. Our own body always serves as a direct link between our consciousness and other bodies of the universe. It may be considered as the only direct object of our sensations.

Hence, motion from a philosophical as well as from a scientific viewpoint, is a necessary link between our consciousness and the external world; but every motion presupposes space and time. What then are these necessary conditions of external experience? Are they inherent properties of the objects, or are they on the contrary, the inevitable form of the consciousness which perceives them? Or, finally, are they only the necessary, or at least, under certain conditions, the inseparable link between the object that is being cognized and the person cognizing it?

Let us explain this by an example. Let us imagine a person blind from birth, who, after an operation was enabled to see objects, but could not distinguish colours. Let us suppose that all objects appeared to him to be all green. The cause would be in himself, in the structure of his visual organs. Let us further suppose, that after an operation another blind person was enabled not only to see objects, but was also able to distinguish their colour, but for some reason or other, he would only be allowed to look at exclusively green objects, so that his room and all the objects in it would be green. The colour impressions of the second blind person would be identical to the first blind person, although the cause of this identity would not be in himself, but in the objects he was perceiving. Finally, let us imagine a third person also blind from birth, who underwent a similar operation like the second person with similar results, but instead of surrounding him with only green objects, soon after the operation he was given green glasses, or light was admitted into his room through a green glass. The impressions of the third person would be similar to the impressions of the first two, although the reason for seeing everything in green colour, would not be in himself, nor in the objects he was perceiving, but in intermediate conditions which cause him to see these objects.

A somewhat analogous assumption may be made regarding space. Objects may appear to us to have extension, because extension is the property of these objects. They may seem to us to have extension, because space is a necessary form of the perceiving consciousness. Finally, extension may only be a condition for the transition of the influence of the external world into the realm of consciousness. In other words, the idea of space may be inseparably bound up with the perception of the external world by our intellect, because space is an integral property of all bodies, or, because space is a form of this intellect into which all external expressions must flow. Or, finally, since it is not a necessary link either with the reality of the external world, nor with our intellect, it is a necessary relation, a single angle of vision, so to say, through which we can perceive the material world.

The first two hypotheses have received sufficient attention in the history of philosophy; we shall consider only the third hypothesis.

Is it possible for objects that by their very nature have no extension, to appear to have extension when perceived by consciousness, which is not absolutely bound by its own form (space)? Is it possible that the idea of space arose merely through contact with these completely different elements, which, if considered singly, would have no relation to space? As regards consciousness, there is no doubt that it may have a whole series of phenomena which have no relation to space. Even in the material world, although all phenomena occur, or, at least seem to occur in space, it cannot be maintained however, that the substance or principle underlying these phenomena has necessarily extension. On the contrary, everybody is more and more inclined to see in the bodies themselves only appearances at whose basis are units of force without extension. In this case, of course, one would have to assume that space is something real, without it motion would be inconceivable; but motion also is not something independent, or unrelated to that which is in motion.

Hence, it is possible that space is neither a property of bodies nor a form of the intellect, but upon further consideration of the question, it becomes evident that whichever way one looks at it, space is a necessary condition for the perception of phenomena of the external world.

In fact, if there were no space, there would be no motion (even in a subjective sense), and if there were no motion, one could not experience any change of sensation in our consciousness on which we base our consciousness not only regarding changes, but also regarding the very existence of the external world.

Impressions of the external world, even if they were at all still possible, would undoubtedly remain immutable, and would be unable not only to distinguish one from the other, but even to separate them from purely subjective sensations.

An objection may be raised against this definition of space as a form of phenomenon, that in reality it does not exclude the first two hypotheses, and hence, is insufficiently defined. This (objection) is quite valid, but this poor definition is not as great a defect in comparison with the internal contradictions or unsubstantiated statements, besides, it leaves a wide area for further investigation.

Such a broad definition is of still greater importance with regard to time. Time *per se* completely eludes our understanding and there is no room for it in our consciousness. Everything that we know and see, all the phenomena of the external and internal world are either in the past or in the future; they either were or will be. But as soon as they appear to our consciousness they become real. For consciousness as such there is neither past nor future, its only form is the present. The difference can only be in the vividness of the images, but not in their reality. The present is that mathematical point which divides into two halves the infinite line of time; it is a point where not a single material phenomenon can be placed regardless of how transient it may be in point of time, it nevertheless comprises some definite size, even though a very small size.

If there is not sufficient ground for recognizing space as being exclusively a subjective form of our cognition, then we have at least reason to suppose that the clarity and precision with which we cognize geometrical truths, that if real space does indeed exist, then its laws must agree with the laws of our reason. Time is a completely different matter: we are not only unable to imagine what time is, but it is as it were, a virtual negation of the fact that within ourselves we are conscious of it more clearly than of anything else. The only method of measuring time that is to any degree accurate is by measuring the motion of material objects, whereas in fact one does not compare time but the path traversed by bodies, i.e. again it is a matter of space, and the activity of the mind does not consist in the perception of impressions of time as something that is flowing evenly, but consists in fixing in the memory that which was by comparing it with that which is: to make the past into the present, at least within our consciousness.

In any act of consciousness, not only in thoughts but also in sensations, there is a combination of many phenomena and motions, and consequently, these motions are perceived simultaneously. If the difference in colour and sound depends on the number of vibrations in the ether or in the air, it is quite obvious that consciousness grasps as a single whole which in nature exists in an infinitely large quantity. An infinite series of consecutive movements of a mass of individual minute particles merges here into a single indissoluble whole. But even without resorting to more or less complex hypotheses, it is not difficult to arrive at the conclusion, namely, that the simplest daily observations lead to the same idea. One need only look at any moving body to be convinced of this fact. Such a body either gives no distinct impression whatsoever, or it gives an impression that is completely new, which has nothing to do with the motion of the parts or of the whole.

Let us look, for example, at a rotating wheel. The spokes will flash by without giving any clear impression, but when it is rotating more rapidly the spokes will emerge into a single continuous circle and one will get a fully distinct impression of an immobile and semi-transparent body. Let us take a hot coal and move it about rapidly in a dark room; instead of a luminous point we will get the impression of fiery lines and exactly the same impression will obtain, instead of moving the luminous point one moves the eyes. Vision which clearly grasps spatial relations and the shape of objects, is completely incapable of giving us the notion of moving objects, i.e. of motion in the proper sense. If we were to follow a moving object we would be able to see it quite distinctly, but then everything else would fuse into a more or less vague mass. If on the other hand, one looks, without moving the eyes, at the medium where the body is moving, the object disappears from view because each point of the object changes into some sort of line and our vision of individual parts inevitably merges into one. But even if the motion itself, i.e., the continuous shifting, instead of giving a notion of time, sometimes gives the impression of immobility, which has really nothing to do with the actual state of the body, is it not strange to suppose that time is a necessary subjective form of consciousness? It is evident, that a melody, for example, could not exist of those sounds which had already been emitted in reality would not continue to exist in our consciousness while our ear continued to perceive new sounds.

When we pass from sensation to thought, we can even more clearly observe the timeless nature of consciousness. When we read something, our eyes move from one line to the next and we get a whole series of rapidly shifting light-impressions, but as a result of all these impressions we are left but with a single thought. The concepts evoked by the light stimuli do not disappear but continue in our consciousness after the sensations caused by them have been replaced by others.

It may however, be objected that sensations and thoughts also change as do external phenomena which evoked them. It does not follow that this type of change should be the necessary property of thought. It is evident that if phenomena occur in time they cannot remain indefinitely in consciousness, if there is only a correlation between the cognizing person and the cognized object. If we bear in mind that all or almost all of our feelings and thoughts are bound up with our physical organism which itself is only a temporary phenomenon, then it is evident that all or almost all our thoughts cannot occur outside the framework of time. Generally speaking, that continuous change of thought and sensations which we observe in our consciousness is completely different from the change of phenomena occurring in the external world. It in no way corresponds to the notion we have about the material motion and change of phenomena in the external world where one moment sharply differentiates the infinite past from the infinite future, where the present can be compared to a narrow crevice, through which we view the rapidly flashing objects appearing and disappearing instantaneously.

In the psychic world, on the other hand, phenomena do not pass by without leaving some trace. They seem to gradually emerge from an invisible depth, as it were, gradually reach their greatest vividness and then fade away and are overshadowed by new phenomena, continuing to cast their reflection even when they are no longer recognizable. Who, for example, has not experienced some indefinite depressing feeling, where one sees everything in dark colors, without being able to account for it, when one suddenly remembers some strong impression, sometimes even a dream, which brought about this mood? Is it not evident that this impression was not only retained in the depth of the unconscious, but continued to influence our mood while completely different external impressions flashed by before us?

I have said that almost all our notions, impressions and thoughts lie in time because they are all related to the temporal and not because time is a necessary form of consciousness. This is not the only reason; the force of our thinking and the clarity of our consciousness are limited; therefore when we concentrate our attention on one impression or thought, the others fade and almost disappear as if they no longer existed. We only have to turn our attention to them and they appear once more before us. At times this takes place independently of our wishes, and a single hint is sufficient to re-establish vividly before us a whole image which apparently had disappeared from our memory without a trace.

This does not however limit the effect of consciousness on time, since consciousness not only evokes things from the past, but gives us a picture of a present that has not as yet taken place. We constantly foresee the immediate future just as we constantly carry, although somewhat vaguely, impressions of the past. All our actions are determined by such foresight of the future, since their goal lies always in the future; regardless how problematic it may be in itself, it seems quite real to us. Of course, in foreseeing the future based on deduction, errors are more apt to occur in recalling the past, but by and large, this foreseeing of the future has been so well justified, that when an error does occur it creates a completely different impression which the event itself would have evoked. We see it in a completely unique light, as something unforeseeable and it evokes in us a feeling of amazement. Thus, in the inner psychic world the past and the future, at least within certain limits, fuse into a single integral impression of the present, and this present to a considerable degree, depends on our will, on ourselves. Our impressions are not wholly passive reflections or some simple variation of external reality. We see and hear not what strikes our hearing and sight incidentally, but what we wish to see and hear. In a room where a number of conversations are carried on, we can only hear one of them, while the rest fuse into a dissonant din. On a sheet of paper on which a number of figures and drawings appear and where lines intersect, we can follow one of them and see one image so that all the rest lose their meaning for us and hardly reach our consciousness.

The act whereby we select, secure and perceive a small quantity of an infinitely large number of phenomena around us and objects flashing by, is a unique kind of inner creation. It requires a particular act of psychic inner principle to convert a series of infinitely small sensations received simultaneously from the external world into one distinct image corresponding to a given object which seems to us to be the cause for all these sensations.

The entire universe insofar as it appears to us, exists for us in space and in time: this is not only a fact of experience but also a logical necessity. We would however, be hardly justified to draw the conclusion that space and time are only subjective forms of consciousness. When we say that space is a subjective form of consciousness, we prejudge the question, and presuppose that there is nothing in the object that corresponds to space. If we hold the same view regarding time, we not only commit the same error, but we also encounter a certain contradiction vis-à-vis our inner experience that tells us that in consciousness there is no past nor future, but only the present. Ideas of space and time could not have been acquired from experience, since they are already assumed to be data in every experience. In observations we see only the real, hence, only the present. On the other hand, and by the same token, in none of our sensations is there any notion of three-dimensional space, it is only a logically necessary conclusion, though an unconscious one, drawn from our observation of motion. In view of this, it must be admitted that the idea of space is inherent in our intellect, although it does not follow that there is nothing which corresponds to it outside us.

In fact, without innate ideas we would not have the slightest idea of the external world, and consequently, no idea of observation and experience. If we did not inherently possess the idea of causality, there would only be a series of sensations and impressions in our consciousness, which we would never think of objectifying by projecting them outside ourselves. All logical truths constitute such innate ideas, which does not necessarily follow, of course, that an infant would recognize them in the same form and with the same clarity as would a philosopher or mathematician. Even a child who has not learned to talk, is guided by them unconsciously: when he stretches out his hand to grasp some object, he does not, of course, stop to consider that a straight line is the shortest distance between two points, but instinctively extends his hand along a straight line toward the object, although he does not have the slightest understanding of a three-dimensional aspect of space, nor is this third dimension given to him by his sensations. Similarly, when a child asks for something or is afraid of something, it does not occur to him that the object of his wish or fear does not depend on his will and therefore is something real and non-subjective, hence, it must have another cause. However, both the wish and the fear are undoubtedly based on an unconscious application of the law of causality which alone brings both the child and the thinker out of the realm of purely subjective ideas. One can of course, doubt the law of causality in which case the only firm link between thought and the external world is destroyed, this leaves no grounds for experimental studies, and our consciousness has only room for unlimited fantasy. On the other hand, by recognising not only the subjective, but also the real significance of innate ideas, we have the only real basis for the existence and development of the mathemathical as well as all the other exact sciences.

Even though at times the most obvious A PRIORI truth which are the foundations of all our thinking give rise to seeming contradictions and incongruities, it is nevertheless simpler to doubt the accuracy of the logical process which led to such a conclusion than to doubt those axioms which serve as bases for all our thinking process. Even if we assume that the thinking process is absolutely valid, it is still without any meaning, since the thinking process itself leads to the conclusion that these bases which were all the time presupposed, were invalid.

Our consciousness can grasp with any degree of clarity only finite objects including our own bodies, which occupy space and time and are in continuous motion; this produces the illusion that the cognizing subject himself is located in time. In fact, while he experiences a continuous process a series of images and impressions, it seems to him that he himself changes exactly like the external images. When however, he is faced with the idea of death and the impossibilty of re-uniting with his own body, which is the direct but still temporary object of knowledge, with the cognising object, then the question involuntarily arises, what will become of this subject when the bond with his body is severed, will consciousness itself then disappear, or will it have some other medium, or will it be able to contemplate the eternal after it has been released from all contact with material objects occupying space and time? Neither philosophy nor the positive sciences can answer these questions, which belong to the realm of religion. Science, religion, and philosophy however, agree on one thing, namely, that time can change and destroy only phenomena but not the inner essence of things, and that he who recognizes and believes that he himself is not an accidental collection of chance phenomena, is something real, and identical with himself, then death for him, which exists only in time, cannot be the end of his real being, and the disintegration of his body which binds him with the world of objects that have extension cannot serve as proof that consciousness in general cannot be conserved.

Section IV
ETHICAL PROBLEMS

— — — — — — — — — — — — — — — —

BIOGRAPHICAL SKETCH

Nikolai Yakovlevich Grot (1852-1899) was the son of the wellknown Academician Yakov K. Grot. Young Nikolai received his higher education at St. Petersburg University and was very active in university life. He was interested in psychology and philosophy. He studied in Germany for a while, and upon his return he was appointed to the chair of philosophy at the Institute of History and Philosophy at Nezhin. His master's dissertation "The Psychology of Feelings" as well as his doctoral dissertation "Toward a Reform of Logic" were published soon after his appointment at Nezhin. He later accepted a position in the field of philosophy at Odessa, and soon after he was offered the chair of philosophy at Moscow University, where he remained until his death. He became the President of the Moscow Psychological Society and the editor of the first philosophy journal, *Voprosy filosofii i psikhologii* (Problems of philosophy and psychology).

Grot was greatly influenced in his earlier period by men like Herbert Spencer and other positivists. In his later period he became interested in metaphysics and he tried to bring about a reconciliation between metaphysics and positivism. In his ethical views he was influenced by Lev Tolstoy.

In his quest for a 'scientific philosophy' he gradually abandoned his earlier positivistic views by admitting that metaphysics is valid subjectively, while science is valid objectively. He arrived at the position of a moral universe, which inevitably led him to acknowledge freedom of the will. While adopting Schopenhauer's metaphysical voluntarism, he did not regard the 'universal will' to be the ultimate essence of reality, but something that is 'injected into nature' by God's will. Due to a chronic illness, he was unable to complete his newly-developed ideas. Most of his writings are on psychology, although he wrote a number of articles as well as books on philosophical subjects. His "The General Tasks of Philosophy" is especially useful for a proper evaluation of his philosophical views.

N. Ya. Grot

THE FOUNDATION OF MORAL DUTY*

In their discussion of moral duty, moralists rarely draw a clear distinction between two very different questions: (1) "What" must one do to be a moral person, and (2) "Why" must one act morally.

Schopenhauer was the first to underline the difference between these questions in philosophical ethics. Even Kant in his famous doctrine of the categorical imperative of duty confuses the concepts of "principle" with the "basis" of ethics in his concept of "law". According to Schopenhauer, the "principle", or the highest law of ethics, is the most concise and exact expression for the mode of action which it prescribes, or in which moral value can be found. The "foundation" of ethics is the basis of obligatoriness or of desirability or laudibility of virtue, i.e. of the moral mode of action.

According to Schopenhauer, most moralists deliberately (I would say inadvertently) avoid this difference, since it is quite easy to point to the principle of ethics, but very difficult to show its "basis". Indeed, in deciding the question of what behaviour is moral, not only the moralists, but practically all people of the same cultural level are in agreement. The various nuances in the solutions offered for this problem are not so much determined by the differences in philosophical schools and abstract principles, as by the Zeitgeist and the degree of cultural development. At the present time, for example, all educated people consider the following to be immoral: slavery, violence, egoism, while the following qualities are praised as moral or morally-obligatory:

* This selection appeared in *Voprosy*, Vol. 3, Bk. 12, pp. 146-164.

respect for personal freedom, love for one's neighbour, self-denial. In earlier times, even Christian nations saw nothing immoral in slavery and violence – and even the shedding of blood in war and the intolerance of the beliefs of others in the name of one's people, is at present considered to be moral, there will no doubt come a time which will, from an ethical point of view, frankly regard these actions immoral.

The fundamental and most difficult question in ethics is "why" one should love one's neighbour, hurt no one, but on the contrary, help everyone as much as possible, in other words, why in general should one act morally. The utilitarian answer is: for the sake of one's personal benefit, while the Kantians would say, in the name of the idea of duty, i.e. regardless of any personal consideration. There are many intermediate and compromising solutions between these two extremes.

English moralists of the last century accepted as the basis for moral behaviour man's inherent "love" or "sympathy", while Schopenhauer considered "compassion" as the highest basis of morality, depending on the metaphysical identity of the nature of all living beings. Sympathy, as the basis of moral behaviour is, so to speak, a refined understanding of benefit. The violation of the principle of sympathy threatens the acting personality with suffering only if sympathy is a law of man's nature. Moreover, sympathy as a basis of morality, is higher than the direct inspiration of vulgar egoism, higher than the idea of personal benefit in the real meaning of the word. The same can be said about the altruism of the positivists and Spencer.[1] Schopenhauer's compassion is in principle opposed to the idea of benefit and egoism, because he does not recognize any value in the personal life of man, and the denial of life as a good. It is quite obvious, that if we are to have compassion for the sake of reducing our own suffering vis à vis the misfortunes of others, we are, in the final analysis, seeking our own personal benefit and happiness.

The problem of the foundation of morality and virtue should generally be stated as follows: can one find a basis for moral behaviour which would have no reference to the personal happiness of a man acting or wishing to act morally? Man aspires to happiness and tries to avoid suffering, this is unquestionably so. This is the fundamental law of life not only of man, but of all living beings. Can we and should we avoid this law in advocating moral behaviour?

For many centuries theological morality was considered the highest type of unselfish morality, but Kant had already pointed out that the

---

[1] Herbert Spencer (1820-1903), English philosopher, who formulated the principle of evolution before Darwin, and forms the fundamental conception of his "System of Synthetic Philosophy".

outstanding feature that was gradually adopted by theological morality was the idea of rewards and punishment in life after death. In advocating the most unselfish love for God and for one's neighbour and personal self-denial in a world of wrath and sorrow, religious morality nevertheless promises as a reward for virtue, bliss in a world free from sorrow and suffering.

These historical examples of a "careful" search for a basis of morality without reference to the morally acting person, are extremely edifying. If religious morality said, "do good to your neighbour in the assurance that you will be unhappy not only in this life but in life beyond the grave, i.e. that the more virtuous you are the more you will suffer for acting morally, not only temporally, but eternally", then one could say that this type of morality does not have in view any personal benefit. If Kant had said that the moral world order is such that virtue and happiness will "never" meet, and the more faithful you are to your duty the more you will suffer, then such morality would be unique, free from any consideration of personal happiness.

These moral doctrines, of course, never did and never could make any such absurd promises. On the contrary, all of them, like other moral systems, always offered salvation and deliverance from evil and suffering – either in one's lifetime, or in the future. It follows from the above, that a search for a basis or sanction of a morality which would have no reference to the happiness of the moral person himself, is completely fruitless, i.e. it is a misunderstanding and a self-deception.

In spite of this, the proposition that moral activity based on egoistic motives and consideration for personal benefit is not moral behaviour, i.e. that it has no moral value, is still valid. This proposition issues directly from the idea of "moral" activity, in contrast to "immoral" activity, since this presupposes the idea of the complete contrast between egoism as a principle of behaviour, and some other higher and better principle of activity which excludes it and is in conflict with it.

We thus arrive at the following contradiction, or, in philosophical terminology, antinomy, whose solution is the main task of ethics as a science.

On the one hand, consideration of personal happiness and benefit, or egoism, excludes any moral activity, any moral value of one's behaviour. On the other hand, it is obviously impossible to find any basis or sanction for moral behaviour and the idea of moral duty without reference to personal benefit to the moral being.

The task of the following analysis will be to solve this basic contradiction as simply as possible.

PRELIMINARY REVIEW OF THE PROPOSITION

Let us first of all state outright where the solution to the problem is to be found, and then we shall attempt to justify the individual propositions which form the elements of this solution.

First proposition. – There can be no inner sanction or final basis for human behaviour and activity other than the feelings and sensations accessible to man. The feelings and sensations which man strives to experience are defined as "pleasant", and in their general totality and connections are, what we call pleasure, enjoyment, joy, happiness, bliss. The feelings and sensations which man tries, consciously or unconsciously, to avoid in his life, or which he tries to eliminate or obviate are "unpleasant" components which people call, pain, suffering, sorrow, unhappiness, misery.

Second Proposition. – None of man's activity, including therefore, his moral activity, can, in the final analysis, have any other basis than his striving toward pleasant sensations and feelings and his aversion for the unpleasant. It is therefore completely hopeless and fruitless to try to eliminate from ethics as the guiding principle of man's moral behaviour any eudaemonism, i.e. the only possible principle, namely, happiness and bliss which alone can govern a living being in its activity.

Third Proposition. – The above statement does not imply however, that the guiding principles of pleasure, enjoyment, egoistic benefit, individual happiness, and animal pleasures, etc., should govern man's moral behaviour. Man has two natures: one is low, animal-like, irrational, extremely individualistic, and most of all, egoistic. The other nature is higher, uniquely human, rational, social, and most of all hostile to egoism and pure individualism. Hence, man may achieve happiness in a two-fold manner.

Fourth Proposition. – The duality of man's nature is peculiar to his whole existence, and is reflected in the dual, partially conflicting order in his mental, volitional and sensual functions. In the realm of thought, individual perceptions, notions, and concepts, limited by time and space, contrast with universal, stable and eternal ideas and ideals. In the realm of will, personal, temporary, transient attractions and wishes contrast with the universal constant and unchanging striving toward truth, beauty, goodness, freedom and eternity. In the realm of feelings, temporary and transient joys and pleasures connected with man's animal nature, contrast with the sum of ideal, uniquely human feelings which stem from the perception of beauty, truth and goodness and are connected with the awareness of realizing these principles in ourselves and outside of us in the world, whose pulse beats palpably in our own ideal and general well-being.

Fifth Proposition. – In accordance with the duality of man's entire spiritual existence and self-consciousness, there are two forms of well-being in which man can formulate the purpose of his life and the task of his activity. The following possibilities are open to man: (1) animal happiness of a physical organism, fully enjoying all its functions and forces, and (2) human happiness of a spiritual being fulfilling all its functions and all its inner purposes.

Sixth Proposition. – Both forms are incompatible, as they are opposed to each other. Man's powers are limited. Any conscious aspiration or action which tends toward the satisfaction of the needs of animal happiness, inevitably diverts man's powers from aspirations or actions which lead to the satisfaction of the needs of spiritual happiness, which is uniquely human. Hence, there results the inevitable struggle of attractions of a dual order, and the experience of profound suffering in trying to combine the incompatible.

Seventh Proposition. – A physical or animal life for man as an organism, is inevitable, and a certain degree of animal satisfaction is therefore a "sine qua non" for man's very existence as a living individual. But as soon as animal satisfaction is transformed from a necessary law of the unconscious physical nature of our being into an object of conscious physical nature of our being into an object of conscious human efforts aimed at increasing and intensifying animal feelings and material well-being, there inevitably results that egotistical activity which is detrimental to our universal and higher ideal nature, which is essentially opposed to moral activity.

Eighth Proposition. – Moral activity is that activity which is aimed at curbing, suppressing and limiting the instincts of our animal nature, at decreasing and weakening sensual pleasures with a view to increasing and intensifying ideal joy, spiritual feelings, along with the meditation and embodiment in life the eternal and immutable universal principles of our own being and the being of the whole world. The foundation of moral activity is therefore, the striving toward a happiness and bliss that is spiritual and ideal and alien to any temporal and spatial limitation, or to any individual existence.

Ninth Proposition. – As a consequence of the above proposition, we inevitably arrive at the postulate of the possibility of moral activity which presupposes the independence of the universal substance – the soul. It is the soul that enables us to discover in ourselves a personality that is capable, in its highest ideas, aspirations and feelings, to renounce the individual and temporal conditions of animal or physical existence.

Tenth Proposition. – It is only in this manner that one can explain why moral activity presupposes not only a struggle against every kind of egoism, sensuality, considerations of personal benefit, and prosperity.

It also presupposes a complete renunciation of the animal personality, i.e. man's readiness not only to experience every possible suffering connected with the limitation of his animal nature, but also, if need be, a complete readiness to sacrifice it in the name of a higher spiritual happiness, even when it involves his individual life, which is a temporary and incidental form of the being of that universal principle which is the essence and basis of the ideal existence of the individual.

These propositions require some elucidation.

It is obvious, that moral activity even excludes any spiritual pleasure when it is absolutely necessary to be realized. It excludes the preservation of the animal personality, and generally its individual well-being, i.e. it excludes any intellectual and aesthetic pleasure that is bound up with egoism, that insists in upholding in any personal, animal individuality a privileged position over other individualities. Because of the fundamental contradiction of the temporal animal nature of the individual, namely, its universal and spiritual basis, a man does not have the right to place his individual existence above other individual existences. He must not base his happiness in the preservation of himself as a physical organism, but in the preservation and multiplication in the entire world of that ideal well-being and in the strengthening of that spiritual power which he recognizes in himself, and in whose name he acts morally.

Hence, the command to love God as a higher, eternal ideal, and the command to love one's neighbour as one's self, i.e. as that higher spiritual principle, which every person possesses and which can be realized in others in the name of God, no worse than in himself. It is the task of embodying spiritual principles in life, if only he set the example of self-denial, i.e. of the moral development of the spirit to such a level where the animal existence is wholly sacrificed to the eternal and absolute spiritual being. But the command to love our neighbour and to deny ourselves in no way excludes the peaceful hope or even assurance for the continuance of our spirit beyond the limits of the temporal and spatial existence of our animal personality. It does not exclude that eternal bliss which we have already tasted here in the advancement of love and which belongs essentially to our higher moral nature.

In stating the problem of the foundation of moral activity, the "categorical imperative of duty" is, at first glance, turned into a hypothetical imperative or a conditional command: "If you wish to attain the highest and eternal bliss, then act morally, i.e. serve the higher and universal ideas and ideals of a human being and not the lower and temporary interests of your animal individuality." The conditional nature of the moral imperative would not be prejudicial or harmful to the nature of the moral essence of man, since the very condition that determines moral activity, namely, the striving toward spiritual satisfaction and bliss, presupposes the natural sublimity and nobility of a human being. The conditionality of the moral imperative is nevertheless completely "relative". It is conditional only from the standpoint of the entire human personality, considered as a whole, which includes the animal individual. The spiritual aspect of this personality knows no such conditionality. If man as a whole being who is striving to achieve both temporary happiness for his animal existence and eternal bliss for his spiritual being, can still be asked to choose between the two forms of happiness, the truly spiritual being can only strive toward the highest spiritual bliss and satisfaction. For such a person the expression "if you want spiritual satisfaction, then act in such and such a way . . ." has no meaning. For him the hypothetical imperative has the following "categorical" meaning: "you, of course, want higher bliss and satisfaction, you must therefore act morally, selflessly, serve the eternal interests and not the temporary and incidental – mortify your animal nature bring about the triumph of the spiritual", etc.

The crux of the problem is then, that the human personality should be fully conscious of his spiritual essence, and should understand the real supreme law of his life, and should realize the brevity and relativity of all the distractions of animal pleasures and the fears of animal suffering which control his life on the lower level of its development which are very harmful to his true happiness. The masses of people learn this, sooner or later, from life itself and from its cruel and merciless lessons. But it may also be the result of scientific experiment and scientific demonstration. This is precisely the task of ethics as a science, namely, to give this demonstration and to prove beyond doubt that the law of "human" life consists of man's irresistible striving toward a higher spiritual bliss, that any violation of this law is sooner or later severely punished, and that a spiritually-moral life is in itself the highest reward which gives complete satisfaction.

In summing up our position, we dare make the assertion that we have fully reconciled the above antimony in which, on the one hand, moral activity excludes any animal egoism, and on the other, one can only find support when the moral person is striving to attain his own happines. A person's real happiness consists in the renunciation of his animal isolation, and in recognizing himself to be a link in, and embodiment of the universal, the whole, the eternal. It is in the realization of this consciousness that one finds that happiness and bliss, are the true basis of man's moral behaviour, and therefore his moral duty as well.

We have nothing to fear in ideal eudaemonism for which happiness is still the true aim of man's activity, and not the happiness offered by transient animal pleasures. True happiness consists in the complete renunciation of personality, in the act of self-sacrifice during which "eternity" is embodied in a "moment" of joy (since eternity is timeless and not an infinity of time). Generally speaking, time has no place in a higher spiritual act. Eternity for it is the present, so that the future bliss of the next world offers no reward and no increase over the present happiness, but only a possible "continuation", which is, however, not necessary for the present absolute satisfaction. Whether this continuation will take place or not, is a matter of faith.

Man "now" dies for the good and for his brethren. He experiences something incomparably high – an eternal eternity; in this one moment of being he experiences the satisfaction of the absolute and general well-being of the world which is now completely embodied in him. He does not need any reward, since his reward is to experience God in himself, to feel himself to be the embodiment of absolute power and the inner focus of all things, to realize clearly that his external animal nature is an incidental appendage. He does not know what will be beyond the limits of the temporal. But what can tempt or seduce him, when he feels within himself "everything", that higher, universal and eternal which is in us and is everywhere and in everything. Even if you cut him, stab or burn his animal body, he must still love you, since your better part is in him, and his better part is in you, and you gave him the opportunity to experience the higher level of which he is capable and to which he can rise.

This is how the Christian martyrs or martyrs for any idea or ideal must have felt and reasoned on their crosses, stakes and gallows. Who does not envy their happiness and who does not recognize in comparison with themselves, the utter meaninglessness of everything with which people daily amuse themselves in life, suppressing God within themselves and scorning the eternal principle?

We have presented the general outline for solving this problem. We must now prove the individual propositions which are the components of the whole problem, since nearly all of them, in spite of the fact that they sound in part, old and familiar themes, are nonetheless one psychological or philosophical "hypothesis" which are not only unacceptable, but are in the main directly contradictory to the leading psychological and philosophical theories of the present time. Without mentioning the philosophical hypothesis of a spiritual substance, even the fundamental and far from uniform concepts of personality and individuality which we intend to defend, are so unusual that they necessarily require special philosophical analysis and justification. Just as unusual is the theory concerning two poles of feelings, which we posit as the foundation of our ethical system. Each thesis therefore requires special study.

FEELING AS THE ULTIMATE BASIS FOR HUMAN ACTIVITY

The first premise in our ethical system is of a purely "psychological" nature and is the conclusion derived from all our previous psychological studies to which we would refer the reader.[2] We shall mention only the most important results of these studies.

We perceive everything within ourselves and outside ourselves in a dual form of spiritual states: (1) objectively, in the form of sensation and ideas, and (2) subjectively, in the form of feelings and senses.

The senses of sight, sound, touch, smell, taste, contact, heat, and purely organic senses, are in themselves indifferent and do not lead to any action. Equally indifferent are all the notions we form of things and about our own states as well any ideas and concepts that are more or less abstracted from individual and particular images. If some sensations become the leading thread of our actions, they may then be only pleasant or unpleasant, i.e. depending on their accompanying sensations. If some concepts and ideas are to become the guiding principles of activity, they may be good and bad; but the goodness of ideas is determined solely by feelings which they evoke in us.

In every mind there is a great number of notions and ideas which are drawn from intercourse with other people and from interaction with things which are completely useless in the sense of being motives of activity. They become bases for activity only as a result of the approval or disapproval which manifests itself in the form of feelings. The ideas of liberty, fraternity, equality and progress are "known" to all educated people, but become the guiding principles of behaviour only for people in whom they evoke feelings of approval, enthusiasm and hope. Other people are indiffernt to these concepts and their activity is guided by other principles; still in others they evoke feelings of repulsion, anger and fear, and these people are guided by opposite ideas which produced anger, fear, repulsion even those who respect these principles and are guided by them. It is obvious, therefore, that feelings alone can arouse aspirations and desires and are the point of departure for man's conscious activity.

This does not, of course, prevent feelings from at once perfecting and refining the development of man's ideas and concepts. One must

[2] See N. Ya. Grot, "The Psychology of Sensations" 1880 on the subject of the psychology of sensation, also "On the significance of sensation in man's knowledge and activity" (Moscow, 1881).

not place "only" the development of feelings in direct dependence on the development of ideas. It is generally recognized that people who are intellectually undeveloped often reveal the finest and most sublime feelings, while highly intellectual people, on the other hand, sometimes display remarkable coarseness and base feelings. It is unquestionable however, that the source of inspiration and the point of departure for mental activity and intellectual development is the feeling of truth, the feeling of mental harmony, which is an object for which the human soul yearns.[3]

The proposition that feelings "empirically" direct man's will does in no way contradict the other psychological truth that they themselves are to some extent expressions of will or indications of its tendency, i.e. they measure the intensity of the various aspirations.[4] The questions of the relation of will to feeling will be discussed from a metaphysical point of view later in more detail. At present it is sufficient to know that sensations and feelings, being the results of satisfactions or dissatisfactions of desires, are at the same time their only "point of departure", hence, their "purpose", inasmuch as will is capable of being guided by conscious motives extraneous to it. The will is always striving toward "satisfaction", and since feeling is the only form in which man can realize this satisfaction, it is obvious that the will finds its realization and conscious purpose in feeling. Generally speaking, sensations and feelings are those inner states which give a particular sense of meaning, and therefore, significance to our lives, consequently, they are the only motives of will in man's consciousness.

If one could imagine a person whose organs of sensations and feelings have been atrophied so that he could not experience any feelings, even intellectual ones, but could only perceive shapes, images and representation of things, it would be incomprehensible how such a person could act consciously and realize what meaning there was to his life. Indeed, even the weakening of the intensity of feelings under the influence of life's forces results in the loss of all living energy and frequently ends in suicide. Even suicide as an "active", conscious and arbitrary act presupposes some feelings – those of despair and satiety.

If however, the first proposition is valid, namely, that only sensations and feelings can be the basis for man's activity, then the supplementary assertion is equally valid, namely, that all these "psychic states are divided into only two categories – pleasant and unpleasant". The

---

[3] See, N. Ya. Grot's article, "The significance of feeling in man's activity and knowledge".

[4] See, N. Y. Grot's article "A critique of the concept of freedom of will in connection with the concept of causality", in *Works of the Psychological Society*, 3rd issue.

former we try to experience, reproduce and intensify, the latter we try to avoid and to weaken at any cost. The indifferent feelings about which some psychologists speak, are absolute nonsense.[5] An indifferent feeling is simply the absence of feelings. Indifference is thus not a feeling but an indication of the absence of feelings where they should be. Amazement until it becomes a pleasant or an unpleasant emotion, is not a feeling but a certain intellectual state (a relationship of sensations or ideas), the basis for the emergence of a feeling, i.e. an embryonic but as yet undefined pleasant or unpleasant emotion.

In any case, even if indifferent feelings and sensations were possible they could not determine the will to action, but on the contrary, it would lead to inaction, and this is the best proof of the inner contradiction inherent in the concept of indifferent feelings. There cannot be indifferent feeling, but in the sense of feelings, there are indifferent psychic states, such as sensations, notions and ideas mentioned above.

Pleasant feelings by category, are defined by the concepts of pleasure, satisfaction, happiness and bliss. All these concepts, are of course, relative, but they can be used in psychology and ethics for a more exact designation of feelings of a different order and degree. It is, for example, very convenient to understand by the term "pleasures" the purely physical and organic, (i.e., animal) pleasant sensations; by "satisfaction", we understand semi-animal, semi-spiritual (i.e., mixed) feelings, such as tender, aesthetic and partially intellectual sensations as a more or less permanent state of the subject, then "pleasure" will be the sum of separate pleasures; "happiness" will be the sum of the satisfactions which constitute the content of life, "bliss" is usually taken to mean the sum of spiritual joys, "eternal bliss".

The same relationship may be shown to exist in the realm of unpleasant sensations and feelings, between the concepts of pain, sufferings and sorrows and pain (illness), misfortune and torture or torment.

We repeat, that the distinctions we have made are relative and conditional, and that another definition of concepts is possible, although it may be less convenient. It is remarkable how many terms there are in different languages to designate the various orders of pleasant and unpleasant, and we think that this variety of terms is the result of the correct awarenes of the various sources of feelings, such as physical, spiritual and mixed. We never speak of the "bliss" of animals. When we speak of their joys and torments, we mean their pleasures and satisfaction, their pain and suffering, and we attribute to them, perhaps without adequate basis, the higher feelings peculiar to ourselves.

[5] See, N. Ya. Grot, "Psychology of Sensations", chapter X, pp. 444 fol. for an elaboration of these ideas.

After this brief psychological analysis of the cognitive basis of the human will and activity, we must now examine the first two purely ethical propositions.[6] Any activity, including therefore, moral activity, can have no other basis than man's aspiration toward pleasant states and his aversion for unpleasant ones. This does not mean, however, that the striving toward pleasure and satisfaction and the aversion for physical pain and suffering can be the motive and basis for man's "moral" activity. It is neither necessary nor possible to eliminate from ethics any eudaemonism, even though it be "ideal" (eudaemonism); but one must be able to find the border between animal and truly "human" eudaemonism. All moral theories and ethical systems in the world were always eudaemonistic, whether obvious or hidden, frank or disguised. There can be no other moral system, since man will always remain man, i.e. a being who is striving toward the highest possible happiness and bliss. The task of ethics is to find and justify a higher human good, even if it involved a voluntary renunciation of one's individual animal existence. Man is a link between two worlds, and the question is in which of these two (worlds) should he seek for the satisfaction of his thirst for a complete being, his lawful yearning for bliss.

A review of the ethical systems of the past gives us an excellent basis for the assertion that every ethics is an ethics of "feeling" and "happiness", and it also enables us to classify more exactly the various foundations for human activity found in the realm of sensations and feelings and which would lead to the establishment of various moral systems.

---

[6] Grot continues to analyse in greater detail these problems in a subsequent article in *Voprosy*, which we omit from our present selection.

BIOGRAPHICAL SKETCH

Nikolai Ivanovich Kareyev (1850-1931) was Professor of History at St. Petersburg University and a famous historian. His numerous works made him very popular in academic circles in Russia. He is often labeled a semi-positivist and personalist. He was greatly influenced by Mikhailovsky's 'subjectivism' and he was a staunch defender of the subjective element in the historical process. His approach to the philosophy of history is based on concrete historical data rather than on speculative philosophy.

Karayev regards the historical process as a blind, unsystematic and alogical flow of events. History takes on meaning only when man 'intrudes' into the historical process. It is this 'intrusion' which constitutes man's freedom of the will. Kareyev places great emphasis on the 'individual principle' in the philosophy of history. History is chiefly concerned with progress toward the achievement of human destiny. History, thus, finds its supreme meaning not in its 'absolute', but in its 'significance for man'. The philosophy of history is for him a 'judgment of history'.

His chief work "Fundamental Problems of the Philosophy of History" is a thorough critique of the Hegelian view of history. His other major work is "The Essence of the Historical Process and the Role of the Individual in History". He also published a number of important articles on relevant subjects. Unfortunately, his works, like most of other Russian philosophical works, are still unavailable in English translation. Kareyev is another example of 'lay' philosophers in the history of Russian thought. It would be very useful to make a comparative study of his philosophy of history with those of Arnold Toynbee and Oswald Spengler.

N. I. Kareyev

ON THE QUESTION OF FREE WILL FROM THE POINT OF VIEW OF THE THEORY OF THE HISTORICAL PROCESS *

It has long been my desire to share some of my ideas with the members of the Psychological Society to which I have the honour to belong. I not only wanted to show that I belong to the Society by actively participating in it. There were also personal reasons for wanting to deliver a paper at one of its meetings in order to confirm my personal views in a discussion with representatives of various specialized fields who are united by their mutual interest in psychological questions in the hope of finding in them a solution to some of my perplexities, and partly to get some information.

Unfortunately, I had not succeeded in doing this, thus far. This is my first opportunity to visit the Psychological Society, and my old wish is now being fulfilled. I ask your indulgence for a brief period to air some of my views on a question to which the Psychological Society has devoted considerable efforts. It considered this question (and quite rightly so) to be of tremendous importance for all sciences in general whose object of study is man and the world of human phenomena.

The choice of this theme for today's discussion can be explained on my part by the following reason. I had just completed and published a work "On the Essence of the Historical Process and the Role of Personality in History", when I chanced upon a book which is well known to you, containing essays and articles by members of the Psychological Society on free will. There is a very close connection between

* The above selection was originally read at the Moscow Psychological Society on April 10, 1890, and was published the same year in *Voprosy*, Vol. 2, Bk. 8, pp. 113-142. Certain brief paragraphs were omitted from the selection because they were either repetitious or were irrelevant to the main theme.

the questions with which I am concerned in my new work and the question dealt with in these articles and essays, and I cannot tell you how I regret that I have only become acquainted with them after the publication of a large part of my work. At any rate, I read the book on free will, published by the Psychological Society, although I did not read it while working on the investigation of the historical process and role of personality in history, nonetheless I read it at a time when my thoughts were not quite fully settled. Hence, I felt it necessary to contribute something of my own to the work undertaken by the Psychological Society, entitled, "A Collection of Experiments for Stating and Solving the Problem of Free Will", and at the same time to offer a point of view on this question for consideration by competent experts, a view which I call the theory of the historical process. I dare say that it will not be a waste of time, and I hope that basically it will withstand the test of scientific criticism.

I shall begin by stating, that during the reading of the above essays on free will, I was struck by two circumstances which are very important to me. First, not a single specialist on the historical process is listed among those who participated in the discussion on free will. Secondly, nothing is indicated in the essays themselves that this question which is of interest to the philosopher and psychologist, the moralist and the criminologist, could be of equal interest to the historian. Only in one article by P. E. Astafyev some mention is made to the effect that this question is related to the laws of history and to the activities of separate personalities, but this was only mentioned casually with no apparent intention of solving it on the basis of any consideration drawn from 'the philosophy of history'.

These two considerations would have passed unnoticed, had they not confirmed two ideas which I have expressed several times. In an essay which I had read recently before the Historical Society in St. Petersburg University, entitled "On the Development of Theoretical Questions of Historical Science"[7] I pointed out that in this work the historical specialists participated in a much lesser degree than they could and should have done, and less than the representatives of other scientific fields.

In my new book, "The Essence of the Historical Process and the Role of Personality in History" I partly remarked that the question of causality about which different points of view have been expressed by authors on philosophy, the logic of science, psychology and criminal law, remains unelaborated from the point of view of historical science, although the latter states that the combination of the facts it studied as

[7] See N. I. Kareyev, "The Essence of the Historical Process" in the March issue, 1890 in *Russkayea Mysl* [Russian Thought].

one of its tasks, and although the solution of the question from the general philosophical, logical, psychological and criminological points of view are either insufficient or inapplicable to the needs of historical science.

The concept of free will with which the members of the Psychological Society have been so preoccupied, is closely bound up with the concept of causality whose theoretical elaboration completely escaped the attention of the historians, in spite of the fact that the causal nexus plays such an obvious role in all their scientific constructions, and in spite of the fact that both philosophers, logicians, psychologists and criminologists set a good example for them from various points of view in a series of essays on causality. And even now, when the Psychological Society, in several of its meetings was busy considering the question of causality, and especially causality in human affairs, not a single historian said a word on such an important subject. Furthermore, even the representatives of the various scientific fields, who were here discussing free will and causality, failed to see its significance in the study of human action which are within the scope of the pragmatic process of history, and I do not consider it to be a mere accident.

In my second volume *The Fundamental Problems of the Philosophy of History* [8] I had already pointed out, that in regard to the general importance of psychology for history and sociology, its particular importance should not be individual psychology studying the psychic processes which occur within a separate personality, but rather a so-called collective psychology, whose objct would be embodied in the spiritual phenomena arising in human society. I am still strongly convinced of the need for a scientific investigation of collective-psychic phenomena and processes. Hence, I pointed out once again in my new book on the importance of a collective psychology where I initiated a discussion on what psychology can and must contribute to the theory of the historical process. [9] Incidentally, I touched on the fact, that the theory of historical causality could borrow from psychological theories on this subject. I understand the matter as follows. From the point of view of pragmatic history, the actions of some people, in one way or another, are determined by the actions of other people. But from the point of view of psychology, they are determined by the concept of motive as being the cause of an action, which hardly enlarges upon the question of actions being the causes of actions, since this can only be considered outside the realm of individual psychology. At one time, an

[8] See N. I. Kareyev, *Osnovnyey voprosy filosofii istorii* [The Fundamental Problems of the Philosophy of History], Vol. II (1883), where this subject is discussed in great detail. Available only in Russian.
[9] See Kareyev's "The Essence of the Historical Process", pp. 209 foll.

historian regarded the actions of some people to be essentially the causes (or enter into the composition of causes) of the actions of other people. And it would have been very important for the theory of the historical process to make use of such a psychological theory which would examine man not in isolation, but along with other people, i.e. in their psychic interactions.

Unfortunately, psychology pays very little attention to this sort of problem, when under the influence of one person (i.e. under the influence of any of his actions, or a number of actions) another person commits one act or a series of acts. This extremely individualistic view on "the science of the soul" was expressed both in essays as well as in the discussions on the question of free will, which is appropriate in a Psychological Society. Both the protagonists and opponents of free will in its various aspects, considered man, his soul and his will in isolation, outside the pragmatic and cultural dependence of a single personality upon other personalities and outside pragmatic and cultural influences to which it itself points. It seems to me, that this is the reason why it never occurred to those who read papers on free will at the Psychological Society to devote themselves to something which could lead to an understanding of the subject, by examining the historical process, which in its pragmatic aspect deals with the motivations of the actions of some people by the actions of others. Hence, I am inclined to think, that it is no accident that none of the historians participated in the discussion of free will which took place in our meetings, and that in this discussion, and in the discussion of that aspect which concerns the problem of historiology was completely forgotten. In other words. here is an example of the indifferent attitudes on the part of the historians toward an elaboration of certain theoretical questions which are of tremendous importance to their particular field of study. It also shows the absence of any special interest on the part of psychologists in those phenomena which occur in the psychic interactions of individuals.

At this juncture I shall not elaborate on any one of these points. My essay, of course, includes a certain accusation against the representatives of the scientific community to which number I belong by virtue of my profession. I have already presented this accusation in the abovementioned work which I read at the Historical Society (in St. Petersburg). At this point, on the other hand, I shall take the liberty of dealing with the side of the matter, which is, if you please, of a mitigating nature for historians. Although we as historians can raise certain objections in regard to the contemporary state of psychology. Of course, the psychologists will have a great deal to say in their defense, and I am prepared beforehand to agree with a substantial part of their arguments with which they will defend themselves, but in one respect I intend to maintain that I am unconditionally right.

The general non-participation attitude on the part of the historians toward an elaboration of the theoretical problems of historical science, which incidentally concern problems of psychology, is partially explained, in my opinion, by the fact that psychology in its present state, as the science of the individual soul can offer very little to historical science in the present phase of its development. The days when the biographical element in history was central, have gone never to return. Biographical history has become sociological (history), but unfortunately, the broadening of individual psychology in psychology, which would study man individually and people in their psychic interactions did not correspond to this evolution. Taine,[10] one of the influential historians of our time, declared more than once that the present theory of history is nothing but psychology. While I do not completely agree with this idea, since history has another side apart from the purely psychological, namely, a sociological side, which Taine completely ignores. I cannot avoid pointing out here, that the truth in his assertion would still be truer, if he meant by psychology not a simple psychology of the individual. Having read a fairly large number of major and minor discussions about the importance of psychology in history, I found precisely this gap. As soon as one goes beyond the limits of the biographical side of the historical existence of personality, and as soon as one begins to think about the spiritual processes which occur in individual human groups and in whole societies, at that very moment one often fails to see that the historian could utilize very successfully the psychological theories which constitute the main core of modern "science of the soul", without being concerned with a psychological analysis of separate individualities, similar to that with which for instance, the novelist is concerned. In a word, the general nature of modern psychology which remains individualistic, does not at all correspond to the general character of history, which by its very nature, is a science dealing with something that is collective. Hence, present-day historians have much greater points of contact with representatives of the social sciences, i.e. with politicians, jurists and economists, than with psychologists who still study man in isolation.

I have a positive basis for stating that the dominant philosophy of history is unfavourably disposed toward the idea of a personal element in history, and to a certain degree I can explain it by the fact, that historical science in its study of reality does not encounter anywhere an individual isolated from other people, which is the chief concern of psychology.

---

[10]   H. Taine (1828-1893), French historian. Author of *Philosophie de l'Art* (1865) *De l'Intelligence* (1870).

The scope of the present paper does not, of course, permit me to examine thoroughly even that aspect which the theory of the historical process rightly demands of psychology, since it broadened the scope of its authority, or failed to discover why the attempts which were consciously made to establish a basis for a collective psychology (such as Volkerpsychologie by Lazarus,[11] and Steintahl,[12] Psychologie der Gesellschaft by Linder,[13] etc.) have at least thus far produced no important results for the theory of history. Finally, they failed to consider what aspects of psychic interactions should be studied and how they should be studied. I shall only take the liberty of giving an example of the particular problem of free will which is of interest to the Psychological Society, the sort of omissions which are made, in my view, in solving this problem. Consequently, the object of investigation is regarded here as an individual will outside its interrelation with other wills, both in the course of ordinary life and in the course of history.

As a matter of fact, when the question of freedom or non-freedom of the will is stated and being solved, the individual person is considered in isolation from other persons with whom he is closely bound by thousands of invisible bonds. There is, to be sure, an area where this question is considered from the point of view of man studied not in isolation, but in groups and en masse. But in this area problems of a non-psychological nature are being solved. In saying this, I have in mind a series of social phenomena which are subject to mathematical calculation, because they can be expressed in numerical data, i.e., they become the object of statistics. Recently, a certain regularity was under observation monthly and annually in certain statistical numbers. For example, it was observed that a number of letters were undelivered with constant regularity. This was due either to the absence of an address or for some other omission. This incident was almost regarded as a definite argument against freedom of will. It would be erroneous to assume that while I intend to raise the question of free will on the basis of a collective psychology, that I am advising to use the method employed by statisticians for centuries.

I have not as yet mentioned the fact that among the phenomena with which statistics are concerned, is the moral phenomenon, which is the external expression of the will; it occupies an unimportant place (in statistics). Statistics do not only offer a diagnosis of social conditions, but in addition, deal with the changes of one state to another – important for history, which in turn is concerned with the study of

---

[11] M. Lazarus, German Psychologist of the 19th century.
[12] H. Steinthal, German psychologist of the 19th century, author of many books.
[13] Lindner belonged to the same German school of psychology as Lazarus and Steinthal.

processes which occur in society (incidentally, processes also of a spiritual character). I wish to draw your attention to the fact, that in studying people en masse, statistics regard individual human numbers as components of certain aggregates, and not as living people, who are in constant interaction with each other. To put it in other words, statistics show in figures certain general causes for this or that event, and that they act in such and such a way on such and such aggregates of people, but they have no means of tracing the nature of these causes, conditions, means, methods, forms, purposes, results, etc. of the actions of certain people on others and the dependence of their behaviour on each other.

It is not a matter of imagining a certain sum of people, whether statistically, i.e. "in abstracto", or artistically, i.e. "in concreto", which have something in common. It is rather a question of grasping the processes which occur in social groups, of a less homogeneous composition, to imagine separate persons which form these groups, not as items of a certain sum in which there is manifest an act of some general cause, or as non-homogeneous examples of some common type, but (must be imagined) as living persons, each one with his individual physiognomy and specific role; each in his special dependence upon others and with his special influence on others. That is the reason why I think that psychology must not learn from the statisticians how to take for its study "man not in isolation". This method will not go beyond a statistical characterization of separate nations, or a psychological analysis of the so-called collective personality, such as this or that social group is in history, which differentiates itself by its peculiar features. That which passes for the concept of a national spirit, or the character of a social group or some such thing, is nothing more than the result of a complex psychic interaction between individuals. It is precisely this interaction which should have been the fundamental object of that aspect of psychology which one should employ in the study of man, namely, "not in isolation".

While actually insisting that one must bear in mind when solving very many psychological questions of this nature, that man is "a living social being", I am far from insisting that because of this, one must regard a single personality as a simple product of society. What I have already said on the subject of the statistical relation to the individual, as a homogeneous component forming certain sums, and what I had to say about the psychology of groups or masses, which regards separate individuals only as different examples of a certain general type, should make it sufficiently clear that I wish to preserve the concept of an independent personality in my Weltanschauung. Furthermore, I should generally like to separate this idea from the scientific views, which reduce it to zero. The latter leads at the present time mainly to two trends, with different points of departure, but with the same result. The one trend leads to a division of the individual Self into a series of events occuring in it, and makes personality the sum of a collection of designated minute psychological processes. The other trend, on the other hand, makes every such Self one of the reflections of the Zeitgeist, or the nation, and regards personality as a simple creation of the social environment, which is wholly explained by it. Thus, from both points of view, personality is not something unique and a whole. It is either the sum of separate psychic phenomena, or a part of some higher spiritual whole, as can be seen in Taine's general historical concept.[14]

In my present paper in which I devote a great deal of attention to point out the inadequacy of one individual psychology, I consider it of course, very important to state that I have no intention whatsoever of regarding the individual personality as a product of society. In order to save time, I shall refer you to what I stated in my book "The Essence of the Historical Process and the Role of Personality", where I subjected to criticism the position of the sociologist Gumilovich (Grundriss der Sociologie) who regarded human personality, without any remainder, as the product of the social group to which it belongs.[15]

Due to lack of time I cannot stop to consider what is valid in both views, which destroy the concept of the individual and whole personality, and also where the error lies in the conclusions made concerning the nature of the individual soul. But in advocating a personal principle from the standpoint of the concept of personality in the name of the latest results of individual psychology, or in the name of data which are the point of departure of modern sociological theories, I cannot agree with the former view of personality, viz., that it is an individual spirit which can be studied apart from physiological and psychophysiological processes which occur in the organism, and apart from the collective-psychic processes occurring in society. However, while the first of these truths has already found its way into science, the second one is only now beginning to blaze a path toward its general recognition. This was also stated in the reports read at the Psychological Society regarding the methods of posing and solving the problem of freedom of the will. When the problem is discussed, one very often refers to the dependence of the spirit on the body. They completely lose sight of the fact that one spirit is dependent upon another spirit. They devote their attention to find out how the will is conditioned by something or other, which is in itself another will, completely ignoring

---

[14]   Cf. V. I. Gerye's article on Taine in *Vestnik Evropy*, Jan. 1890, pp. 54 ff.
[15]   See N. I. Kareyev, "The Essence of the Historical Process", pp. 169 ff.

the occasions when one will is determined by another will or its manifestations. In a word, they talk about the relation of the Self to the non-Self, but do not talk about the interrelations of the Selves.

One cannot of course, regard man as a being in his life and activity when he is in contact only with objects and phenomena of one material world. Man lives and acts in a society with people like himself. He is bound to them by many and varied relationships, subjecting his behaviour to a number of influences from other people, and through his own personal behaviour exerts his influence on their behaviour in his own particular way. Basically, the problem of freedom of the will viewed from its practical relation to the problem of human existence, is closely bound up with the social life of people. Both ethics and criminology which play an active role in exploring the problem, do not consider man individually, but in a certain relation to other people. This subject should have also been considered from a purely theoretical view. They should not have lost sight of the fact that causality in human affairs is more or less dependent upon the actions of certain persons upon the action of other persons. Hence, in solving the problem of free will theoretically, it is very important to view man in his interrelation with other people. The latter cannot however, take place until a theory of causality in human actions is established on the basis of a collective psychology. I think that the matter would have advanced more rapidly, had a theory of the historical process come to the aid of psychologists, which of course, is the prerogative of historians being their field of specialization.

The idea of causality plays a very important role both in philosophy and in other sciences, but it seems to me that its general theory is not sufficiently elaborated, especially in its applicability to human behaviour. The idea of causality whose nature is being studied by philosophers, is also of interest, from various points of view, to logicians, psychologists and criminologists, and plays an important role in the systems of historians. Nevertheless, there are very important gaps in their scientific investigations.

I have already mentioned earlier that historians unlike representatives of other scientific fields, who are interested in the problem of causality, have failed completely to subject it to a scientific study, but were merely satisfied to state a general principle, viz., that historical facts must be connected with cause and effect. I pointed out also that individual psychology is incapable of covering the problem in its totality, because it does not make a study of psychic interactions which take place within human relations. The manner in which the question is raised by logic and criminology, does not remove the gaps due to the inattention paid to it by historians, and also, because of the one-sided interpretation by psychologists. In logic, the idea of causality is mainly bound up with the theory of induction. Also due to the concept of the uniformity of nature, which is at the root of the concept of scientific laws discovered by the inductive method, all considerations centre in the idea of causal connections in the world of material phenomena. The question of internal causality in connection with spiritual phenomena as well as causality in human action does not play any role in the logical sciences, so that they do not fill the gap in the theory of causality, due to the fact that thus far the representatives of the historical sciences have not been interested in this question. Similarly, the criminologists are unable to remedy the desideratum inherent in the question of free will, when dealing with it from a psychological point of view.

The fundamental question which criminology can solve is, to define when the action of a person may be regarded as the cause of a certain event, and under what conditions must this be considered an event or deed which is prohibited by positive legislation, and also how to define the relation of criminology to such criminal actions, and what indeed are the actions prohibited by law (for example, in the case of an instigation to commit a crime). Hence, criminologists take only certain actions from human behaviour, ignoring all the rest, and out of all the actions of man upon man, they concentrate only on one specific aspect. Both philosophy, psychology, logic and criminology have a great deal to offer toward a correct formulation and even solution of the problem of causality in human affairs. But it seems to me that the most important conclusions must be expected to come from the theory of the pragmatic process of history whose formulation has hardly begun.

The facts constituting the material for historical science are either events or forms of material, spiritual and social mode of life, in which case the first may be termed pragmatic facts, while the second, cultural facts. Hence, we may distinguish two trends (or directions) in historiography. Leaving aside the cultural aspect, we must first of all point out that the pragmatic historians have always considered it their task to connect events as a cause and effect relationship, so that the words 'pragmatism' and 'causalism' may be regarded as synonyms. From this point of view, one may be permitted to consider the scientific ideal of the pragmatic historian as knowledge of the past in which all events follow from preceding events, as effects from their causes. What are the pragmatic facts of history? In the final analysis they are reduced to separate human actions, which become events. This is expressed in the designation of history as "historia rerum gestarum", and in the term 'actions' as it was called in Russia in ancient times and as it is still called among the Poles and Czechs (*dzieje, dêjiny*).

Since however, the task of pragmatic historiography is to deduce one set of events from other (events) as effects from their causes, and since the events themselves consist of human deeds as primary elements of every pragmatic fact, a conclusion is "ipso facto" arrived at concerning that general concept which is the basis used by pragmatic historians to express the course of history. Indeed as far as our task is concerned, which the Greek historians have already posed for our science, man's actions are regarded as deeds occasioned by the action of other people.

It seems to me that such is the basic conception of every pragmatic historiography, and I think that it would be difficult to raise any objections against this assertion. Furthermore, if this main idea of historians were invalid, or at least did not contain a significant portion of truth, then everything that has been written on the course of events in various countries and at different times, would necessarily have to be regarded as nonsense, and in the future, astrology or alchemy which are based on false premises, would threaten historical science. No matter how much they criticized and from whatever standpoint, the fundamental concepts and methods of our science, it has never occurred to anyone to doubt the right and duty of historians to connect pragmatic facts as they had always done throughout the existence of historical literature. I do not know what basic objection could be raised against this idea, not to mention the fact, that one could adduce a positive argument in favour of the idea of man's action in history. It is a different matter to apply the principal idea to an examination of actual facts: here mistakes of various kinds could have been made and were actually made, and these have been more or less noted by those dealing with the historical method. It may be asked, are the historical activities unique, i.e., are those actions the only ones which historians single out for analysis and description in their works, are these the only ones which are subject to the general rule, viz., that the actions of some people are motivated by the actions of other people? Of course not: the distinction between actions of historical significance and those of non-historical significance must be sought elsewhere, and by no means in the method of their origin.

In social intercourse which embraces all aspects of man's life, his entire behaviour as well as his individual actions cannot be wholly insolated from his behaviour or from the individual actions of other people. It is here that a complex network of various interrelations among separate human activities takes place, which has at its basis whole systems and isolated instances of the psychic interactions of individual members of one and the same social group. Since this psychic interaction should have constituted the object of collective psychology, and since the mechanism of the pragmatic process of history, should in the final analysis, be applicable to it, hence, the theory of the latter and collective psychology should have worked in one direction, although using different materials and different methods.

If human events are essentially the results of other historical events, and if human acts are subject to other acts, then the process in relation to this idea may be regarded as basically true, and this easily leads to mechanism in the literal sense of the word. Events and their elements, i.e., separate acts, may be compared from this standpoint, with wheels of a complex machine, which transmit movement from one of its parts to another, without introducing anything of itself into this movement.

Elsewhere I have examined the various shades of the idea of the role of personality in history,[16] originating in the mechanistic view on the pragmatic process. This view is explained by the fact, that in considering the external aspect of this process, i.e. by examining the motivation of certain events by other events, the important point is overlooked, viz., that events consist of separate acts, and that between the causal-act and effect-act, there is no direct contact, since these are formed into a single link of the pragmatic process by a certain moment – the psychic act, which consists in the transforming of an external influence into the motivation of a new act. Individual psychology which studies man in isolation, systematically disregards all those instances – and they are infinite in number – when a certain action or actions of people enter into the composition of the cause which gives rise to a certain human act. Without a scientific analysis of the most important categories into which similar phenomena could be divided, the internal psychic aspect of the pragmatic process will always be obscured by the external aspect, which is of a mechanical nature, and the historical actions of a person, without exception will lead to the historical actions of his predecessors, so that there will be little place left for personal action in the historical process. In the case of the latter, it has happened that a number of general views on history failed to allot any role to the personal views very instructive, both for the theory of historical causality as well as for the problem of free will, but it is instructive only from a negative aspect. From the same standpoint numerous protests by historians against the mechanization of the pragmatic process in the name of free will, also seem to me instructive. Unfortunately, the lessons and other historiological views have, thus far, been of negative importance.

Theologians, philosophers, psychologists and moralists as well as criminologists, have written on free will, analysing and discussing the

[16] See N. I. Kareyev's *The Essence of the Historical Process and the Role of Personality in History*, where he discusses this subject in greater detail.

question from various aspects setting forth arguments both for and against (free will). Even here, as in the question of causality, the historians who expressed theoretical views on the fundamental understanding of their science, limited themselves to a simple declaration in favour of 'human freedom', or in defense of 'historical laws' without taking the trouble to enter deeply into the subject. Generally speaking, it seemed to certain historians, who were always only slightly interested in the problem, that negation of free will in history would lead to a fatal elimination of personality from history, and in order to escape such a conclusion, they were often ready to preach with firm belief the absolute freedom of will, failing to see that the application of such a view to pragmatic facts of history, would basically destroy the science which seeks causes for the facts it studies precisely in other facts, and hence, cannot conceive of causeless facts. It seems to me that under a better elaboration of collective-psychic phenomena, the recurring mistake would have been eliminated. The defenders of what they themselves called free will (incorrectly so), defended a true concept, that act-effects cannot be reduced wholly to causal-acts, i.e. that human action motivated by the actions of others, have their cause not only in these latter acts, but in man himself who performs the act. The results of individualistic-psychic processes are constantly intruding upon the mechanical process of the motivation of deeds by deeds, the engendering of events by events, each having its own origin, its own personal causality, inexplicable by any one historical pragmatism. It is precisely this constant introduction of new forces into the pragmatic process, which the opponents of the mechanistic point of view called human freedom, without taking into consideration the fact that the amount of freedom with which we participate in the pragmatic process of history, does not play the role of transmitting instruments which receive and transmit movement not motivated by them, but that this portion of freedom is the result of our submission to other causal ends but are independent of the causality of pragmatic facts.

Without wishing to be an exception, I shall not insist that the former statement of the problem of free will was useless. I only think that it is incomplete, and that the necessary completion occurs only when we pay attention to the form the question of free will and causality should assume, when we fulfill the requirements of defining the role of personality in history, or as a result of this (or independently) we arrive at the idea of studying the psychic influences of man on man, which becomes the motivating force in influencing the acts of others. It is precisely on this basis alone that the conditionality of our actions can be studied from a point of view which has generally received little attention in the examination of causality in human action, and the concept of freedom takes on a new meaning, – a sense of freedom from the fated courses of history, often taken as a fatalistic law of history which completely governs all human behaviour.

It would require a great deal of time, if I undertook to give even a short account of my theoretical views on the role of personality in history and on the degree of possible freedom for us, which in my view are incorrectly termed historical laws. I shall only say one thing. The theory of historical causality as I understand it, may be equally far from the fatalistic conclusions, which certain writers derive from the fact that the pragmatic process leads to a causal connection of human actions produced by people, and also from an excessive exaggeration of the notion of human freedom. Certain historians also arrive at such a conclusion without accepting a negative view of a personal principle in history. They are more ready to admit the existence of a complete miracle in its course, i.e. a constant incursion into this course of cause-less acts which become causes of new events, rather than agree with the deterministic concept. The question of the role of personality in history, which is usually not stated theoretically when discussing the problem of free will, is only touched upon when the question is raised regarding its importance "for the practical evaluation of our daily problems".

On the very first two pages of his paper, L. M. Lopatin begins his discussion in this vein, proving the importance of the problem under discussion. "Every one of us, no matter how simple his goals are, hopes to produce something which would somehow modify its (life's) deter-ministic course, by doing something "new" which would depend only on ourselves, even though we have had to choose for this (purpose) a very narrow sphere of activity".[17]

In one way or another we consider ourselves called upon to struggle with the external world in order to exert a distinctive influence upon the elemental and merciless course of its events by our reason and will. We instinctively look upon ourselves as the source of creative forces, which we can manifest, if we seriously desire to do so. Every "predetermination" is in conflict with this natural self-consciousness of personality. Most of all it is in contradiction with the view according to which our Self, because of its independent opposition to external nature, becomes its passive continuation, and from a free source of energy becomes a bundle of processes, predetermined by the general life of the universe in all its minutest details. And to this view, the author adds the idea that determinism leads to complete inevitability. If I am not mistaken, this is the only place, in all the published papers

[17]   L. M. Lopatin, "On Freedom of the Will", pp. 97-98.

by the Psychological Society, where this question is raised in connection with the problem of the role of personality in history.

L. M. Lopatin points out that everyone of us hopes to produce something new in life, i.e. something which it hitherto did not have, something which depends on us alone, and that we therefore hope to modify the fated course of life. From this viewpoint he sets forth the idea of the personal awareness of our creative forces which oppose the elemental and merciless course of events in the world. By the latter, he obviously understands only one external nature, about which he speaks in the above work, which stands in opposition to the independent Self. We thus have, on the one hand, the creative forces of the independent Self, and on the other, the elemental and fated course of events of external nature. The individual Self is here thought of along with external nature, which is a purely individualistic statement of the problem, and he ignores the fact that besides the individual self there are other selves distinct both from the individual Self and from external nature, which is in opposition to the Self.

Everything which is created in life without my participations, is actually either the result of a purely spontaneous and determined course of events, (if my personal right refuses other "selves" that privilege to modify the fated course of history, a privilege which I recognized for myself), or it is only the result of a spontaneous and fated course of events, provided I accord the same privilege to others. In other words, in L. M. Lopatin's discussion the fact is overlooked that along with the single Self as an independent opposing force to external nature, there are other selves, each one having its own importance, but are for us the same external forces with which we will have at times to struggle on the same level as with forces of the external world, but which, as it appears, act like ourselves, i.e. quite independently, once we recognize in this independence our distinction from natural phenomena. Hence, the processes occurring outside my Self are essentially or actually purely spontaneous processes, if only I alone exist as an independent principle, or they are not essentially purely spontaneous processes, if I admit that there are other independent selves participating in these processes.

No one, of course, will support the first proposition, and once we are obliged to adopt the second point of view, our investigation must be concerned not only with the question of the relation of the individual self to external nature as opposing forces, but to other selves as well which possess the same independence as we do. We have the right to accept L. M. Lopatin's point of view, so long as we regard man as a being who is placed in the midst of various mechanical, physical, chemical and physiological processes, which take place outside his spiritual Self and which condition his life, and determine his behaviour. But as soon as we consider the individual in his relations to some phenomena of a psychic and social nature, which occur outside his spiritual Self, this view turns out to be unsatisfactory in all its defects. Leaving this question aside, let us suppose that everything which is created in life not by myself, seems to me to be equally determined and spontaneous, regardless who created it, be they natural forces or other personalities. Also, let us suppose that I consider myself and have a right to consider myself, as a force upon which something depends, a force that is unique and independent. We may still ask whether determinism, with its complete inevitability, leads to the view that my independent interference in the course of world affairs is pure illusion.

L. M. Lopatin holds the view that 'not everything in the world is a consequence', but that there 'are causes for which there are no other causes'. My mind positively refuses to understand how this can be, but if by determinism is meant a theory which assumes that everything in the world is an effect of something else, in that case I declare myself without hesitation to be the strictest determinist. This however, does in no way interfere with my recognition of the importance of personal interference in the fatalistic course of events, and in no way compels me to arrive at the deterministic conclusion, which, in the words of L. M. Lopatin, results from determinism with complete inevitability.

I am not undertaking to prove this in detail for one reason only – lack of time. I shall endeavour, however, to point to the manner of my proof, by taking L. M. Lopatin's words as my point of departure, a view with which I frequently agree, when he affirms universal phenomena and does not merely accept its explanation. For example, I fully accept the following description of what in Lopatin's view, the active force accomplishes teleologically which he contrasts with the causality of external phenomena (in his case they are only 'natural' phenomena). "It directs them", says Lopatin; "it supplements that which they lack. But this means that it interrupts their blind course, and in forms of a future result it introduces into them the moment of activity, independent of their fated cohesion".[18]

It is that much easier for me to agree with such a position, since I myself understand the role of personal action in history, precisely in history, which from the purely-mechanical viewpoint is not far from "the senseless, elemental natural movements", which L. M. Lopatin alone takes into consideration.[19] Events do not in themselves 'flow' in

---

[18] This is how Lopatin formulates one of his ideas in his paper, "Freedom of the Will", p. 191.
[19] See N. I. Kareyev, "The Essence of the Historical Process", Bk. I, Ch. V & VI.

certain directions: we direct them. There is a constant intrusion of personal activity into their elemental and fated flow, which interrupts their blind course and which is itself independent of them. Does this mean that the direction which I want to give and even do give to the flow of events, is a result of a causal action which does not require any further causes for its existence, but is not the result of some other causes, without whose actions things would not proceed in the order which I would like to give them and actually do give? Intrusions into the blind course of events which assume meaning because of my activity, are naturally achieved not without a cause. But if my activity, instead of being subject to the events, subjects the events to itself. Does this imply that my activity, which is independent of the direction in which things proceed without me, would generally be independent of anything else? The historical process is formed by the causal connections of human actions, but it is the biological process which provides the agents for this uninterrupted drama, independent of the pragmatic process of history, and if the act of one person motivates the act of another person, then the first is not the entire cause of the latter, since in the origin of acts by other acts, which constitutes the mechanism of pragmatic history, there is a constant intrusion of separate acts of the psychic life of individuals, i.e., separate moments of such processes which are completely independent of this mechanism.

My appearance in the world as a being endowed with certain natural propensities, does not on the one hand, depend upon the turn of events at this particular moment. That is to say, it is as though I intrude myself into them like an alien force. They are not my cause, but generally speaking, I am not without a cause. On the other hand, in the separate acts of my behaviour, which exert their influence on the course of events in this world, not everything is explained by the previous moments of this course, since a great deal of these acts does not depend on what happens outside myself, but on what takes place in me and on my relation to them. In turn, one should look for explanations in my psyche which is independent of external events and which takes place simultaneously with the processes of my personal, spiritual life. This is the reason why, having declared myself to be a determinist, I deeply believe in the reality of personal interference in history. The role of personality in the processes of the latter is not determined by it alone, but by many other factors which do not constitute it and do not depend on it. The more a personality is determined in its behaviour by such forces, the freer is its will from the fated course of events, the more is this will self-determined and not conditioned by what other persons are doing.

This is not all. Since not everything in human behaviour is determined by history, personality cannot therefore regard itself as the slave of history, hence, there is no place for a fatalistic view of history. The fatalistic formula is as follows: What is to be one cannot escape, no matter what one does to avert it. But such a formula could only make sense if everything occurring in history were determined only by history alone. If the biological process of the changes of generations did not introduce into it new agents, and if each agent did not introduce into the process something which is new to him, not as a result of his previous moments, but that which has its genesis in the processes of the individual being. Nature creates new individuals which enter the arena of history. We create new facts which are related only to old facts of history in one aspect, the other aspect is the result of our personal life.

L. M. Lopatin connects quite thoroughly the idea of freedom of the will with the idea of creativity, and the latter plays a very prominent role in his essay. On page 113 [20] for example, he expresses doubt in the fact that "we must limit ourselves to a physical interpretation of causal connection and reject its universal idea of a 'creative' relationship". On page 119 he shows that the psychic force is related to its products, viz., sensations, in a creative sense, since "even here we have to do with products which constantly come into being anew, and not with the simple rearrangement of the qualitative and quantitative immutable elements".

L. M. Lopatin regards every purposeful deed as a "certain transference of the general and the indefinite into the concrete, and the individually-completed", and this he calls creativity.[21] I agree with this and with similar views, but not without reservations. The chief reservation may be expressed by the aphorism, "ex nihilo nihil fit". Even so, personal creativity cannot be studied on the basis of individual existence. As in his behaviour so in his creativity as well as in pragmatic history and in cultural history, human freedom is limited by the behaviour and creativity of other people. I think that not only the question of freedom of the will, but also the question of the essence of human creativity must be formulated on the basis of a collective psychology and the theory of the historical process. No matter what uniqueness man may have brought into the world and no matter how independently he would refashion the external impressions and influences, he creates everything, beginning with language and ending with the highest products of philosophical thought. He begins with the establishment of the simplest relations with people around him and ends with the greatest social reform. This he achieves not alone, but with the help and results of other people. He tries out one or another set of impressions and in-

[20]   See L. M. Lopatin, *ibid.*, p. 113.
[21]   See L. M. Lopatin, *ibid.*, p. 136.

fluences, not arbitrarily, but by submitting to the conditions of the historical moment, and by fulfilling (although spontaneously and originally) the demands of cultural evolution. Unfortunately, even this question had not hitherto been formulated on the basis of a collective psychology, as a result, the interests of the theory of the historical process suffer.

BIOGRAPHICAL SKETCH

Nikolai Aleksandrovich Berdyaev (1874-1948), was born in Lipky, a suburb of Kiev. On his father's side he was descended from a long line of military men, while on his mother's side he is a descendent of a French noble family, the Choiseuls, who were given asylum by Catherine the Great. Berdyaev's mother was Princess Kudasheva, who insisted on bringing up her children in the French manner of life.

He was enrolled in the Corps of Cadets in Kiev, and was later transferred to the Corps of Pages. However, a military career was very repugnant to him, and he decided to choose his own life's work. Accordingly, he steeped himself in philosophy. German idealism, as well as Schopenhauer, Nietzsche, Marx, Leontiev, Dostoyevsky, Ibsen, Bohme, Tolstoy, Solovyov and others, all left their influences on him.

During his student days at the Kiev University, Berdyaev became interested in Marxism, and in 1894 joined the Social Democratic Party. He became very active in that movement, but at the same time he was still an ardent Kantian. In 1898 he was arrested along with one hundred and fifty other members of the Social Democratic Party. He was exiled to the northern province of Vologda where he wrote his first book, "Subjectivism and Individualism in Social Philosophy", which was an attempt to integrate idealism with Marxism. The book was intended as a critique of Mikhailovsky's 'subjective sociology'. It was a deviation from orthodox Marxism in that it insisted that only transcendental critical idealism can solve the problem of truth.

After his return from exile in 1901, he went to Germany where he entered the University of Heidelberg and in 1904 he returned to Russia and settled in St. Petersburg. It was there that he embarked upon his literary activity. He and Sergei Bulgakov edited a journal, "The New Way", (*Novyi Put'*). He also co-operated in another journal, "Problems of Life". It was during this period that his ideas began to develop. He was no longer an orthodox Marxist nor a thorough-going idealist. He became more interested in religious and mystical ideas. Merezhkovsky, Rozanov, Nesmelov and Solovyov now became his spiritual mentors. He summarized his Weltanschauung in his autobiography in these words: "My manner of thinking is intuitive and aphoristic rather than discursive and systematic, I am unable to expound or demonstrate anything by way of ratiocination". (*Dream and Reality*, p. 81.)

His spiritual and intellectual odysseys may be divided roughly into four main periods. In his first period his emphasis was on the problem of morality. His second period is marked by a mystico-religious interest. This was his most creative period. His third period centers around the problem of the philosophy of history with special emphasis upon the eschatological element in the historical process. Finally, his *personalistic* ideas which permeated his whole life and thought. The two central ideas connected with his personalism are: (1) the principle of objectivation, and (2) the primacy of freedom over being. He was truly a 'captive of freedom'.

Berdyaev was a prolific writer. He wrote on many subjects. His major works are: *Subjectivism and Individualism in Social Philosophy; Sub Specie aeternitatis; The Meaning of History; The End of Our Time; Freedom of the Spirit; Spirit and Reality; The Russian Idea; The Origin of Russian Communism; Dream and Reality*; and a posthumous work *The Kingdom of God and the Kingdom of Caesar* and other minor works as well as numerous articles. His works have been translated into many foreign languages and his contribution to both philosophical and religious thought has yet to be evaluated.

N. A. Berdyaev

SUBJECTIVISM AND OBJECTIVISM*

The subjective 'method in sociology' *sub specie aeternitatis,* is an original product of Russian thought. Its protagonists speak with pride of the existence of a Russian 'ethico-sociological school'. The 'subjective method' has in recent years been the focus of a lively controversy as a result of the conflict between the protagonists of the old trends with the new way of thought. But this object of pride on the part of the Russian sociologists has not been adequately clarified either by them or by their critics, since neither side touched the real core of the matter, or the philosophical basis concerning the relationship between the subjective and the objective. Meanwhile, this question is at the very centre of our world-view. The haziness which has thus far shrouded this problem clearly points up the weakness of such philosophical grounds, as for example, positivism on the one hand (N. Mikhailovsky)[22] and dialectical materialism on the other (N. Beltov).[23] We shall rely entirely on critical philosophy and shall endeavour to show that it can be a great ally of the social world-view which we profess. The objectivism of which we are justly proud can only be firmly grounded in critical philosophy in which alone can be found a suitable place for our subjectivism of which we should be no less proud and which can be repudiated by a misunderstanding.

* The above selection, Chapter I, pp. 16-141, is taken from Berdyaev's book, "Subjectivism and Individualism in Social Philosophy", and is considerably abridged. It is a critique of Mikhailovsky's 'subjective method'.

[22] N. K. Mikhailovsky (1842-1904), Russian social philosopher and active leader of the Populist movement in Russia.

[23] N. Beltov is the pseudonym of G. V. Plekhanov (1857-1918) wellknown Russian socialist and theoretician of Marxist dialectical materialism.

N. K. Mikhailovsky is undoubtedly the most talented defender of the 'subjective method' and is its chief creator, but it would be futile to look for any strict definition of this original method. It is quite obvious that the nature of this method was far from clear to Mikhailovsky himself: his observations are very inconsistent. Our task is to classify and examine all the possible concepts of the subjective method in sociology. First of all we shall dwell on the general nature of Mikhailovsky's 'subjectivism' and on the fundamental defects of his worldview.

In the foreword to the new edition of his works, Mikhailovsky describes very beautifully the motivating force behind all his literary work: "every time I visualize the word 'pravda' (truth) I cannot but marvel at its striking inner beauty. There is no such word, it seems, in any European language. It would seem that only in Russian are truth (*istina*) and justice (*spravedlivost'*) called by the same word, forming, as it were, one great whole. "Pravda" in this broad sense has always been the goal of my searchings. *Pravda-truth* (*pravda-istina*) separated from *pravda-justice* (*pravda-spravedlivost'*),[24] the truth of a theoretical heaven cut off from the truth of a practical earth, not only failed to satisfy me, it always outraged me. On the other hand, the noble daily practical aspects of life, the highest moral and social ideals have always seemed to me offensively impotent, when they turned away from truth (*istina*) and from science. I never could believe, and do not believe now, that it is impossible to find a point of view where *pravda-truth* (*pravda-istina*) and *pravda-justice* (*pravda-spravedlivost'*) would go hand-in-hand, the one enriching the other ... To be able to look unflinchingly into the eyes of reality and its reflection – *pravda-istina* or objective truth, and at the same time preserve also *pravda-spravedlivost'* or subjective truth – this is the task of my entire life. It is no easy task."[25]

The prevailing impression left by all Mikhailovsky's discussions on the 'subjective method' is as follows. Every living person should be subjectively related to social phenomena and can only evaluate them from his own preconceived point of view. Hence, cognition in social science is complicated by a new element – the subjective element which basically distinguishes sociological cognition from all others, from the cognition of the so-called natural sciences. In social science the objective method is therefore not sufficient, whereas the subjective method is essential.

[24] Pravda-truth (*pravda-instina*) represents objective truth while pravda-justice (*pravda-spravedlivost'*) represents subjective truth. Whenever these phrases are used in the future, they will have the above meaning.
[25] See N. K. Mikhailovsky, *Sochineniya* [Collected Works], Vol. I, Foreward.

Here are Mikhailovsky's own words found in the opening pages of the first volume of his works: "In sociology . . . a preconceived opinion is necessarily complicated by the moral element. Besides the objective truth which is sufficient for the naturalist, a sociologist's preconceived idea ought to reflect in itself his ideal of justice and morality, and depending on the sublimity of this ideal, he should more or less approximate an understanding of the meaning of phenomena of social life." [26] We shall try to discover Mikhailovsky's fundamental epistemological error. First of all, we must ask what is the meaning of the concept of the subject and to what extent can it be contrasted with the concept of the objective? Mikhailovsky nowhere analyses the concept of the subjective and the objective. His initial point of view remains very naive and uncritical, since he completely ignores that discipline of thought which alone can investigate objectivism and subjectivism in cognition. We shall try to show that Mikhailovsky's 'subjective method' rests primarily on an epistemological confusion – a gross confusion of a logical and a psychological nature. This also makes it difficult to discern the small portion of truth which undoubtedly exists in Mikhailovsky's work.

Before discussing subjectivism and the subjective method and the peculiarities in sociological cognition, it is essential to answer the question, what is objectivism in cognition. The concept of objectivity first assumed profound meaning in the philosophy of Kant. Cognitive objectivism can be based only on transcendental philosophy. The term 'objective' here denotes that which is universally obligatory, that which has universal application (allgemeingültig). Kant's greatest historical merit lies in the fact that he discovered the firm foundations of the universally-obligatory, i.e. the objectively-valuable in transcendental apperception. We state categorically that if we admit the empiricists view, only the existence of psychological consciousness which draws its content from experience, then the whole idea of the universally-obligatory is destroyed, hence, everything that is objective (is destroyed) and we arrive at sceptical subjectivism. Only inconsistency and intellectual cowardice keeps the empiricists from this unpleasant but inevitable conclusion.

What then is this transcendental, universal consciousness and wherein does it differ from the usual psychological consciousness? Every cognitive act presupposes a cognising subject. In every cognising subject we discover elements obligatory for all cognising subjects; they are the logical conditions of cognition, its necessary premises. All our cognition is experienced, but cognitive experience is possible only because it is logically preceded by such necessary conditions, as for example, the law of identity, the forms of time and space and the category of causality, etc. We do not say that the "a priori" chronologically precedes experience. There is nothing in the cognising subject prior to experience. The transcendental cognitive elements exist only for experience, and are meaningless without them; they are applicable only to our empirical world. In each cognitive act we only discover a definite logical sequence. We discover, for instance, that the category of causality has a universally-obligatory nature, a universal applicability in cognition; we say therefore that it logically precedes experience. An experienced phenomena of this cognitive category would not guarantee its universality. We could not be certain that future experience might not present us with causeless occurrences, and in fact, any sort of surprises. Such conscientious empiricists as J. S. Mill arrives at a sceptical view of causality. Besides, the changeable and unstable psychological consciousness, we must take as the objective fulcrum a more transcendental and logical consciousness, otherwise the world would become a complete chaos without law or knowledge, and would become a subjective game without any objective knowledge. The theory of knowledge (epistemology) is concerned with universal transcendental and not with subjective psychological consciousness. The position that is concerned with development is wholly applicable to psychological consciousness (the object of psychology), but it has no place in the theory of knowledge, which is concerned with only the logical and not with the origin and development of knowledge (this again is the concern of psychology), but with its composition and general applicability, i.e. its value (Gultigkeit). We proceed from the assumption that there is normal cognition. The objectively true is the epistemologically normal.

The most outstanding representative of philosophical criticism Alois Riehl [27] says that the logical, like the ethical has a social character, that it arises in spiritual intercourse. If only a single consciousness existed there would be no "a priori", no logical or ethical norms. How must this be understood? This important idea has the following meaning: the basic sign of logical and ethical norms is their objective value, their obligatoriness and applicability to every consciousness. They therefore presuppose the existence of several consciousness, since only in intercourse with others does the individual consciousness realise that it has something of the universal, i.e., something objective in the only possible sense of the word. The usual criterion of objective truth in cognition, namely, correspondence with eternal objects, is not sufficient philosophically. It is necessary that this correspondence should be the same for every consciousness, should apply equally to every consciousness, but this is possible only by recognising the transcendental elements of consciousness, and these are precisely the supreme criteria. In this sense, truth is indeed social.

Thus, the source of objectivism in cognition is the transcendental logical consciousness, while the individual psychological consciousness is the source of subjectivism. We recognize the existence of an objective truth; its logical bases are absolute and unshakeable, the main sign is its universally-obligatory nature. Epistemological scepticism – the fatal result of empiricism, removes the basic arguments of its supporters and leads to intellectual suicide. We are in need of an organically – integral positive world-view, and the role of such scepticism at the present historical juncture can only be reactionary.

In "The Notes of a Layman", Mikhailovsky discusses the question of the criterion of truth, and offers a definition of truth which in his opinion "unites the theoretical and the practical aspects". Mikhailovsky defines truth as "the satisfaction of the cognitive demands of human nature"; he considers it possible to substitute this phrase for the word 'truth'.

It is here that the whole unprincipled Comtian positivism in which Mikhailovsky finds his philosophical support is affected. He circumvents the correct viewpoint and sees only a small portion of the truth.

Mikhailovsky, in his attempt to establish the criterion for truth, bases it on the concept of human nature whose cognitive demands must be satisfied. What then is this human nature, this MAN who is at the centre of the subjective-anthropocentric or anthropological world-view? There is no need to prove the truth that human nature is deceptive, and that to satisfy its cognitive demands at different times and at one at the same time in various strata of society are in the highest degree different things. There is no need to prove that abstract man does not exist, but only the concrete historical man with his psychological peculiarities, as a result a lie will at times be more preferable to him than the truth. Mikhailovsky himself feels this and wishes to find a firmer support than merely falling back on human nature. It is not in vain that he says that the person who wishes to penetrate into the essence of things "will be satisfied in a non-human way, i.e., he will seem peculiar, abnormal, i.e. to ordinary people he will appear deluded". But why? Wherein does the nature of such a person differ from Mikhailovsky's nature, who regards the metaphysical attempt to penetrate into the essence of things as "a sin against mankind"? This means that not every satisfaction of cognitive demands is a sign of truth; which means that some special human nature is required. In order to get out of this predicament

Mikhailovsky employs his favourite fiction like a *deus ex machina,* which comes to his assistance in difficult moments.

There exists man who is essentially normal. He is a harmoniously developed whole personality in which the physiological division of labour is developed to the highest degree. He is Mikhailovsky's layman, the symbol of the people – the labouring masses. The normal, differentiated personality is Mikhailovsky's initial and final point of utopian thinking, which is the criterion of truth. It is as clear as daylight that Mikhailovsky bypasses the criterion of truth, by confusing the epistemological problem which is concerned with the logical criterion of truth, with the psychological and sociological problem, which seeks the conditions, (psychic and social) which give rise to truth for man.

We have already seen that truth is not found in the nature of man, i.e., not in psychological consciousness which is always changing, and thus gives rise to subjectivism, but in transcendental logical cognition in which lie the roots of the universally-compulsory norms of thought, and, therefore, the sanction of objectivism in cognition. This is a more reliable basis than Mikhailovsky's abstract "personality", since it alone provides the logical criterion of truth which differentiates objective truth from falsehood. Critical philosophy actually examines the whole world only in relation to the subject, but it is precisely here that the strictest objectivism is to be found, because the experience in which the world appears to the subject is the product of norms common to every cognition. That is why we can say that human truth, in ordinary terminology is relative and subject, but is nevertheless absolute and objective. The subject of the theory of cognition knows no subjective whims or moods – being formal and logical it has no psychological content. The logic of the cognising subject is as absolute and firm as the psychology of man is relative and changeable. Mikhailovsky is not saved from subjective irregularity by that biological abstraction, the normal personality which he attempts to restrain. We must bear in mind that logic which is concerned only with the categories of cognition and not with the psychological (aspect), only that is subjective which is false, truth can only be objective.

When we think of truth we think of the universally compulsory which cannot logically be accepted without violating the norms of our thinking. A theory may be relative or temporal, it may arise historically as something useful and be rejected as something harmful, but truth is always absolute, always equal to itself. Our common terminology concerning the temporary truth of today which tomorrow may be seen as false, requires considerable revision. In refuting a former truth we do not say that the truth has changed, but that we erred in considering it to be the truth. It is logically and psychologically impossible to renounce the truth, i.e., it is inwardly impossible. Outwardly of course, it is possible to use words of renunciation, yielding to the powers of darkness which threaten us with torments. All our ideas and theories are born, mature and die because man's psychological cognition is in perpetual historical motion, it is subject to the laws of evolution, but logic remains eternal, firm and unchangeable, and A must always equal A.

Even if mankind should perish and our solar system along with it, and even if new worlds completely different from ours were populated, if there should come into being forms of life and cognition which have nothing in common with ours, the logical law of identity would remain in its former force and transcendental cognition would not change one iota; its elements will be as eternal in the future as in the past. It will be equally obligatory for every consciousness in the world wherever and whenever this consciousness may exist. Transcendental cognition creates the world, but truth, which is logically obligatory for everyone need not necessarily be useful, but can even be harmful, and therefore psychologically inaccessible. For example, the concept of capitalist society which considers capitalism historically a transcient form of economy is doubtless harmful to the social classes interested in the preservation of capitalism. For them therefore, it is psychologically inaccessible. The scientific and astronomic ideas which today are regarded by everyone to be true, were harmful, and therefore inaccessible psychologically to the clergy of the middle ages. Inversely, falsehood need not always be harmful, but can sometimes be useful. Man often needs an illusion to make life tolerable; history is full of useful lies. As a result of our analysis of objectivism, we arrive at the following conclusion: in sociology as in any science, the objectivity of cognition and in accordance with the strictly regular (*zakonosoobraznost'*) [28] nature of the cognized object (in this case the social process) is guaranteed by the logical "a priori" introduced by the cognising subject into the act of cognition.

We shall now turn to an analysis of the concept of subjectivism. Mikhailovsky does not subject this idea to philosophical analysis, but there is much of interest in his work in this respect and we shall try to show that he unconsciously anticipated the correct point of view, although he was unable to substantiate it and establish a suitable relation between the subjective and the objective. Mikhailovsky's favourite idea is that it is impossible to relate oneself subjectively to social phenomena, that they give rise to love or hatred, admiration or indignation, that the objective, i.e., that the impartial attitude is self-deception at

---

[28] *Zakonosoobraznost'* means in accordance with a pre-established law or principle. Henceforth, this term will be translated 'in conformity to a definite law or principle'.

which some arrive consciously, others unconsciously. Mikhailovsky's service is to be found in the fact that he forcefully and energetically emphasized this indisputable view. If Mikhailovsky's "Subjectivism" does not solve anything, it at least poses an important problem which is ignored by the bourgeois sociologists, such as Spencer, etc.

The problem may be formulated as follows: A person (be he a professor or an ordinary mortal) approaches any study not only with logical norms common to all, but with the entire content of his psychological life historically moulded under the pressure of various daily conditions and different experience varying from person to person. The cognising subject introduces into every cognition not only logical, but also psychological premises. The former impart an objective character, to knowledge while the latter give it a subjective colouring. This fact is completely inevitable and unavoidable, because the process of cognition takes place in life and not in a vacuum, and no one can stand above life, let alone speak of his objectivism. Psychological prejudices play a special role in social science which is closer to life and affects human interests more than does any other science; this also gives sociological knowledge a specific colouring. Knowledge is subject to social friction, behind it is hidden will and feeling.

Here are some quotations from Mikhailovsky's position. "There must be a certain relationship between the observer and the observed phenomenon. It is also necessary in regard to moral phenomena. Man does not value the ideas of freedom. A politically apathetic person cannot possibly be the true master of the soul of a martyr for freedom." [29] The historical process adds its own special social restrictions to the natural limitations on human personality. Tell me to which social organization you belong and I will tell you how you look at things." [30]

Had Mikhailovsky merely said this, it would be foolish to ridicule his subjectivism. This subjectivism is obligatory for everyone without exception. As we have already pointed out, his (man's) nature is purely psychological and his origin purely social.[31] The points at which Mikhailovsky's view and mine coincide are obvious. The genetic point of view of which historical materialism is very proud, is of only secondary importance for Mikhailovsky, but he relies on the important idea, somewhat neglected by historical materialism, namely, that one should not evaluate phenomena by the category of necessity and that the

[29] N. K. Mikhailovsky, *Sochineniya*, Vol. IV, p. 426.

[30] *Ibid.*, p. 461.

[31] It has already been pointed out that A. Riehl thinks that in transcendental knowledge, the logical, and ethical norms are of social origin. P. Struve is very attracted by this idea and he sees in it a strong argument in favour of historical materialism.

ethical point of view is independent. But how does Mikhailovsky manage to get to the subjective method, to subjective sociology?

Such a transition is logically inconceivable, but in time of need human psychology overcomes and defeats human logic. The crux of the matter is this. Every time psychological subjectivism, i.e., those psychological prejudices which man introduces into the act of cognition come into conflict with logical objectivism, with the universally-obligatory norms of thought, the result is a lie and a falsehood. In the absurd expression 'subjective method', a noun with a purely logical meaning is qualified by an adjective with an exclusively psychological meaning. With Mikhailovsky, we accept subjectivism – psychological "a priori",[32] as an inevitable fact. We regard psychological objectivism as an impartial view of the struggle between social groups, to be a theoretical illusion, a figment of the imagination, which too often conceals 'subjectivism' of the worst kind. Neither an ordinary mortal nor an educated person can be a moral *tabula rasa*. The so-called impartiality of which theoreticians are sometimes proud is merely a *façon de parler,* a completely indifferent person is psychological *non sens*; indifferentism always hides definite feelings, sympathies and aspirations.

How in this case, can there be psychological subjectivism and how is it related to scientific logical objectivism? Since in our view, subjectivism and objectivism are two completely different categories they necessarily are in opposition to each other and contradict each other or are mutually exclusive. Human psychology with its specific subjective relationship to the surrounding phenomena may hinder human logic and scientific knowledge, but it cannot live peaceably with, or even promote, the objective concept of phenomena. The question therefore is, under what conditions does the inevitable human subjectivism not contradict the demands of scientific objectivism? What is needed for the harmonious combination of the subjective and objective? This question cannot be solved by confusing psychological (subjective) with transcendental (objective) consciousness, as Mikhailovsky does, but by a strict differentiation between them. The solution of this problem requires both the theory of knowledge and sociology. The founders of the materialistic view of history have indicated the correct approach, but the philosophical aspect of the problem is as yet undeveloped. The psychology (subjectivism) of any progressive social class creates the most favourable grounds for the objective (in the scientific sense) attitude toward phenomena. Ideologists of the progressive class have nothing to fear; they can face truth, because the historical process

---

[32] The term a priori is not used in a strictly epistemological sense. Psychological a priori in our sense is always the product of experience, it is created by life, but it may be regarded as a premise (not a logical one) of social science.

is their ally. The characteristics of an historically progressive class, a class with a great future, are a distinctive harmony of the subjective and the objective, the desired and the necessary, and a minimum of utopianism.[33] If every psychology is the result of adaptation to the demands of the social environment, then the psychology of the progressive class is the result of the adaptation to the demands of the universal-historical progress. It should always be borne in mind that the ideal and the anticipated overlap, since the ideal always goes further and is imbued with those utopian and romantic elements which cannot be eradicated from man's soul.

One frequently hears that historical materialism [34] is the world-view of only one social class, the class that has a vested interest in it, since this theory predicts victory for this class, while for others it is inaccessible and useless. Learned people pursuing the spectre of psychological objectivism cannot possibly comprehend it. What meaning can this common phrase about the class character of historical materialism have? Can there be a 'class' truth? Does not class subjectivism contradict the materialistic concept of history – the objective scientific approach, which is the most fundamental claim made by this concept? Not in the least. Truth cannot really be a class concept – it logically transcends classes, and is equally obligatory for all, but historically, as a certain theory, can assume a class character and even become the monopoly, as it were, of some class. We may therefore boldly state that historical materialism, in as much as we consider it to be the truth, is logically obligatory for every rational being, but that it is psychologically accessible to only one class.

Let us sum up. Objectivism has a purely logical meaning; its bases are immutable and are rooted in transcendental universal consciousness. Objectivism is obligatory in cognition and there can be no question of allowing any sort of subjectivism. Subjectivism has a purely psychological meaning; it is rooted in psychological consciousness and is conditioned by social environment and the social group. It is obligatory in life, its absence is tantamount to indifference and impartiality, but it has no place in cognition. Subjectivism and objectivism are different categories and must not be confused. Mikhailovsky's basic error is his inability to analyse these concepts and to differentiate between them. As a result we have such an absurdity as the "subjective method".

---

[33] It is self-evident that this harmony is relative, not absolute. Perfection is not man's lot. Man possesses the truth only during the course of the whole historical process, and there is no end to this approximation to truth.

[34] The phrase "historical materialism" is used only traditionally, although it is an unfortunate phrase like another expression popular in Russian literature – "economic materialism".

2

30   N. A. BERDYAEV

A reconciliation of the subjective and the objective, which we consider to be the ideal task of philosophy, is possible on other grounds. The categories of necessity and desirability (we shall speak about justice later in connection with the ethical problem) are not logically connected, but this does not prevent them from having a psychological and historical connection. The historico-psychological grounds for this reconciliation is the progressive class where we find a much greater harmony between objective knowledge and subjective relations to life.

We turn now to another aspect of the "subjective method in sociology". Among the different interpretations given by Mikhailovsky to his "subjective method", the ethical one is particularly important. Mikhailovsky says that "since we do not participate with our heads or hands in the origin of natural facts, we must take them as they are, without passing any judgment on them; we can only use them for our purposes, generally submitting ourselves to them. Still another group, are the facts, which, so to speak, pass through human hands. Basically, they do not of course, differ in any way from natural facts and are regulated by real laws common to them. Erroneously or not, however, man by his very nature feels in their form his responsibility, the need for moral judgment, the opportunity to influence facts in one way or another.[35] In demanding a "high moral level", Mikhailovsky anticipated the great truth, namely that a special psychology is necessary for social knowledge, a special type of mentality which would not allow the sociologist to sell science to the ruling elements of society. We have tried to show that this "high moral level" is created by the psychology of the class which has adapted itself to the demands and tendencies of social progress.

We wish once again to emphasize our complete agreement with Mikhailovsky's view that every man must give a moral evaluation to social phenomena, and that no one can be indifferent to "good and evil". The ethical point of view has an independent value along with the genetic point of view. Not only the category of necessity, but also the category of justice is applicable to social phenomena.

The question may be asked, why that subjective criterion which Mikhailovsky proposes to use in evaluating both the entire historical process as well as separate phenomena should be obligatory for me. Why may I be a good sociologist only when I attain that level? Wherein lies its advantage over any other subjective criterion? That subjective ideal, that 'utopia' which is basic to his world-view, is developed by the life of a given historical moment.

Mikhailovsky wanted to give us a unique "system of truth". We acknowledge this task. Science, with its category of necessity, cannot

[35] N. K. Mikhailovsky, *Sochineniya*, Vol. V, p. 378.

create an ideal and cannot even provide a basis for it, but philosophy must find a point of view which would provide a harmonious co-existence of the scientific and the ethical in relation to the world. We tried to show that one half of truth, "*pravda-truth*" (*pravda-istina*) is obligatory for all, although not accessible to all. The other half – "*pravda-justice*" (*pravda-spravedlivost'*) must also be obligatory for all, otherwise it will not be truth. The question which we put to Mikhailovsky also applies to all those who recognize only subjective morality and the subjective ideal, and who deny the objectively-obligatory. Such subjectivism is prevalent nowadays and is detrimental also to the social world-view which we generally support.[36]

Social materialism is bound up historically and psychologically (not logically, of course) with a definite social ideal, with the most sacred aspirations of modern humanity. For what sort of basis does it provide for the social ideal? This ideal is of a dual nature. First, our social ideal is objectively necessary; the tendencies of social development are such that the social system which we consider to be our ideal will eventually be achieved. It will be the inevitable result of the immanental conformity of the laws in the historical process. Thus, the ideal assumes an objectively-logical scientific sanction which enables one to look boldly ahead. Because of this, the adherents of this social ideal oppose the utopians and pride themselves not so much on their ideal aspirations as on their scientific prognosis. Secondly, social materialism provides a subjective, psychological basis for the ideal. The ideal of communal living, coinciding with scientific foresight is subjectively desirable for a definite social class and this class struggles for its realization. The second basis, while practically important, is theoretically subordinate to the first, because the desires and ideals of social classes are developed by the regular social process. We suggest that this dual basis is totally inadequate. A third basis is still necessary which we will term the objective-ethical (basis). It is necessary to show that our social ideal is not only objectively necessary (the logical category), not only subjectively desirable (the psychological category), but that it is also objectively moral and objectively-just, that its realization will be progress in the sense of amelioration. In a word, that it is universally-obligatory, and that it has absolute value as a duty (the ethical category).

[36] Marxism, in its struggle with bourgeois ideology, became hostile to every ideology. Historically this is perfectly understandable, but theoretically it is quite wrong. Theoretical restating and further development of marxism should lead to the creation of an independent 'higher ideology' which would provide a philosophico-ethical basis for those idealistic appeals to truth and progress to justice and humanity which form the practical activity of the fighters for this world-view.

The materialistic concept of history turns to the following arguments in order to get out of this difficulty. One social ideal is higher and morally preferable to another, because the historical process supports it, because it is more progressive and more accommodating to the demands of social development. The morality of one class is better and more just than that of another, and because it has a future. The bourgeois ideal is bad not only because it does not arouse a feeling of sympathy in us, but also because it has no future and hinders the development of the progressive forces in contemporary society. All this is perfectly true and the benefits of historical materialism are in this respect invaluable. This does not however, offer a satisfactory and exhaustive answer to our question. This question is superficial. In the discussion above we have shown that a given ideal, for instance, the democratic ideal, is not only subjectively desirable, but is also objectively necessary, that social development leads inevitably to its triumph. This is, of course, necessary for me to know, but it in no way increases the ethical value of my ideal. Neither does it follow that it is better, more just and more moral than any other ideal.

It is particularly important to bear in mind that the ethical category of justice has an independent meaning which differs in principle from the logical category of necessity. We shall endeavour to find a philosophical basis for the objective ideal and for objective morality, in a word, for PRAVDA-JUSTICE as we attempted to do for PRAVDA-TRUTH.

Ethics like the theory of knowledge, must take Kant's critique as its point of departure. We have seen that the source of the objectively-true is rooted in transcendental consciousness. It is there also that we must find the source of the objectively-moral and the objectively-just. Objective morality is possible only when we recognize the a priori nature of the moral law which necessarily differentiates between good and evil; in this case alone will the good assume a universally-obligatory character. When something is ethically universally-obligatory, that means IT OUGHT TO BE. All attempts to deduce an empirical concept of good and evil from non-ethical elements, for instance, from the constantly recurring experiences of satisfaction and suffering, results in a fiasco and is unsatisfactory as is the empirical theory of knowledge. We are interested now not in the question of the origin and development of morality, but in its value. Morality is not a subjective illusion as the empiricists-evolutionists wish to prove, but an independent quality which cannot be decomposed into any number of non-ethical molecules. The formal distinction between good and evil, the moral and the immoral, precedes sensory experiences. The category of justice is given A PRIORI to our transcendental consciousness, and this ethical A PRIORI makes moral experiences and moral life possible. It plays the same role in the realm of morality as for instance, the category of causality plays in the realm of knowledge. This does not, of course, prevent us from admitting that only by means of social development does man become conscious of his moral nature.

The formal bases of morality are immutable; there exist the objectively-moral, the good and the just, but the content of morality is highly unstable and is in the constant process of development. The idea of man and mankind as ends in themselves is not inherent in people's psychological consciousness where we often find completely different goals, ideals which preach shameless violation of the human personality and which violate the sacredness of its moral dignity. Mankind will arrive at this eternal idea of the moral good only by means of social progress. Moral ideas not only change radically with the changing of different historical epochs, but we encounter in one and the same epoch several typical moralities hostile to each other.

Sociological ethics studies moral concepts and their crystallisation in social morals, but we wish to turn from that which people consider to be good to that which IS good. Psychological moral consciousness (the source of subjective morality) is conditioned by the social existence of people, their membership in one or another social group; it may be found in different relations to transcendental moral consciousness, to the ethical norm (the source of objective morality). Consonant with the general spirit of our world-view we think that harmony of the psychological and the transcendental consciousness, of subjective and objective morality can only be found in the moral consciousness of the progressive social class.[37] Why is this so? Because the psychology of the progressive class is the result of adaptation to the demands of universal social progress. Hence, it is only here that we find the coincidence of the individual and the universal which constitutes the fundamental sign of morality. Morality, of course, like truth, cannot be of a class nature, but historically it takes on a class form and its bearer is that social class which bears the banner of universal progress.

Our whole argument which is based on historical materialism, rests on one basic premise – namely, the premise of universal progress. The theory of progress is a bridge which unites both halves of truth – PRAVDA-TRUTH and PRAVDA-JUSTICE, and within each of these halves their objective and subjective aspects are united. If we admitted the existence of only the historical process and not its progress, then the

---

[37] Once again this idea must be understood in a relative and not in an absolute sense. The progressive class may, of course, display instances of immoral behaviour, but it is in a more favourable position to encourage moral progress. It is evident, that this harmony is characteristic of a certain class, but not of its individual representatives.

adaptation to the demands of this progress would not necessarily be moral, on the contrary, it may even be immoral, where for example, social development leads to the triumph of more refined forms of exploitation and slavery. Progress is improvement i.e. a transition from the ethicallly worse to the ethically better. The difference between the worse and the better, the good and the bad, is given A PRIORI to our transcendental consciousness. We ourselves introduce into the historical process a regulative idea of the universally-obligatory goal, and on this immutable basis we sanction it as progress. Man as an end in himself, the rule of mankind and of human power and consciousness – this is our guiding star. The truth of this idea cannot be proven, just as the universal applicability of the principle of causality cannot be proven, but without this A PRIORI principle we would be morally blind and would be unable to distinguish in our environment between the just, the humane and the progressive, and the unjust, the inhumane and the reactionary.

We can now answer the question which we posed above. A social ideal may be considered not only from the point of view of its objective necessity and subjective desirability, but also from the point of view of its objective justice and morality. Every social ideal is relative in the sense that it is born for a given historical period, but in another sense it may be absolute if only it is in that epoch it is objectively just, provided it is in agreement with the tendencies of that universal progress which is a transition from the worse to the better, provided it is sanctioned by the ethical norms of the transcendental consciousness. Our attitude to Mikhailovsky is now quite clear. The teleological "system of truth" is to be found least of all where he was searching. First of all, he incorrectly places in opposition pravda-truth to pravda-justice, calling one objective and the other subjective.[38] Truth is always objective; that consciousness is only subjective which constitutes different degrees of approximations to the eternal truth. The psychological premises of every cognitive and moral activity can play both a positive and a negative role. We have tried to indicate the conditions of harmony. There is a group of people in modern society who are placed by circumstances of life in such a morally beneficial position that its practical activity in itself imports into life justice and goodness,

---

[38] Mikhailovsky is quite right in remarking that "where there is no teleology there can be no moral rules, consequently, neither blame nor praise; but he failed to give a clearly-defined philosophical definition of teleology. He did not understand that pravda-justice must be objective, that it presupposes a universally-obligatory purpose (allgemeingultig), that one cannot arrive at an ethical norm on a psychological basis of subjective goals, that the desirable and the OUGHT-TO-BE are one and the same.

because its task is bound up with the task of universal progress sanctioned by the A PRIORI norm as an improvement.

We will adduce several quotations which force us to assume that by the "subjective method" Mikhailovsky means "the psychological method". A thinking subject can only attain the truth when he is completely merged with the thinking object and does not leave him for a moment, i.e., he enters into his interests, experiences his life, thinks his thoughts, experiences his feelings, suffers his sufferings and cries his tears".[39] "The subjective method is that method which satisfies the cognitive demand when the observer places himself mentally in the position of the observed." [40] Such a concept of the subjective method may have a methodological value, but it can have nothing in common with a moral evaluation of phenomena, and Mikhailovsky confuses the two.

There is a science in which the "subjective method" has received the rights of citizenship, namely, psychology. Any course in contemporary psychology begins with a discussion of the psychological method, and only the philosophically-uneducated naturalists can affirm that psychology is a part of the physiology of the brain. But psychology is not a normative science; it does not know the difference between good and evil, between truth and falsehood, it investigates equally the whole process of cognition and feeling. The subjective method in psychology, according to Mikhailovsky, must be recognized as morally indifferent, and in this sense as objective.

We recognize that the social psychology of people is developed by their social existence, and this means the primacy of life over ideas, of practice over theory. Once however, we reject social psychology nothing will be left of the historical process. The entire historical process which presupposes the struggle between man and nature which finds expression in the productive powers of mankind – this whole process is realized in a psychic medium. The human psyche develops in the process of the social struggle for life, but the social struggle for life is a psychic process which can in no way be interpreted in terms of mechanics.

Historical materialism which is monistic in character should not see in the historical process the dualism of spirit and matter, the psychic and the physical, it knows only the whole social (phenomenon), and it is this whole that is psychic from a philosophical standpoint. We do not in the least wish to explain either that which is essentially psychic or any other ideology as being physical or material, since this would reduce human thoughts and feelings, as well as philosophical, religious

39   See N. K. Mikhailovsky, *Sochineniya*, Vol. I, p. 56.
40   *Ibid.*, Vol. III, p. 402.

and moral concepts, to a mechanics of atoms, to the movement of material particles. We regard causality as being entirely psychic, and one psychic event is explained by another, also psychic, i.e., by the social conditions of the struggle for life and by the extent of human power in the struggle with nature.[41] Materialistic sociology, therefore, in its criticism of rationalistic sociology, finds support both in modern voluntaristic psychology which regards cognition as the servant of the will, and in Kantianism which considers theoretical reason the servant of the practical.

Mikhailovsky's subjective-dualistic point of view, strictly speaking, makes sociological science impossible. Is sociology concerned with the "natural course of things" or with "human activity"? In studying the "natural course of things" it bypasses social phenomena and the historical process. This is precisely what Mikhailovsky is doing when he employs biological concepts and "social organisms". In studying "human activity" apart from the "natural course of things", sociology becomes a series of subjective propositions in which Mikhailovsky mainly specialised as a sociologist.

We now come to the great problem of freedom and necessity. Mikhailovsky attaches a great deal of importance to this question and even regards his "subjectivism" as one of the attempts to solve the question of freedom and necessity. He adds little that is original, and here again we see his lack of philosophical training and depth. Here is what Mikhailovsky has to say on this subject. "The importance of historical conditions as factors which determine the actions of individuals is unquestionable, but equally unquestionable is the right and possibility of the individual to judge the phenomena of life without reference to their place in history, but according to the inner evaluation attributed to them by one individual or another at any given moment. This is an inevitable result of the conditions of human nature. The contradiction between necessity and freedom is basically unsolvable, and we must fall back alternatively now on one and now on the other." [42] Mikhailovsky's argumentation on the problem of freedom and necessity is from a philosophical viewpoint superficial and sketchy. The problem cannot be solved on these grounds. The peculiar dualism forces him to move in a vicious circle. But as often happens with

[41] We consider the cliche about "the material foundation upon which the ideological superstructure is raised" to be unfortunate. It is, of course, a figurative expression, but it is a poor one, since it presupposes a dualism of the material and the ideological. Upon analysis it proves to have no definite meaning. From an ethical standpoint, we are inclined to regard the relation between the material and ideological as that between means and end.

[42] Mikhailovsky, ibid., Vol. III, p. 437.

Mikhailovsky, we do meet something valuable here – he instinctively feels the truth. In order to sort out this complex problem, we will first of all consider its epistemological aspect.

Freedom and necessity is one of the Kantian antinomies. It was customary after Kant to regard freedom and necessity as an insoluble contradiction. We are inclined to think that the famous antinomies do not constitute the strong aspect of Kantianism, and may be eliminated by the monistic theory of knowledge. Kant does not always strictly distinguish between the epistemological and the psychological points of view, and this affected his solution of the problem of freedom and necessity.

Freedom and necessity are not basically in contradiction to each other and cannot be placed in opposition, because they are completely different categories. Necessity is an epistemological category. Since all our knowledge occurs on the basis of the formal principle of causality (this is the universally-obligatory A PRIORI introduced by consciousness into cognitive experience), it follows that all the objects of consciousness, i.e., the whole world, is coloured by that bright colour of necessity. Freedom has no place in the cognitive process; the cognising subject does not know freedom. Every cognitive act is achieved according to eternal, immutable laws rooted in transcendental logical consciousness. The monistic theory of knowledge knows no contradictions in our consciousness and within the confines of epistemology there is no antinomy of freedom and necessity, because freedom is not an epistemological category. What then is freedom? Freedom is a psychological category. Our activity is coloured by freedom. When we perform an act in life we do not employ the category of necessity, because practical life is not a scientific discipline. Teleology and not causality is the guiding principle of our life and our activity. The secret of life may perhaps be found in practice, which is the realization of goals. I act in a certain way, follow a certain goal and satisfy a certain need. The process of cognition, of course, reveals the causes of my actions and recognizes them as necessary, but this causal dependence and necessity is beyond my mental outlook, and as an acting being they do not interest me at the moment. The cognising subject and the acting subject do not contradict one another, they merely constitute different spheres, and therefore different categories are applicable to them.

What does psychological consciousness of freedom mean, is it not a simple illusion? Psychological consciousness of freedom is not a consciousness of the non-causality of our will and actions. I consider myself free when I act as I wish, i.e. according to my will. Freedom must not be contrasted with necessity, since free actions, i.e. those dependent only on the will, are also necessary, because they are determined by psychic causes; it should be contrasted with its dependence on forces outside the acting will, those that are inimical to the will. Consciousness of freedom is an illusion which should be rejected, if it is understood as non-causality, as indeterminism, in a word, if it is contrasted with necessity in general. One should eliminate from man's soul the consciousness of the difference between actions resulting from inner, psychic causes, and those that stem from our own will and actions imposed on us from without by mechanical causes which we are obliged to fulfill irrespective of our will.

The possibility of moral evaluation and moral responsibility is based on the psychic causality of the will, while indeterminism of the will would make morality inconceivable. The ancient theory of freedom of the will, which no one would now dare to openly defend, turns our moral life into some terrible chaos where all distinction between good and evil disappears. Freedom is our goal, and not a reason in the sense of being able to begin a series of phenomena without preceding causes. History should create free individuals. Man will freely accept the moral law as desirable, as one stemming from the innermost essence of his being. On this is based moral autonomy of the individual and the sacredness of human dignity. Free will is moral will. But moral freedom is inseparably bound up with social freedom, regardless of what the reactionaries may say, who simultaneously preach indeterminism and violation of the human personality. It is high time to deprive the reactionaries of the right to add any ideal moral force to their obscurantism.

Many people are not satisfied with our view of freedom, or they want some other kind of freedom. It is a strange self-deception which people cannot give up. Man says, "I do not wish to be a plaything of universal forces, but by asserting that my Self is a product of these forces you turn me into a passive instrument, into a pawn. You say all this from the point of view of your Self which wants to be free and independent, but your Self is what the universal forces make it to be. Your Self consists through and through of the aspirations and desires which were determined by a preceding series of phenomena. Your freedom, therefore, can exist only in agreement with your Self, with those aspirations and desires which were placed in you by the universal and historical process. There is nothing fatalistic about this, because the volitional acticity constantly accompanies every living being, and it is precisely in this that we see the original basis of the psychic life.

You may wish to contrast your freedom not with that necessity which called your Self into being, but only with the one which wants to eradicate you from the face of the earth, the one which destroys your volitional activity. Hidden behind the apparent antagonism of freedom and necessity is the actual antagonism of our will to the forces that are detrimental to it. This antagonism diminishes with man's increasing power over nature, with the growth in consciousness, and hence, historical progress is the triumphant course of human freedom. If you want another (kind) of freedom, you step out of your human Self and you begin to speak not on behalf of your volitional activity, but on behalf of some fiction devoid of any meaning or content, and you begin to attribute to freedom a meaning which is neither psychological nor moral, which is the only meaning it can have, any other meaning is completely incomprehensible. If in your yearning for freedom you wish to get rid of determinism, then you are erring by confusing different areas in transferring the psychological category into epistemology.

Historical fatalism errs more or less in the following: it excludes mankind and his will from the chain of causes and consequences in the historical process. The fatalist has something in common with the advocates of free will – the latter also exclude the human will from the regular historical process. The only difference is that the fatalists subordinate man to fate, while the advocates of free will subordinate him to chance, the difference is therefore not very great. As determinists we say that man, human will and activity, of course, play a role in history – they create it; without man there is no history. But this role is not that man may struggle against the historical process as against some alien "natural course of things" and make history only at his peril in defiance of the tendencies of social development. This role amounts to this, that the regular historical process ("the natural course of things") the tendencies of social development, emanate from man's active struggle with man and with nature. In their social struggle for life people are by necessity socially related. We must recognize the power of the social environment over human personality.

Let us now see what objective theory of progress can be offered by historical materialism in conjunction with critical philosophy. In our opinion, there are only three points of view on progress. The subjective point of view offered by Mikhailovsky; the negation of progress and the recognition of process only; finally, the objective view of progress which presupposes a universally-obligatory goal. Only the third viewpoint provides a philosophical basis for the greatest idea that mankind has ever invented. We attach particular importance to the philosophical theory of progress, since it alone is capable of harmoniously uniting the subjective with the objective on the one hand, and PRAVDA-TRUTH with PRAVDA-JUSTICE on the other, in some higher unity.

We can draw conclusions from the historical concept of history which are extremely instructive for the theory of progress, although the founders of this theory offered no philosophical theory on progress.

The theory of progress offered by Marx and Engels may be summarized as follows. At the basis of the historical process lies the development of the productive forces of human society. Everything that is beneficial to the development of the productive forces is progressive, everything which retards it is reactionary. What does this mean? It means that the historical process is nothing more than the process of the social struggle of man with nature for the preservation and development of life. It also means that in this struggle man creates a social environment which stands between him and nature, and defends him from the elemental forces, and whose growth symbolises man's power which distinguishes him from the animals. This means, moreover, that the measure of progress is the extent of man's victory over nature, the force and power of man and that the higher forms of mankind can grow only on this basis. In a philosophical sense this point of view leads to the conclusion that progress is the victory of the conscious over the unconscious, and hence, is in accord with the aspirations of the greatest thinkers of mankind.

Various historico-philosophical trends discussed a great deal the growth of consciousness in history, but only the teaching of Marx and Engels points out the real fundamental nature of this growth. It is not in vain that Engels spoke about the transition from the realm of necessity to the realm of freedom. Even if the utopian idea of a sudden transition from necessity to freedom were discounted, there would still remain the great truth that the historical process is the liberation of man. Man, his power and freedom, is not only a subjective goal set by him for himself, in whose name he struggles with the elemental forces of nature, but it is also the objective result of the historical process and its universally-obligatory goal.

There is in the historical process an immanent teleology which in no way contradicts the principle of regularity,[43] but is simply its other aspect. Mankind is at once both the end of the historical process and its factor, therefore it will always take its own. The teleological inevitably survives in history. Progress does not therefore, depend on any definite ideal, as the "subjectivists" suppose. Ideals always change in man's history and each of them is good only for its own period, while progress transcends all ideals which receive their sanction from it.

Formally speaking, progress is improvement, the transition from worse to better. The historical process is the struggle of man with nature, the growth of human might. Why then is this increase in human

[43] See footnote 28.

might and consciousness, man's eminence, which is the result of the development of the productive forces in society, a transition from worse to better, and why is it an improvement? The answer to this question presupposes the existence of an objective-ethical sanction, a universally-compulsory goal of the historical process, and anyone denying this sanction and higher goal must deny the idea of progress and must be satisfied with poor substitutes. It may be adequate for everyday living, but it leaves a large vacuum in the soul of a thinking person. And indeed, every person denying the absolute nature of the good and the moral purpose in life, must sense this vacuum. The demand for idealism is eternal.

Mikhailovsky solves the above problem from his subjective-anthro-pocentric point of view, based primarily on the negation of objective teleology, i.e. he denies any goals in nature. Objectively, man with his joys and sorrows has no advantages over everything else in the world. Senseless nature, the natural course of things, is indifferent to mankind. Subjectively however, man considers himself the goal of creation, and in the name of his own human ideals raises the banner of rebellion against the "natural course of events" in nature and in society.

We have already said that subjective teleology is incapable of satisfactorily solving the great problem of progress, because progress needs an objective-ethical sanction. Strange as it may sound, we would prefer objective to subjective anthroprocentricism. We rely both on Kant's "Critique of Practical Reason" and "Critique of Judgment", although our point of view differs somewhat from his. It is not only subjectively that man considers himself the goal of the historical process; he often does not even consider himself as such. He is the objective, universally-obligatory goal of the historical process, but man's kingdom should be realized only in the actual world of phenomena and not in the intellectually-projected world as proposed by Kant and the neo-kantians. It is the objective truth, that the growth of man's power, human consciousness, man's freedom, are progressive, moral and just; it is the objective truth obligatory for every consciousness, but it can only be so, because it is not of empirical origin, it is given A PRIORI in the transcendental, supra-individual consciousness. A conscientious, strong, humane and free humanity and not only mankind, but life in general, a higher life than that of humanity, is not some definite, subjective ideal with a certain content, but an objective norm which sanctions progress as a movement toward a higher moral goal. The penetration of a universal, logical, ethical and aesthetical norm into the life of humanity, which follow social progress, is perhaps the triumph of a single Universal Self in the individual Self.

If our principle is only regulative and normative, what guarantee do we have that the historical process is teleological in the sense of approaching the final goal which makes this principle progressive? Is not the teleology and progressiveness of the historical process a matter of chance? Of course not. Why does the historical process follow a definite regular pattern? It does not follow a definite regular pattern by chance; in the object of social science we see an immanent regularity, because transcendental apperception makes it such, by introducing a constitutive principle of causality. The philosophy of the future will ultimately be able to show that the immanent teleology and progressiveness of the historical process (and of the universal process as well) is not a matter of unpredicable chance, which is after all what the mechanistic world-view presupposes. Teleology is rooted in transcendental apperception, is the supra-individual consciousness which regards the world not only as causally-conditioned, but also as moving toward a goal. The historical process creates the most varied ideals, but only those that are in accord with the objective norm of progress are moral, just and progressive. We should remember Kant's great maxim, that form without content is empty, and content without form is blind. Man receives his sight with regard to progress only because he adds to the empirically given content an A PRIORI given form, the ideal of a goal.

We believe that this point of view finally settles accounts with "subjectivism". But man, whom Mikhailovsky places at the centre of his world-view hardly suffers any harm from such objectivism. On the contrary, this objectivism elevates man to such a height of which Mikhailovsky would never have dreamed. It gives man absolute and universal significance. Utopianism is eliminated, but the ethical ideal is revived in spite of the strictly-realistic foundations of the world-view. We regard man as an end in himself, a formal objective norm, whereas for Mikhailovsky he is a material, subjective ideal. The material aims of mankind change; not one of them can claim to be universal, but the formal moment always remains in force and runs right through the entire history of human consciousness. For us, progress goes along "the broad highway of history", and not along the alleys.

We especially wish to emphasize that our ethical point of view differs from the usual ethical point of view in social science which presupposes an eclectic moral mixture instead of sociology. We have already stated a number of times that we view historical morality from the materialistic (or realistic) point of view, and we do not recognise independent moral factors which are called upon to solve the social problem. We combine "scientific realism" with "civil idealism" on entirely different grounds.

People who understand the meaning of formal apriorism may ask: why are the ethical norms which are not always present in peoples' consciousness universally-obligatory? It is precisely because they are ethical norms and not psychological properties. Both ethical and logical norms, according to Riehl [44] arise in social intercourse; they are not born in us, and people's psychological consciousness arrives at them only after a long process of social development. It may or may not be beneficial to PRAVDA-TRUTH and PRAVDA-JUSTICE. Man becomes aware of its universally-obligatory nature only by means of social progress. We must finally come to the conclusion that the whole harmonious truth cannot be attained by the unprincipled confusion of different spheres, but by a philosophical distinction between them.

Let us sum up. There are three kinds of A PRIORI in sociological consciousness: the psychological, the logical and the ethical. Subjectivism is grounded in the psychological A PRIORI, which is not absolute, but relative, subject to constant change. The "system of objective truth" is based on the logical and ethical A PRIORI. The former introduces the principle of regularity (zakonosoobraznost') into cognition, and gives rise to the PRAVDA-TRUTH, while the latter introduces the principle of teleology, gives it an objective criterion of progress, and gives rise to PRAVDA-JUSTICE.

The psyche of the progressive class is the basis on which all the elements are most harmoniously united, and where the unique "system of truth" will emerge which the historical process is called upon to realize in theory and in practice. Progress is in the final analysis nothing more than the attainment of the kingdom of humanity, absolute truth, justice and beauty, i.e. the final goal by the elimination of everything that is disteleological.

---

[44]   See footnote 27, on Riehl.

N. O. Lossky

THE FUNDAMENTAL CHARACTERISTICS
OF VALUES*

DEFINITION OF VALUE

The idea of derivative value can be defined easily as follows: Value is existence in its significance for the realization of the absolute plenitude of being, or for the receding from it. The whole difficulty is inherent in the definition of the super-cosmic, absolute positive value. It (value) is God, as Goodness itself, as absolute plenitude of being. It contains within itself meaning which justifies it, makes it an object of approbation and gives it the absolute right to be realized and preferred above all else. This definition cannot be decomposed into elements, it can only point to the fundamental source and a multitude of consequences, although not complete, resulting from it for both the MIND and the WILL that will to any extent commune with it (such as justification, approbation, the recognition of right, preference, etc.).

Similarly, the definition of derivative value cannot be analysed into GENUS and DIFFERENTIAE, although superficially its grammatical form seems to be the same as in the definition "A square is a rectangle with equal sides". We must not be deceived by this apparent similarity. In the definition of the square the idea of rectangle is the GENUS which contains the square as SPECIES. That is the reason that the proposition "a square is a rectangle", when taken out of the whole definition expresses a truth. Our definition of derivative value has an entirely different structure. "Existence" is not a genus which contains the concept of value. This is evident from the fact that the proposition "value is existence" is false. The superficial similarity of the above definition to

* This selection is taken from Lossky's book *Tsennost' i bytiye* [Value and Being], Chapter III (YMCA Press, Paris, 1931).

the definition by means of GENUS and DIFFERENTIAE is due to the greater discursiveness of language than thought. The fact that we must not separate the concept of "existence" from the above definition and reduce it to a predicate of the concept of value is to be noted in the linguistic expression of the idea by means of the preposition "in", in "existence in its significance". This combination of words shows that value is an organic unity, which includes elements of existence and significance, but while it is based on these elements, it represents a new aspect of the world, distinct from its elements.

Experience, which forms part of value, always contains a moment which in a developed consciousness is given as feeling and finds expression in such words as pleasant, noble, dear, tender, delightful, sublime or disagreeable, vulgar, rude, repulsive, etc.

Significance and meaning is an ideal aspect of value. Hence, every value is either fully ideal, or at least, has an ideal aspect. If valuable existence is itself ideal, then it is fully ideal. Thus, for instance, the substantival agent, as a supra-temporal and supra-spatial source of action, is a fully ideal value. If valuable existence is real existence, then the corresponding value is ideal-real (value), for example, an aria performed by a singer. The idea of an aria, a shrine, an act, etc. is wholly an ideal value capable of being realized. The performed aria, the finished shrine, the completed act, are ideal-real values.

In their meaning, derivative values generally have two possible directions – toward the realization of the absolute fullness of being, or away from it. Hence, they are at opposite poles, i.e., they are either positive or negative. The former are good and the latter are evil, evil in the broad sense (i.e. not in the sense of being merely morally good or bad).

To enable the reader, to follow the subsequent exposition, one should bear in mind, that henceforth, I shall frequently use the word GOOD instead of the long phrase, "positive value" and the word EVIL instead of "Negative value".

Consonant with the ontological theory of value developed by me, existence is not only a carrier of values, but is itself a value, if we regard its significance. It is itself either good or evil. Hence, the distinction between Gutter (good things) and Werte (values) used in modern German literature, to indicate that there is a distinction between existence as a carrier of values, and value itself, is of no basic significance for my theory.

The polarity of values is necessarily bound up as well with the polarity of their symptomatic expression in feeling, primarily of pleasure and pain. Similarly, the reaction of will on value, which finds its expression in attraction or repulsion is also polar.

The possible relation of value to feeling and will does not entitle us to construct a psychological theory of value. Value conditions definite feelings and desires, but is not their consequence.

The necessary connection that exists between values and the subject, due to the fact that every value is a value for some subject, does not entitle us to speak of values being subjective. Just as cognition of the world presupposes consciousness, it does not follow that consciousness wholly conditions the truth that we discover. Similarly, the axiological nature of the world presupposes the existence of subjects, it does not follow that values are wholly conditioned by the existence of the subjects. Value is something that transcends the opposition of subject and object, because it is conditioned by the relation of a subject to something that is higher than any subjective being, viz., Absolute fullness of being.

Value is always connected not only with the subject, but precisely with the life of the subject. This may be shown in the very definition of derivative value by expressing it as follows: Value is existence as experienced by the subject or by other beings in its significance for the realization of absolute fullness of being, or alienation from it. The term LIFE denotes here the teleological activity of the substantival agent existing specifically for him. It is evident then, that this connotation of value is not a biologism. The physical-material life of plants and animals is only one of the forms of life in general. The absolute life of the Kingdom of God requires an ascent from the material-bodily life and the acquisition of a spirit-bearing body.

ABSOLUTE AND RELATIVE, OBJECTIVE AND SUBJECTIVE VALUES

Absolute positive value is a value that is *per se* unconditionally justified, hence, possesses the character of goodness from any point of view, in any relation, and for any subject. It is not only always good in itself, but the consequences which necessarily result from it never contain evil in themselves. Such good, is for instance, the Divine absolute plenitude of being.

A relative positive value is a value possessing the character of goodness only in a certain relation or for certain specific subjects. In any other relation or for any other subjects such value is in itself evil, or is at least necessarily bound up with evil. Values in which goodness is necessarily bound up with evil are possible only in the psycho-physical realm of existence, where the agents are relatively isolated from each other by their greater or less egoistically self-containment.

The phrase 'subjectiveness of value' will be used to denote its significance for a specific subject only; the general significance of value.

i.e. its significance for every subject will be termed OBJECTIVENESS. Absolute value, according to its definition, is simultaneously a value that is significant for all, i.e. it is an OBJECTIVE INTRINSIC VALUE.

The most important task of axiology is the establishment of the existence of absolute values and the overcoming of AXIOLOGICAL RELATIVISM, i.e. the theory which states that ALL VALUES ARE RELATIVE AND SUBJECTIVE. At first sight axiological relativism seems to be firmly based on observation of reality. Wherever we look we encounter relative values. The rapid chase of the greyhound after a rabbit is good for the hound, but bad for the rabbit. Anna Karenina's love for Vronsky means happiness for Vronsky, but unhappiness for Anna Karenina's husband.[45]

The assertion of the relativity and subjectivity of values is not only based on empirical observation of reality as mentioned above, but is also based on certain theories regarding the structure of the world, as for example, the theory deduced from an inorganic conception of the world. In fact, according to the inorganic view of the world, the world consists only of elements separated from each other, self-contained in their existence, capable of uniting into temporary wholes only on the ground of the external relations of spatial contiguity and external actions, such as push and pressure. In such a world there are no common experiences; intuition as an immediate insight into somebody else's existence is impossible, nor are love and sympathy possible as an immediate practical acceptance of somebody else's existence. In such a world is also impossible to have an identical common good in which everybody could equally participate. In such a world every good is torn into shreds, is consumed and destroyed by separate individuals, each in himself and for himself, and is detrimental to others. There too, communal life and communal action are not possible as well as the absolute fullness of being.

In such a world, regarded as an aggregate of self-contained fragments of existence, there is nothing that possesses the character of self-justification or is of common value. Each self-contained subject accepts the positive value of his limited life, or even some separate manifestation, of it, and he evaluates everything in the world as either positive or negative only in accordance with his personal life or its manifestation. But this personal life itself, viewed in its inevitable limitation and self-containment, is, according to this world-view devoid of absolute worth. The subject is aware that he advances it as a supreme value not because it is intrinsically justified, but only because it is HIS LIFE, and hence, he has a reason for accepting it as a supreme value ONLY FOR

[45] Anna Karenina is the central character in the novel by that name, by Lev Tolstoy.

HIMSELF. And every other subject accepts something else as the supreme value, namely, his own self-contained and limited life or some manifestation of it. Indeed in such a world there would be no absolute values of universal significance. Every value would be subjective and relative, i.e. it would exist only from the point of view of a particular subject and only in relation to him.

A consistent development of such an inorganic world-view negates the ideal aspect of the world; consequently, it negates the universal as well as the partial meaning as a special ideal aspect of the world. It recognizes only the existence of facts, (events in space and time) as subjectively pleasant or unpleasant. In such a structure of the world it would be impossible to find a rational basis for the preference of one type of behaviour over another, or to establish norms of behaviour of which could be said that they contain within themselves intrinsic justification which is significant for everybody.[46]

Fortunately, however, the inorganic concept of the world is false, it is a world-view which leads to axiological relativism and subjectivism, which admits in the world only self-contained fragments of irreformable and imperfect being. In reality God and the Kingdom of God actually exist as absolutely worthy and justified beings. And even our kingdom of psycho-physical existence, although imperfect, nevertheless is an organic whole. No being is self-contained; there exists intuition, genuine sympathy and love are possible and heroic feat and heroism are also possible. Every being can have genuine and immediate communion with the life of beings like himself as well as with beings of a higher order, of nations, humanity and the universe. Moreover, every agent can become a participator in the Kingdom of God with its creative activity and absolute plenitude of being, in comparison with this fullness of being intoxication with narcotics is a pathetic impoverishment of life.[47]

Freedom is the greatest worth of personal agents, necessary for the realization of absolute positive values, but it also contains a hidden possibility of pursuing the negative way of life. Different degrees of loving harmony as well as different degrees of separation; of conflicting opposition and hostilities are spontaneously realized in the world. There exists collective action in the Kingdom of God, where concrete consubstantiality, perfect organic wholeness and deification are realized – that offers absolute fullness of being. On the other hand, there exists also a psycho-physical kingdom of beings with various degrees

[46] The imaginary dialogue between the Moralist and the morphinist is omitted here, pp. 85-86 (Russian text).
[47] A short paragraph on p. 87 was omitted as it was considered to be redundant. The idea is developed in subsequent paragraphs.

of disruption in the organic wholeness and a diminution of mutual immanence. However, even in the most extreme cases of egoistical self-containment, there are at least preserved some abstract consubstantiality and some remnants of participation in the common life of the world, as well as the possibility of regeneration and of becoming worthy of entering the Kingdom of God. Hence, absolute values exist even for the agents of the psycho-physical kingdom and constitute the ultimate of their activity. Any attempt to negate absolute values leads to self-contradiction, since the absolute value of God and the Kingdom of God is the *sine qua non* of all relative values and even of existence itself.

The fact that absolute value is always a value, experienced by any subject, in no way contradicts its absoluteness, i.e. its self-justification. The concept "absolute" when it has the meaning of a predicate or a definition, is applicable to such objects as are found in A SYSTEM OF RELATIONS. For example, in asserting the absolute movement of body A, moving toward body B, we do not deny that this movement is in relation to body B, we deny only those theories, according to which the approach of two bodies, viewed in its concrete fulness, could equally be expressed as "A moves toward B" or "B moves toward A".

ALL EMBRACING AND PARTIAL ABSOLUTE INTRINSIC VALUES

God is the Good itself in the all-embracing meaning of the word. He is the True, the Beautiful, the Moral Good, Life, etc. Hence, God, and especially each Person of the Holy Trinity is the All-Embracing Absolute Intrinsic Value. The full mutual inter-participation of God the Father, the Son and the Holy Spirit in their mutual life, entitles us to affirm that the All-embracing absolute intrinsic value is not divided into three parts and does not exist in three exemplars: it is one in three Persons. Moreover, every created member of the Kingdom of God is a person worthy of communing with the Divine plenitude of being by virtue of the fact that it has chosen the path of goodness, and has actually received the grace of God which would enable him to be fit to enter into God's eternal life and to actively participate in it. This personality has reached the stage of deification by grace, despite the fact that it is a creature, it nevertheless possesses an all-embracing absolute intrinsic value. Each of these personalities is a created son of God.

Finally, even each agent of the psycho-physical kingdom of being, despite the state of his alienation from God and the poverty of a relatively isolated existence, is nonetheless an individual, i.e. one who possesses a unique normative idea, by virtue of which he is a potential member of the Kingdom of God. Hence, every substantival agent, every actual or even potential personality, is an absolute intrinsic value, which is potentially all-embracing. Thus, all agents, i.e. the whole protoplastic world created by God, consists of beings who are not means for some ends or values, but are absolute intrinsic values, and for that reason are potentially all-embracing. To be worthy of God's gracious help in raising their absolute intrinsic value from the potentially all-embracing state to the level of the actual all-embracing, i.e. to attain deification, depends on their own efforts.

Only a personality can be an actually all-embracing absolute intrinsic value: only a personality can possess absolute fulness of being. All other forms of being which are derivative from the existence of personality, i.e. the different aspects of personality, the activities of personalities, the products of their activities, are indeed derivative values, that have their existence by virtue of the all-embracing absolute good. We have indicated earlier the following definition of derivative value: it is being in its significance for the realization of the absolute fulness of being or alienation from it.

Consequently, it would seem, that every derivative good is reduced to the level of only a means. In this event, one would have to think, for example, that the love of man for God, or the love of man for his fellows, is not a good *per se,* but is only a means of attaining absolute fulnes of being. This would also apply to beauty and truth, which would not be good in themselves, but only as means.

A full apprehension and exact understanding of this thesis necessarily leads to a sense of repulsion for this view, and such a feeling is a true symptom of the falseness of this thesis. In fact, love toward any being deprived of intrinsic value and reduced to the level of only a means, is not genuine love, but a falsification of love behind which is hidden hypocrisy or treachery. The falseness of this thesis is also to be seen in the fact that the goodness of the Absolute All-embracing Good, becomes itself incomprehensible. If love, beauty and truth, which are undoubtedly present in It, are only means, then what is the inherent good in the Absolute Good itself? Fortunately, we do not have to oscillate between the two alternatives, namely, the all-embracing absolute value and instrumental value (the value of means).

Adopting the concept "radiated value" developed by Stern [48] we will have to modify it however, in accordance with the system of philosophy which we are developing, and at the same time change the

[48]   The theory of values developed by W. Stern, in his *Wertphilosophie,* p. 127, where he calls these values Strahlwerte. Lossky modifies this idea to suit his own axiological system.

name to correspond to our meaning, in distinction from absolute all-embracing intrinsic values, namely, "partial intrinsic values". In spite of their derivative nature, in the sense that they cannot exist apart from the whole, they remain intrinsic values. In fact, we place at the apex of axiology the all-embracing fulness of being as the absolute perfection. That indefinable goodness and self-justiciation, which is thoroughly permeated with the fulness of being, also belongs to every moment of it by virtue of its organic wholeness. Hence, each necessary aspect of the fulness of being is perceived and experienced as something which is good in itself and is justified in its own content as that which ought-to-be. Such values are love, truth, freedom, beauty. All these aspects of the kingdom of God with the Lord God as the Head are impressed with the marks inherent in the Absolute Good. The characteristics of the Absolute Good are: it is not self-enclosed, does not commune with any hostile conflicting opposition, is compatible, and communicable, has existence for itself as well as for others, and has the capacity for self-surrender.

There are thus only intrinsic values in God and in the Kingdom of God as well as in the protoplastic world (first-created): there is nothing that is merely a means. Intrinsic values are all absolute and objective, i.e. they are of universal significance, since here there is no isolated separated existence. The classification and correlation of these values are expressed in the following table:

	All-embracing	*Primordial*	Actually All-embracing
Absolute intrinsic *values*	Partial	Created	Potentially All-embracing

RELATIVE VALUES

Those values are relative which are in one relation good and in another evil, because they are at least necessarily connected with evil.

Such double-faced values are possible only in the psycho-physical kingdom of existence, which consists of agents that are in a state of separation from God and are to a greater or lesser degree separated from each other. To understand the nature of relative values and to establish their basic forms, we should distinguish the possible kinds of relations of creatures to God and to the Kingdom of God.

All beings strive for the absolute fulness of being. To achieve this goal two diametrically opposed courses may be chosen. The first course is the all-surmounting love to God as the Primordial Absolute Good, and love toward all created agents as the potentially all-embracing good. This results in a voluntary subordination and voluntary harmony in the communal activity of all those beings who follow God. Agents who were guided from their initial existence by this ideal, are worthy of deification and entered from the very beginning into fellowship of the Kingdom of God, without having to follow the course of evolution, which gradually leads to the highest degree of good. The other course, which is diametrically opposed to the first, is the proud aspiration to personally become God and attain absolute fulness of being by subjecting all other beings to oneself. This is the ideal of Satan. It leads to rivalry with God. In its attempt to realize this ideal, it meets with unsurmountable obstacles, and in case of impenitence, there results a burning hatred for God and for every genuine good. In following this course, the result is a progressive perfection in evil and a greater alienation from God and the Kingdom of God; this is SATANIC EVOLUTION.

However, a less decisive defection from God and the Kingdom of God is possible. Aspiration toward absolute fulness of being may be bound up with greater love for oneself than for God or other beings. This aspiration is not the proud desire to take God's place; it is rather a preferential interest for one's self, in the sense of concentration on one's own experiences at the expense of inattention for and absence of interest in the life of others. This is egoism, not Satanic, but earthly. This leads to the separation of agents from each other, and results in a state of being where each agent is left to himself. This leads to such poverty of isolated existence as is known to modern science, for example, in the state of a single separated electron.

As was indicated above, the poverty of the isolated life, can be overcome by means of the evolutionary process. In this process the agent learns gradually to leave his self-containment, at least partially, and to enter into union with other agents, forming with them organically united wholes which enables them to attain a greater complexity and variety of life than in isolated existence. However, the increase of power and the creative activity of life acquired in such organic unities is used to a great extent for selfish purposes, specifically for an energetic struggle for existence against those who are not within this unity. The good which results in the raising of the level of life in one group of beings is accompanied by the evil of oppressing other beings. This unfortunate relativity of good in the evolutionary process is highly significant. The moral evil of alienation from God, i.e. the evil of isolation of agents, leads as a natural consequence, to all possible kinds of evil, such as sufferings due to the poverty of existence and the mutual restriction of life of those beings who found themselves outside the Kingdom of God – in the kingdom of psycho-physical being. This lower type of existence is the result of an incorrect, but voluntary act of choice. Similarly, in accordance with the theory regarding the nature of the Kingdom of God, the rational perfection of this existence, and the forsaking of the lower type of existence by acquiring holiness and by communion with the Kingdom of God, are possible only by a free search for the right way by means of free creative acts. Hence, the whole evolutionary process in nature from the agent who is on the level of existence of an electron, up to man and even beyond that, must be understood as a voluntary creative process, and not as a necessary process subject to a definite principle of law. All these qualities necessary for the possibility of the creative process for the regeneration of fallen agents are preserved, as indicated above, even on the lower level of natural existence. Each substantival agent possesses a super-qualitative creative power; there is a connection between the agents in the form of abstract consubstantiality, capable of teleological creative activity, etc.

Every gain in normal evolution, every activity in its course, is a positive value in so far as it is significant for the ascent to the absolute fulness of being. Each manifestation of life in this normal process is not only A MEANS of ascent, but also an INTRINSIC VALUE FOR THE SUBJECT WHO IS CREATING AND EXPERIENCING IT. It is the moment of SUBJECTIVE fulness of being.

The number and variety of such intrinsic values is very great in such a relatively highly developed agent as the human Self, which has gone a long way, comparatively speaking, towards the liberation from egoistical self-containment. Man lives a life which is partly common to the life of many agents of a lower level that are subordinated to him, which enter into the composition of his body. Similarly, he lives a life which is partly common to the life of many agents who are nearer and higher than himself and to whom he is subordinated, such as his family, his nation, his church, etc. Many activities in each of these areas possess the character of intrinsic values for the subject. Biological functions of a healthy organism, for example, in the partaking of food with a normal appetite and the digesting of it, physical work, rest after normal work, etc. Each one of these activities, as well as the objective contents themselves that they produce (a healthy body, a well-made chair, a good snapshot, etc.) may be intrinsic values for a person. On the other hand, each one of these activities and each object produced by them may also be reduced to the level of merely a means. Moreover, each of the above activities and their objects may be reduced to the level of merely a means not only in relation to absolute intrinsic values but also in relation to values which are likewise relative.

The above-mentioned activities in the kingdom of psycho-physical existence must more or less struggle with beings who are outside of the agent or outside of that union in whose interests he acts. In one way or another all these activities are connected with the struggle for existence, and even within each union harmony among its members exists only in certain relations, but in other relations they are in conflict with each other. This conflict may find expression for example, in certain diseases of the organism, in competition in trade and industry, in exploitation of labor by capital, etc. There is no love relationship among all beings, no full harmony of interests, no communal activity. Hence, the experience of some one agent or a group of agents could not be the object of full active co-participation of all the others. While these experiences and their object are intrinsic values for some individual, they nonetheless belong to the realm of relative and not absolute values.

Perfect love, beauty, truth, the moral good, are universally valid intrinsic values, while the relative good is universally valid, not as intrinsic value, but as something instrumental, as a necessary moment in evolution which leads to the threshold of the exit from evil. The various forms of the relative good may possess the character of intrinsic values only for the bearers themselves and those agents of the psycho-physical kingdom near to them, who struggle together for the preservation of life and the raising of its level. Hence, these are SUBJECTIVE INTRINSIC VALUES.

NEGATIVE VALUES

A negative value, i.e. the character of evil (in the broad and not the ethical sense), possesses all that which serves as an obstacle toward the attainment of absolute fulness of being. It does not follow however, that evils, such as illness, aesthetic ugliness, hatred, treachery, etc. are in themselves indifferent, and are regarded as evil only in so far as they fail to attain fulness of being. Just as the good is justified in itself, so is evil something unworthy in itself, deserving condemnation; it is in itself the opposite of the absolute fulness of being, as the Absolute Good.

In contradistinction to the Absolute Good, evil is not primordial and not independent. First of all, it exist only in the created world and not in its protoplastic essence. It has its origin in a volitional act of the substantival agent and derivatively, as the result of this act. Secondly, evil acts of will are committed under the guise of good, because they are always directed toward a genuine positive value. However, in this correlation with other values and means of attaining it, evil is substituted for good. Thus, to be God is the highest positive value, but the usurpation of this worth by a creature is the greatest evil. Thirdly, the realization of the negative value is possible only by utilizing the powers of good. This dependence and contradictory nature of negative values is particularly to be seen in the sphere of Satanic evil. We shall now proceed to examine this problem.

Satanic evil is the pride of the agent who cannot tolerate God's supremacy as well as that of other agents above himself, and one who aspires to take God's place, and to occupy a preferential position in the world higher than that of other creatures. This basic characteristic of Satanic will is expressed in various forms, for example, in Satanic ambition, Satanic love for power, in manifestations of hatred, envy, cruelty, etc. Such acts and conditions, which in themselves and not merely by their consequences and prior circumstances cause damage to other beings, possess intrinsic value for the Satanic will.

The difference between Satanic evil and evil of earthly selfishness is briefly this: From the point of view of the Satanic will evil acts, are themselves positive intrinsic values, in as much as they SATISFY HIS PRIDE. For earthly selfishness, however, evil acts possess only INSTRUMENTAL value, but are *per se* undesirable. In either case, the evil caused other beings is not the primary goal, but is only the result of selfishness. In this sense, even Satan is not a being who strives to cause suffering to others just for its own sake.[49] The nature of Satanic selfishness is such that his aims include oppression of other beings by analytic necessity, while the aims of the earthly selfishness are bound up with the acts and conditions that oppress the existence of others by synthetic necessity. The first is absolute evil, the second is relative evil.

The difference between these two forms of will may be explained by the distinction between Satanic and earthly ambition. For Satanic ambition, SUPREMACY as victory over the other agents is an INTRINSIC GOAL, whereas for earthly ambition, the attainment of supremacy is not an INTRINSIC GOAL, but A MEANS. To be more specific, it is either an indication of an act performed, or the source of securing for oneself some good, (such as a position in society favourable for free development of all activities of life, etc.).

Theoretically it is not difficult to differentiate between Satanic and earthly ambition, but in actual practice it is often quite impossible to

---

49 See my article, "The Nature of Satan according to Dostoyevsky", in a collection of articles, *F. M. Dostoyevsky* (in Russian) edited by Doleening, Vol. I, 1922 (St. Petersburg). Scheler solves this problem differently. See N. Hartmann's *Ethics*, Vol. II, pp. 176 ff. *The Teleology of the Anti-Values and the Idea of Satan* (London, George Allen & Unwin Ltd., 1931).

know with which of these ambitions we have to do when we encounter the concrete manifestations of a person. Competition, in a gradual and imperceptible manner leads to the development of envy and hatred, which, according to Scheler [50] rejoices in the faults of the one hated, and grieves at any worth in him. Having embarked upon this course, a person moves along the edge of a precipice and is ominously illuminated by reflections from the Satanic evil. The lives of great men and important historical persons provide many examples of such a dangerous position.

Selfishness both Satanic and earthly, is the FUNDAMENTAL evil. It is a moral evil, realized in different variations. As a result, insofar as it leads to the relative isolation of agents from each other, there appear all possible forms of evil, which may be called derivative evils: such as physical suffering, illness, death, mental suffering and mental illness, aesthetic ugliness, lack of the full truth, errors, etc.

If the world is the creation of a benevolent Creator, a world that is rational in all its details, then the question arises, why does evil exist in the world, and what is the meaning of the different forms of evil. This question was answered in my book, "Freedom of the Will", and it is also briefly indicated in this book. The highest worth of the world, for which alone it has the right to exist, that is, its capacity to create the Kingdom of God, is only possible when agents have FREEDOM. But freedom is bound up not only with the possibility of good, but also of evil. An agent who uses his freedom wrongly, because he has embarked upon a selfish course, introduces evil into the world. The good for the love of God and for his creatures presupposes the possibility of the evil of selfishness, although it does not require its actual existence. The actuality of selfishness, is thus a free and independent manifestation of the agent. He was not forced to commit this wrong, it is a sin which leads as a natural and necessary consequence to his isolation with all the resulting evils, such as poverty of life, illness, death, aesthetic ugliness, etc.

The fundamental evil – the evil of egoistic selfishness, is an act of a free agent which leads to its own kind of 'antitransfiguration'. Hence, evil is not merely a deficiency in the good, or non-fulness of it, i.e. non-being. Evil is a certain kind of content of being, it is an *esse*, of which it may be said that it is *male esse* as distinct from *bene esse*. However, it does not appear in the world except through the wrong use of the great good, namely, of free creative power. Moreover, it does not appear except in the pursuit of the greatest positive value,

[50] Max Scheler (1874-1928) modern German philosopher author of *Der Forma-lismus in der Ethik und die materiale Wertethik*, etc. He was one of the leading exponents of the phenomenological school of the Husserl circle.

namely, deification, but is pursued along the wrong course. Hence, this *male esse* can never be thoroughly evil. It always contains at least some remnants of positive values.

The correlation of all beings and all events which form a single world, is explained by the fact that at the head of the world there is a World Spirit, a substantival agent who co-ordinates all the activities of all beings, without isolating anyone from Himself. Hence, He belongs to the composition of God's Kingdom. The spirit alone can be the source of such a whole, such a system whose parts lead to the realization of a truly-all-embracing, unchangeable, eternal and absolute purpose. This purpose, in consonance with the Spirit, is to make the whole structure in the world and every event in it subservient to the development of spirituality in the beings of the psycho-physical realm and thus educate them for reunion with the Kingdom of God. Hence, the inclusion of every event in the all-embracing cosmic bond, which result, from the viewpoint of the individual being, the most capricious and unexpected combinations, is not the result of blind chance, but contains a most profound meaning which possesses the nature of moral necessity. As a result we have a world in which every "great cosmic event is adapted to the fate of many thousands of beings, to each in its own way". "The currents of life of all human beings in their interconnection must have as much agreement and harmony, as a composer adds to many voices in a symphony, who apparently interrupt one another." [51]

In this rational whole every evil which painfully touches those beings who themselves bring evil into the world, serves them as either a punishment, a warning, an inducement, or repentance, etc. In this sense, even evil has instrumental positive value. In the realm of evil beings, it is used as a means of curing them from evil.

INSTRUMENTAL VALUES

In our psycho-physical world there are an endless number of actions, events, content of being, which possess only the nature of means for the realization of some positive value. The sweeping of a room, the removal of a grease spot from a dress with a cleaning fluid, the daily trips on a streetcar, the filling out an application form for the purpose of receiving a passport, etc. all these are instrumental values. They are only possible in a world of being where there is separation and impoverishment of

---

[51] See Schopenhauer, *Parerga und Paralipomena*, Vol. I, also Lossky, *The World as an Organic Whole* (Oxford University Press, 1928), trans. by Natalie Duddington, pp. 161-167.

life. These actions and contents of being, have no inner relation to the whole complex system of life, but only to some limited element of it. They are repeatable and replaceable, and are valued not for their relatively-individual content, but only for their connection with the purpose understood as an abstract conception. The more actions there are in the behaviour of a being that have the character of merely a means, the more often they are repeated, the more the tone of such a being is lowered, and the greater is the boredom of life.

As culture continues to develop, man, quite often sets for himself goals whose attainment requires a long series of means. It does not follow from this, that the development of culture must inevitably be accompanied by a lowering of the tone of life. The art of life consists in the ability to complicate interests and to deepen its organic aspect so that means cease to be merely means, at least in some respect contain intrinsic aims, or at least are permeated and alluringly illumined by that intrinsic goal for whose sake they are being realized. Thus, a scientist preparing for a number of years for a difficult expedition, a far-sighted politician like Bismark, an ardent reformer like Peter the Great, could with enthusiasm realize means for a distant goal, seeing in each one of them some intrinsic purpose, or at least, a reflection of that distant intrinsic purpose.

THE DRAMATIC NATURE OF NORMAL EVOLUTION

In the psycho-physical world even in the process of normal evolution the greater part of the activities is directed toward the realization of the relative good. My self-preservation and the preservation of my family, my nation, humanity, as psycho-physical wholes, are a good for these beings, but is in some way bound up with evil for others. Hence, the higher the degree of freedom from egoistic self-containment attained by the agent, the more sensitive he is to the introduction of evil into the world, the more often does his position become tragic.

Even absolute values under conditions of psycho-physical existence, often require, in order to gain access to them and to preserve the conditions which makes it possible to use them, the type of actions which destroy relative values which are of intrinsic value to some subjects. The assassins of Paul I, the highly gifted reformers, such as Peter the Great, who destroy the old modes of life, the participants in civil wars during great revolutions – those who fight for absolute intrinsic values, are experiencing a painful tragedy because they introduce evil into the world in the struggle for the good.

Taking monastic vows does not offer a radical liberation from evil, which is inevitable in a psycho-physical world. Life in a cloister, even in great seclusion, only lessens the number and variety of manifestations of evil, but does not remove them completely.

One may try to calm one's conscience by denying the Christian ideal of the absolute good by a theory which asserts the absolutely IRREVOCABLE LAWS of existence conditions the modes of life in which the relativity of good is inevitable, i.e. the bond between good and evil is irremovable. Such self-justification is Satanic temptation. In reality, the absolute good is realizable, and in the Kingdom of God it is realized, but we have fallen away from it and have created such an atmosphere of existence which "lies in evil" and without transformation cannot contain in itself a pure good. To face this truth courageously, without concealing from oneself the admixture of evil and imperfections which is inherent even in the greatest heroic actions in the psycho-physical world, is possible only on the basis of a Christian world-view. The Christian world-view alone points the way to the ideal kingdom of being, where complete freedom from evil is attained not by the extinction of life as Buddhism maintains, but on the contrary, by the acquisition of the fulness of life, and not through the annihilation of the individual peculiarities, but through the all-embracing disclosure of them.

The sight of evil that penetrates all aspects of life in the psycho-physical world will not lead us to despondency and unbelief in the benevolence of the Creator of the world; it will not lead us to the "revolt" of Ivan Karamazov,[52] and to the return of our "ticket", if we bear in mind that absolute values are not destroyed by any external power. The Kingdom of God, as already shown, is not subject even to the blows of Satanic wrath. Even in our psycho-physical world only imperfect aspects and manifestations of existence, are destroyed, die, and disappear into the past, and not the absolutely valuable existence. These imperfect aspects must perish sooner or later in order not to interfere with the more perfect realization of the absolutely valuable nucleus that lies in their foundation. The love of Agnes [53] for her child Alf does not terminate with his death. Genuine personal love is an ontological binding together by growth of one supra-temporal and supra-spatial being with another, which is not destroyed by that profound change of body which is called death. The death of a loved one may even enhance the quality of the communion with him. It begins to take place as if immediately, in the heart of the one who remains

---

[52]   Ivan Karamazov, a character in Dostoyevsky's *The Brothers Karamazov*, who offered to return his "ticket" to God who allows suffering of innocent children. Ed.

[53]   Agnes, a character in Ibsen's *Brand*.

alive. The conjoining of loves, particularly in the organic union of the family, determines the future destiny of both persons without interruption until they commune with the Kingdom of God, where personal love for the first time receives full realization. The absolute love for one being because of the ideal connection of all individual peculiarities, potentially includes in itself love for other being. Hence, only in the Kingdom of God can love be realized in all its purity where egoistical bias diminish it.

Like love, beauty and the true experience of it, even in the form accessible to us in the psycho-physical world, are also indestructible. Let us recall how Olenin [54] reacted as he approached the Caucasian Mountains and saw for the first time in all its grandeur the range of snow-capped mountains.[55]

The beauty of the snow-capped mountains, their grandeur, harmony, and virgin purity, is only a SYMBOL of absolute beauty, grandeur and purity. Therefore, the mountains themselves are not eternal and should not be eternal, but the beauty expressed by them is eternal, and the experience of this beauty is preserved in the heart for ever, not of course, in its psycho-physical concreteness, which really is not concretenes but only a fragmented abstractness. It remains in its SIGNIFICANCE, like an overtone continues to sing in the soul leaving on everything a new mark of solemnity and greatness and invariably supporting, at least in the subconscious or super-conscious sphere, the Eros for beauty.

The indelible trace left in the soul as a result of the experience of absolute values, will never allow the agent who deviated from the normal course of development, to be satisfied with his condition. He will always be tortured by the contradiction between his behaviour replete with evil, and the "eros" of the pure good, vaguely revealed to him in the earthly experiences of absolute values. Sooner or later, this contradiction will lead the erring ones out of their dilemma, and will induce them to leave behind the "sad songs of earth"; and even Satan, tortured by his duplicity and deception, will perhaps become disappointed in the gloomy grandeur of hell.[56]

[54]   Olenin is a character in L. N. Tolstoy's *The Cossacks* (ed.).
[55]   The passage quoted by Lossky from *The Cossacks* is omitted.
[56]   Johannes Scotus Erigena (circ. 810-880) says, in reference to St. Gregory the Theologian, that wrath is limited, therefore, having exhausted it to the limit, the sinner will sooner or later turn to the course of good, so that in the end there will be no evil left in anybody. (*De divisione naturae*, vol. V, 26). This hope of universal salvation cannot be based on the theory of evolution in accordance with law, but in the expectation of a voluntary conversion to the good on the part of all beings who have experienced the vileness of evil and who have condemned their behaviour.

Evil arises in the psycho-physical world not only in the process of realizing relative values but even in attempts to actualize absolute values. There is however, a great difference between these two cases of the appearance of evil. The relative good, by its very nature, is connected with evil for some beings. The absolute good, on the other hand, by its very nature is a good for everybody, and if under the conditions of psycho-physical being it is connected with evil for some agents, such evil arises from the imperfect nature of these agents themselves, or from the imperfect actualization of the absolute value. In fact, even such an activity as the performing of one of the greatest symphonies of Beethoven might entail suffering for a scientist in an adjacent apartment if it interfered with his concentration on important and difficult work. Similarly, it may be disagreeable to a person not engaged in any activity, if he lacks ability to perceive music and hears only disorderly combinations of sounds, without apprehending the beautiful whole. In both cases evil is not due to the nature of the beautiful music itsef, but is the result of the limited nature of the afflicted persons themselves who are responsible for their own limitations. To be sure, there is a third possibility: the performance of even a beautiful composition by the best artists cannot be absolutely perfect in the psycho-physical world of existence. Disagreeable squeaks, rattles and noises are inevitably mixed with the music and torment a sensitive ear. In this case evil is not due to the nature of absolute value, nor is it due to the limited nature of the afflicted beings, but is due to the imperfection of the performer and the means of performance.

The theory that absolute values are indestructible and that the nature of absolute value itself will never give rise to evil, might lead some uninvited "benefactors" of humanity, people with a revolutionary character, to believe that they have a right to sweep away all obstacles in their way without any scruples for the sake of absolute values for which they are fighting. (Actually, they usually do not fight for absolute values, but for relative values which they absolutize). Naturally, this idea is a Satanic temptation. Although only relative positive values are subject to destruction and the process of normal evolution is impossible without such destruction, nonetheless a sensitive conscience forbids many forms of such destruction, or if it permits such destruction it experiences them as tragedy. We cannot discuss this question here in more detail, since it belongs in the field of ethics and not in the general theory of value.[57]

---

[57] See B. Visheslavtsev's *The Heart in Christian and Indian Mysticism* (Paris, YMCA Press, 1929), regarding the inevitable tragedy of the sinful life.

FALSE ARGUMENTS IN FAVOUR OF RELATIVISM

There are many circumstances which help to make the relativistic theory of values, more acceptable, i.e. the theory which maintains that all values are relative. First of all, we should bear in mind, as was already pointed out, that an inorganic view of the world necessarily leads to a relativistic axiology. Moreover, experience helpfully presents us with a number of facts which seem to be a very convincing confirmation of this conclusion from an inorganic view of the world. In point of fact, in the realm of psycho-physical existence the greater part of activities and contents of being actually belong to the realm of the relative good, i.e. they are necessarily bound up with evil. Moreover, for the agents of the psycho-physical world the absolute values themselves are not objects of striving (as well as contemplation and faith) without the possibilty of being realized only in the Kingdom of God. The attempts at the realization of absolute values in the psycho-physical world are bound up with evil. Those who do not see that this evil is not due to the nature of absolute value itself, but is due to its imperfect realizaton or the imperfect use of it, may arrive at an erroneous conclusion that absolute values do not exist at all.

Finally, there is still one more important factor that provides a reason for relativism. A distinction must be made as M. Scheler [58] has pointed out, between the norms of behaviour and values corresponding to them, and we must keep in mind that under different circumstances they can be the source of different opposite norms. For example, the premise, that "the personal value of one person is equal to that of another person", may under different conditions give rise to two opposite norms: "take care of others" and "take care of yourself".

HIERARCHY OF VALUES

From the definitions adduced above and the theories expounded in connection with them, it follows that positive values are not equal; there are differences between them, differences in rank and in merit. First of all, it is evident that instrumental values are lower than intrinsic values. Furthermore, in each of these groups there are peculiar differences in rank: among the absolute intrinsic values the all-embracing values are higher than the partial ones; among the all-embracing

[58] See M. Scheler, *Der Formalismus in der Ethik und die materiale Wertethik*, p. 219. Also other arguments by Scheler against ethical relativism and scepticism in ethics, pp. 306-320.

values the primordial values, that is, God the Father, God the Son, and God the Holy Spirit stand higher than the created values.

Among relative values the ranks are determined by the steps of normal evolution. Thus, for example, here on earth biological values are generally considered to be higher than the values of inorganic nature, the values of the social process stand higher than biological values. To classify values into groups by rank can be achieved only by having a thoroughly developed theory of the system of value such as the one given by Münsterberg in his "Philosophie der Werte".

Since I do not propose to develop such a system, I shall simply limit myself in the theory of ranks, by defending Münsterberg's view. Many aspects of the problem have been elucidated by M. Scheller in his "Der Formalismus in der Ethik und die materiale Wertethik", as well as by Nicolai Hartman in his "Ethics" and by W. Stern in his "Wert-philosophie".

Heyde rejects completely the distinction of rank in values. He says that every value can possess different degrees. I may prefer a restful vacation to a small moral act; I may prefer a pleasant walk to an insignificant aesthetic value of a theatrical performance, etc.[59] The examples offered by Heyde do not actually compel us to refute the theory of ranks in values, i.e. the difference in their inner merit. These examples only point out that in choosing between several values under the conditions of psycho-physical existence, we should be guided not only by ranks, but also by other qualities, as for example, the non-realization of some inferior positive value (let us say, nutrition) leads to the appearance of destructive negative values (such as illness, death, etc.).[60] It follows that the preference of a value must be determined by its rank only when other things are equal.

[59] See Heyde, *Wert*, p. 186.
[60] See N. Hartmann's theory of the presence of two laws of preference: the preference of value of its position in the hierarchy of values and the preference of value because of its strength, by which is meant "strength of value", the character of disvalue (unwert) which arises when the value is not realized. (*Ethics*, English Translation, Vol. II, p. 455.)

BIOGRAPHICAL SKETCH

Venyamin Mikhailovich Khvostov (1868-1920) was born in Moscow where he received his education. He graduated from the Law Faculty, Moscow University. His dissertation on "The Concept of aequitas and aequus jus in Roman classical Law" was published in 1895. In 1898 he was awarded the Master's degree in Roman Law. His dissertation was on "Natural duties in Roman Law". He was later appointed professor of Roman Law in Moscow University. Publications in the field of Jurisprudence and Philosophy are listed in the Bibliography.

V. M. Khvostov

THE EUDAEMONISTIC SIGNIFICANCE
OF THE MORAL GOOD*

The dual nature of man in which contradictory tendencies are constantly clashing, now reaching to the stars and now delving into the musty atmosphere of vulgarity, we are bound to conclude that in defining the general nature of our existence, each one of us is at the crossroads. A person must either follow the voice of his vocation or go against it, or, lastly, ignore his vocation and immerse himself completely in the bustle of life. It may be asked, what criterion should be used in making this choice? Why should we attach so much importance to the mysterious voice of our vocation which lures us into uncertainty without guaranteeing any apparent happiness? If one may distinguish in man two opposing principles, good and evil, the rational and the irrational, why should we especially value those principles which are called rational or good and not the opposite values?

I have already pointed out in my article on the pluralistic world-view that a solution to this problem is offered by supersensory religious experience which imparts to the GOOD cosmic significance, which enables us to apprehend directly the presence of a secret force that inspires us with vital courage and strengthens our spirit. "The joy which mystics experience in such states", says James, "clearly surpasses the joys which normal consciousness can give us. Such joy, obviously, also arouses our physical nature, because this feeling of rapture is always spoken of as something difficult to endure, bordering on physical pain. But this is too refined, too unusually profound a pleasure to be expressed in ordinary words. The immediate contact

* This selection is taken from *Voprosy*, Vol. 22, Bk. 110, pp. 187-233, abridged in certain passages.

(nearness) of God, the wounds of his spears, the ecstasy of conjugal union, are the usual expressions which describe this joy. In these transcendent states of ecstasy feeling and reason die away." [61]

But besides this evidence of a mystical feeling, one can produce proof of a purely eudaemonistic nature in the ordinary meaning of the word, which will show that the cultivation in oneself the principles of rationality, while serving the moral good, are at the same time our only true way to happiness, insofar as they are generally accessible. The pessimists generally err by not paying sufficient attention to the evaluation of those emotions which are experienced by man in this type of moral action.

I will point out, first of all, that there is in man a feeling of PRIDE which would suffer a great deal, if he were to regard himself irrational, evil and bestial. The very feeling of pride, can of course, no more be logically substantiated and deduced from something that could serve as its basis than can the feeling of mystical perception. But first, as has already been stated, no perception in general can be substantiated logically or deduced from something else. It is always a *datum* of our consciousness. Similarly, the presence of the feeling of pride in man is just a simple DATUM. Nevertheless it is necessary to take it into consideration. If man were to ignore this demand it would cause him extreme suffering. Nothing can be more difficult for many people who possess this feeling to a high degree than the realization that because of their behaviour they become the object of merited scorn on the part of others as well as themselves. It is no comfort to people in such cases to argue that the feeling of dignity and pride which are responsible for their suffering, is a simple fact whose value cannot be proven logically. The only way out is to stifle the voice of dignity or pride by an artificial lowering of the standard of consciousness. That is why people in such a state so frequently resort to drunkenness or debauchery, hoping thus to rid themselves of the consciousness of their degradation. The hedonists pay little attention to such states of man when they start proving that the fulfillment of moral duty has no meaning for human happiness, or that it is even of negative importance.

When asked, what moments in their lives they considered to be the happiest, many people would reply without any hesitation, "those when I forgot myself, when I stopped noticing the passing of time". We shall examine this rather common expression, and we shall arrive at some useful conclusions.

Upon examination, it turns out that the moments when people "forget themselves" are either moments when they are enraptured by

[61] Wm. James, *Varieties of Religious Experiences.*

aesthetic pleasure, or when they are gripped by feelings of deep sympathy, or by love for one's neighbours, or finally, when wholly engrossed in activity.

These authors [62] thus value both aesthetic pleasure, love and activity only as a means of forgetting oneself as well as all the miseries of life. But it seems to me, that one should not stop here: one should go further and ask the question, what does it actually mean to forget oneself? since this expression does not mean that man ceases to exist in such moments. Indeed he does exist and he also forgets himself. How then can one exist and at the same time forget his existence? I think that it will all become clear if we recollect what was said in the article on the pluralistic world-view about the dual nature of man. It will be seen that in these moments of self-forgetfulness, *man's higher Self, the bearer of higher spirituality and reason which is peculiar to people, renounces the lower egotistical Self, and thus attains that peculiar state which goes under the name of self-forgetfulness.*[63]

We have seen that this higher Self is not actually bound by space and time; it is capable of infinite expansion and intimacy with something that is cosmically great and eternal. In such moments of intimacy we forget those narrow limits of space and time in which our small physical Self is immersed as well as that aspect of our spiritual experiences which is closely connected with and dependent upon our mortal body. We are then actually raised to cosmic infinity and are delighted by the positive elements which are revealed to us in great purity which constitute the basis of our higher spirituality, and we cease to notice those sufferings and miseries which are born of the states of our lower Self. The Spirit is victorious over the body and is liberated from its limitations. Here then is our merging with cosmic infinity, with those elements of the universe which are at the basis of our rationality, our propensities towards the good and the adoration of beauty and which affords us the highest bliss accessible to us.

Such states are of course, accessible to man only occasionally, since the demands of our lower Self, do not fail, sooner or later, to announce themselves with great insistence, and take us out of the ecstasy by which we are possessed. The highest bliss accessible to man could be the constant presence of the feeling of union with the infinite which characterise such moments of elevation. The person who experiences such a state, cannot but aspire to it again and long for it. From this point of law, even the phenomenon of boredom, which is so distasteful

---

[62] The authors referred to are Arthur Schopenhauer and Leopardi, who claim that aesthetic pleasure provides for man at least a temporary state of happiness.
[63] The italics are the author's.

to Schopenhauer and other pessimists, receives a different interpretation.

The pleasure which is obtained from activity in the spirit of higher reason is increased still more, if this activity is of a social nature, imbued with the spirit of fellowship and love of one's neighbour. The point is, that fellowship is such an important aspect of man that ignoring it would *ipso facto* lead to suffering. On the other hand, the cultivation of the social aspect of human existence is a new source of pleasure. The modern scientific view of society and man has established quite clearly and convincingly, that man is essentially a social being. Man's very rationality whose cultivation is his highest task, can only develop on social grounds. It is fellowship alone that created articulate speech, and it is only on the basis of speech that we can form abstract thought which differentiates man from the animals, and enables him to deal with such abstractions as the very concept of moral duty. That is why the preservation and development of rationality is only conceivable on the basis of social science. Both science and art are essentially products of organized social collaboration, without which any accumulation of knowledge or the evolution of aesthetic experience would be conceivable.

It is obvious, that social science is the *sine qua non* for rationality, and is at the same time a necessary means of achieving all moral goals. That is why SERVICE TO SOCIETY and its happiness is part of moral duty. Basically, moral duty is first of all every man's obligation to himself — an obligation to cultivate his higher Self at the expense of the lower Self. Another aspect of moral duty is to cultivate in ourselves and in others sociability, which is one of the most important prerequisites for the rationality of the individual. I cannot therefore construct a morality based exclusively on the idea of service to society as many representatives of moral philosophy are doing. The fact that society is stronger and more lasting than the individual is not the only decisive factor in this problem. On the other hand, I do not see how one can avoid the idea of social science in the construction of moral duty, since man is inconceivable in a society without other beings like himself.

In view of the fact that since neither the individual can exist apart from society, nor can society be conceived apart from the individuals who make up society, I suggest that the conflicts between the individual and society are not basically insoluble. These conflicts must be solved in the spirit of the moral ideal, i.e., from the point of view of respect for the dignity of every rational individual constituting society, and respect for society itself as a *sine qua non* for the individual's rationality.

It follows from this that society must not do anything that would violate this respect for the individual as the bearer of the moral law, or that would impede the free cultivation of one's higher Self. The individual on the other hand, is obliged to develop social attitudes to repress any antisocial emotions. Society is so much stronger than any one of us, that even from the point of view of practical realization of our intentions, we must constantly reckon with it. The person who in fulfilling his plans has constantly encountered opposition from his environment, will ultimately be broken by this opposition. This fact alone would compel us to attach to the maxims of our behaviour as general a character as possible and acceptable to others, if this did not arise spontaneously from man's gregarious nature.

Fellowship in its highest manifestation becomes LOVE. Love is generally recognized as the source of the highest pleasure accessible to man. We are interested in love because it contains a clearly expressed broadening of the individual beyond its limits, and therefore is in complete agreement with our general view of man's higher Self. In the feeling of love for one's neighbour, the human Self tears apart the narrow frames of its corporeal seclusion. In the presence of love, according to Dostoyevsky, the heart of one person begins to embrace the infinite source of life for the heart of another. Love of the above kind does not contain any egotistical elements or feelings of ownership in relation to the loved one.[64] Such love conquers any egoism, and in compelling a person to impartially serve another person, greatly broadens his personality, and is evident proof of the fact that living beings are something unique. That is the reason why love usually plays such a great role in moral systems

Having established that rational and social activity and the cultivation of man's higher Self based on love for one's neighbour, is itself the source of the greatest pleasure accessible to man, and it is also a tremendous counterbalance to human suffering. This provides a basis for a CRITIQUE OF PESSIMISTIC AXIOLOGY.

All pessimists regard happiness in a state of REST, herein lies their great error. This argument goes against the very nature of life, since life is activity, and activity by its very nature, is unrest, a struggle with obstacles. Rest is possible only in the grave. Regarding activity as suffering, the pessimists ignore the pleasure which is found in the very

---

[64] Naturally, we do not have in mind every type of love. There are two types of love: EGOISTIC LOVE and SELFLESS LOVE. The difference is, that the first (love) issues from the lower, organic Self, whereas the second one is a manifsetation of the infinite Self. Actually, egoistic love consists in the fact that someone makes himself the centre of his attention and demands that another individual belong to him and serve his wishes. Selfless love on the other hand does not demand anything from others.

process of activity, in the process of free application of efforts, in the free and unhindered expenditure of energy. But they also ignore other elements of pleasure which are inherent in the process of activity and struggle, and again betray their ignorance of human nature. They fail to take into consideration the fact of the force which is manifested in man as a result of his struggle in the overcoming of obstacles. Kowalewski [65] in his studies of the psychology of pessimism, deduces from these elements a particular concept, which he calls the PLEASURE OF DEFENCE (Abwehrlust). Man may derive joy from the pleasure of destroying his enemy by force. He may derive joy from the fact of being very clever and cunning to enable him to rid himself of some threatening danger. He experiences a special feeling of security, when he is able to avert misfortune by taking appropriate measures. Finally, he derives pleasure from his psychological stability, when he is able heroically to endure his misfortunes. And this joy is so great that it generates in man a special LOVE OF RISK. There are many people whose love of risk attracts them to undertakings which they could quite easily avoid. This love of risk explains dangerous journeys to distant lands, which cannot be motivated by any tangible gain; it also explains the attraction of hunting wild and dangerous animals.

History clearly shows, that people only gradually arrive at a conscious evaluation of this enjoyment of life, which is found in life itself, as a process of courageous activity. At any rate, every decisive fruitful activity natural to human nature found its own standard of values almost at the very beginning of cultural development. The lower the level of culture, the less respect is given to different forms of activity which has long since been regarded as being unworthy of a free citizen and the lot of the lower species of men, namely, slaves. Ancient culture was to a considerable extent undermined by this lack of respect for labour, especially strenuous labour that requires discipline. The great service that modern culture has created is a completely new concept of the "knights of labour".[66] A corresponding change of views has taken place even in philosophical thought. Philosophy for a long time has valued generally the universal, the immutable and the stable, and seldom have voices been heard defending the principle of the mutability of all things.

In modern philosophy consonant with the manifestation in practical life of the concept of "knights of labour", the trends of voluntarism, evolutionism and energism have been greatly advanced. Even the epistemologists no longer focus their attention on the universal and the im-

---

[65] See L. Stein, *Der Sinn des Daseins* (1904), especially 1-21.
[66] *Ibid.*

mutable, but rather on the creative and the individualizing, on that which creates something new and original. I think that the appearance at this juncture of the Rickert-Windelband's theory of ideographic or individualizing sciences,[67] is not purely a matter of chance. Obviously, in such areas of thought, completely divorced from practical life is reflected the pulsation of the epoch, for whom the ideal becomes more and more not the imperturbable and calm stoic sage of antiquity, but the eternally active and seething Faust. It would seem fatal to Faust to say to a moment of time, "stop, you are beautiful". Amidst the seething life of humanity, the philosophy of pessimism with its exaltation of rest and inactivity, with its cowardly fear of suffering and boredom, there is a malaise, a symptom of the weakness and degeneration of its preachers and disciples. The courageous human soul will always be guided by Faust's basic idea; this immortal poem offers salvation only to those "whose life was a striving".

Is not the chief answer to pessimism to be found in the idea of the PURIFYING FORCE OF SUFFERING? Suffering very often turns out to be man's best path to the moral good.

Here again we must repeat that we do not know why man is so constituted that he arrives at a knowledge of the good only by means of suffering. In my opinion, this fact refutes the purely optimistic view of the universe, since it confirms the fact that the good cannot be discovered without obstacles or without sacrifices. But the fact itself is quite clear: personal grief and suffering are the best means of overcoming man's finite self, which makes itself the centre of life and which is prepared to sacrifice everything to its narrow interests. Grief and suffering enable the higher self to triumph which is immersed in real altruistic love and clearly recognizes its unity with the world by means of the active good. Only the person who has experienced such sufferings can comprehend the sufferings of others, can value people not for ulterior motives, but quite dispassionately, by paying attention to their suffering and to the moral greatness which is possible for them to attain.

Suffering of course, can have other results. It is not always a school of the good. There are cases when under the influence of suffering,

---

[67]   Heinrich Rickert (1863-1936) German philosopher, and Wilhelm Windelband (1848-1915) German historian of philosophy. Windelband's main position is that whereas science determines facts, the task of philosophy is to determine values. This was later worked out by Rickert, who pointed out the fundamental distinction between natural and historical science: the former seeks to establish general laws and considers particular facts only insofar as they are like others. Rickert stated in contrast to the 'nomothetic' type of science, that history is 'ideographic', i.e. it is interested in the particulars insofar as they have some significance from the point of view of value.

especially undeserved suffering, or suffering beyond endurance, people, may become bitter and fall into despair. Man, without encountering any justice, or encountering the egoistic and apathetic attitude of his fellowmen, and being aware of his impotence as well as that of others to avert the undeserved misfortune that has befallen him, and being unable to make any sense of the trouble or getting any explanation for it, one can easily arrive at a most hopeless negative and pessimistic attitude.

But there are people whom grief not only fails to shatter, but on the contrary, tempers and strengthens them. Any major shock in life produces in them the kind of upheaval which definitely directs them along the path of active service to the good, and compels them to find support for life in precisely these higher spiritual aspects of their nature. A person who experiences such a state is not afraid of suffering for himself, but by merging with the whole world, he experiences in his sufferings the suffering of the whole world, and sees in the sufferings of others his own suffering. Sometimes these experiences lead to the idea that there is some inner meaning in these sufferings, that they are the due desert for that which is base and sinful in man.

People who have passed through such an ordeal and have come out of it morally regenerated, are usually imbued with the idea of THE IMMORTALITY OF THEIR soul, as Dostoyevsky illustrates in the person of the Elder Zosima.[68] They have renounced their small and finite self to such an extent that the force of a higher self is quite evident in them, a self which is close to universal infinity, free from limitations, and therefore approaching eternity, so that the immortality and indestructibility of their soul is for them a self-evident truth which requires no justification nor proof. For such people, personal immortality is not an abstract idea, is not a subject for discussion, speculation and argumentation, but is a completely evident truth given in the depths of human consciousness, verified by supersensory experience.

Suffering is a favourable ground not only for the development of the feeling of love, but also for the development of other higher spiritual qualities. There is no doubt that suffering promotes literary and artistic genius. A great many gifted composers, artists and poets, were very unhappy people. It was only because of their suffering, that they were able to develop those sensitive emotions which enabled them to display their creative capacities in all their force and brilliance. We can therefore say without fear of contradiction that suffering opened the door to them for the highest happiness inherent in creativity.

On the other hand, happiness commonly understood as SATISFACTION

---

[68]   Zosima is a character in Dostoyevsky's *The Brothers Karamazov*.

and TRANQUILITY, undoubtedly spoils people and closes the road to that higher form of well-being toward which the moral good leads us. A satisfied and well-fed person is usually distinguished by his egotism. Not suffering himself, he remains indifferent to the grief of others, and not being in need of sympathy himself, he feels no sympathy for others. Such a person is usually inclined to ascribe his well-being to some special gifts of his own, and treats the unfortunates with arrogance, ascribing their suffering to their inability to adapt themselves to life.

What we have said above can be applied to whole nations. Tranquility and the unperturbed life corrupts the masses and causes them to immerse themselves in the base concerns and interests; politics which does not find for itself a worthy goal degenerates. In place of a principled struggle there develops political intrigue, a race for influence, based entirely on personal ambitions. Only a few, who see in a political career a livelihood, are concerned with such matters. The general mass of people show complete indifference to politics; they are concerned with their personal affairs and lose interest in the common cause.

Our whole argument regarding the spiritual and rational nature which constitutes the good as it is manifested in man, enables us now to define the term 'evil'. If the higher rationality in accordance with our definition contains all the higher spiritual emotions of man which elevate him above the level of the rest of the animal kingdom, and is the manifestation in man of the infinite and eternal cosmic principle of the good as expressed in the striving of the human spirit toward the infinite, then evil is the LIMITING FORCE, THE SOURCE OF ALL FINITENESS, WEAKNESS, AND EVANESCENCE. This force consists in the inability to understand the infinite, and is shown in man's stupidity, ignorance, dullness and narrow-mindedness. The same limiting force manifests itself in the form of obstacles to any manifestation of the infinite principle of the good. In human relations it manifests itself in the form of an evil will, which thwarts any attempt toward goodness, truth and beauty; it appears in the form of physical impotence, frustrating the brave activity of our spirit; and in the form of death, absurdly and mercilessly impeding, at least, our earthly activity.

If the good consists of man's higher rationality, and evil is the result of his limitations, then the person who is less controlled by his lower self and limited nature is more capable of serving the good. In order to serve the good it is necessary, as far as possible, to overcome his lower nature and to subject it to his higher nature. The duality inherent in man is then equalized and he is able to achieve a more or less integral, harmonious state. Man, of course, cannot wholly rid himself of his limitation. An incorporeal existence of spirit may be the object of a zealous faith, but, to argue about it, and to try to visualize such a state, is quite impossible. Our discussion must be within the bounds of empirical reality, where we know only the physical man, and hence, the finite and limited man. But within these limits man can achieve a state of eternity and boundlessness insofar as he does not encounter insuperable obstacles. This does not mean that he must mortify his body. On the contrary, I think that since man must necessarily act only by means of his physical organs, his immediate task is to cultivate his physical health in order that his spirit may become a suitable instrument to influence his environment. Care of the body should go as far as is necessary in the above sense. It becomes harmful only when it leads to the neglect of spiritual tasks.

Thus, the ideal is first of all, a harmonious development of physical and spiritual capacities where the body is the obedient and suitable instrument of the spirit. Not only does it not by its states hinder the work of the spirit, but on the contrary, it readily obeys its commands and fulfills all the necessary movements purposefully and without any difficulty. This state in man is called GRACE. But there are instances when physical limitation is a decisive hindrance to moral duty. One can only harmonize the limited sensuous nature of man with the limitless aspirations of reason to a certain extent. It will then be necessary to sacrifice the requirements of the body and dispense with them for the sake of the requirements of the spirit. The person who is capable of such behaviour manifests that property which Schiller no longer calls GRACE but DIGNITY (Würde).[69] The aesthetic concept alone corresponds to this form of moral behaviour. Kant differentiates between the BEAUTIFUL and the SUBLIME.

There is undoubtedly an aesthetic element in man's moral state, and in this sense Schiller was right in his discussion of *The Beautiful Soul*. It should be noted that those who emphasize the close relationship of the moral state to the LOGICAL UNITY of the human psyche are also right. In point of fact, beauty in moral behaviour is very close to its logical unity. Beauty consists in the fact, that the whole of human nature assumes a certain wholeness. Above all are the demands of pure spirit, the infinite self, to which the body, the finite self, is subject, and in an emergency, is sublimely sacrificed. In other words, such unity of personality may be reduced to the fact that all the goals pursued by man are in mutual agreement and do not interfere with each other. A strict choice is made between conflicting goals on the basis of a guiding principle, i.e. the higher rationality or spirituality of man, and hence, all goals are arranged in a strictly hierarchical order. Among them are the lower goals which we must necessarily sacrifice, if they conflict

---

[69] See Schiller's "Ueber Anmuth und Würde".

with the higher ones. We thus arrive at what may be called the logical unity of behaviour.

Moral duty cannot be based on logic, and the whole content of moral principles cannot be arrived at by means of formal deductions alone. But it should be stated that logic determines the form of man's moral behaviour. The person who wishes to achieve a harmonious state necessary for the service of moral duty, must of course train himself in this direction. Morality is not merely knowledge. It is not sufficient to understand what the moral principle is in order to be actually moral. It is necessary so to influence one's will that it should be imbued with moral beauty, and that our moral convictions should not merely be a matter of thought, but also facts of our entire behaviour.

As a matter of fact, if people can learn to walk the tight rope with great facility, or perform the most difficult balancing acts with great dexterity, surely they can learn to regulate their spiritual movements and become masters of themselves both physically and spiritually. There is no doubt that the achievement of such control over oneself is possible for everyone; there is therefore no justification in blaming one's innate nature or the conflicting influences of the environment; for it is precisely with these excuses that weak-willed people try to justify themselves. If the character is poor, it should be trained, and if the environment is poor, it should not be allowed to devour man. A strong person himself overcomes his hostile environment, and is not afraid to swim against the current, if his convictions demand it. If everybody was helpless in the face of his environment, then there would not have been a Socrates, a Galileo, or a Copernicus, and in general there would be nothing that could be called progress or the moral dignity of man.

We now understand the psychological sources of pessimism. Pessimism is man's lack of enthusiasm for what we call, truth, goodness and beauty. These forces are therefore not sufficiently strong, and thus fade before the force of evil. In his evaluation of the world, the pessimist underestimates its positive aspects and exaggerates its negative properties. By this action, he is actually only projecting his own spiritual state on the entire world.

It seems to me that all pessimists can be divided into certain types, depending on the precise cause of the inner disharmony which is the source of their pessimistic frame of mind.

First of all, pessimists seem to be people with weak wills and strong passions. Being carried away in all directions by their passions without realizing the force which they possess to give unity to their behaviour, to make a proper choice and remain loyal to it, such people are a typical example of the pathological will, projecting his picture on the entire world without any grounds. In the second place, pessimists are people of a highly reflective nature, which poisons every moment of pleasure for them and prevents them from realizing that joy of life, which, as we have seen, is the true basis of the good and man's state. Thirdly, there are those who are subject to excessive suffering, both physical and moral, who do not possess a sufficiently strong will to successfully combat it. Such people reach a pessimism of extreme suffering which can easily lead to suicide.

Such, in my view, is the eudaemonistic meaning of the moral good. The above arguments were an attempt to show that the only way to human happiness is active service of the good. Only a courageous and cheerful person who finds pleasure in the very process of widening his spiritual forces, can find satisfaction in life. Those people who are capable of immersing themselves in the world of music, or in the beautiful forms of art and sculpture, or in the work of abstract scientific-philosophic thought, or in the active service of the good, are capable of happiness, which is especially valuable, since it is found in themselves. These people utilize their actual freedom of spirit and independence from the external environment, which is so dear to man, and through which he alone can preserve his dignity.

But of course, in spite of all these eudaemonistic elements inherent in the moral good, it can in no way insure us against suffering. SUFFERING REMAINS INEVITABLE, and we have seen how, because of the strange incomprehensible constitution of human nature, the very road to virtue is usually to be found in suffering and deprivation. It would therefore be wrong to regard us as advocates of eudaemonism. The purpose of this article was to show that there are indubitable eudaemonistic elements in virtue, and to show from this standpoint the one-sidedness of the purely pessimistic interpretation of the world. I definitely remain an opponent of any shallow optimism which I find a completely unacceptable theory, no less erroneous than pessimism. Generally speaking, I transfer the whole question of morality from both the optimistic and pessimistic premise to a more suitable basis for its correct representation, i.e., on the basis of HUMAN DIGNITY. For me the decisive examples are neither happiness nor unhappiness in the usual sense of the word, but are specifically the dignity and greatness of human personality. Of all the Kantian formulae of the categorical imperative (to which I give my own interpretation), I attribute the greatest importance to the second, which prescribes that one must act in all circumstances in such a way that mankind as embodied in oneself and in everyone else, should always be an end and never just a means. I see the solution of the moral problem in this absolute respect for human personality, by which is meant the highest spiritual self of every person.

Man with his dual nature can never, in my opinion, achieve happiness in the sense of satisfying all demands and of eliminating suffering. But the path to dignity is usually more or less readily accessible to him. For me at least, there is no doubt that this road is the only true one corresponding to man's position in the world, and is the most preferable even from the eudaemonistic point of view, insofar as it can be taken.

As I have persistently pointed out, EVIL is for me an absolutely REAL FORCE. Its importance is unfortunately not confirmed by the fact that it is a *sine qua non* for the disclosure of the inherent goodness in man. The most terrible thing about evil is that it blocks man's path to the achievement of dignity. A sick person can even lose his reason. External circumstances of life can place man in such a position that he cannot cultivate properly his reason in spite of his desire to do so. Who knows how many Lomonosovs [70] have perished under the yoke of social conditions without being able to extricate themselves from the harsh conditions? Man under the pressure of external circumstances and in the name of the same dignity is compelled sometimes to renounce work which was his vocation and which he had carried out successfully, and which without him could be ruined, thus causing hundreds of people to suffer.

As regards happiness in the usual hedonistic sense, i.e., a tranquil and secure satiety, this type, as has been stated, is inaccessible to people. We cannot avoid physical and moral suffering, and we cannot turn our life into shallow pleasure on the basis of our finite and limited nature, which we emphasized many times, and which is a constant barrier to the infinite aspirations of our spirit. Man's life is a process of active struggle against recurring obstacles, and it must be regarded as such. It has its pleasures and very valuable ones, but it cannot continue without suffering.

The surest way for man to achieve tranquility would be the greatest possible LIMITATION OF HIS NEEDS AND ASPIRATIONS. Such a method has been repeatedly proposed by various philosophical schools. But this method definitely conflicts with our sense of human dignity. In this way, irrational people are deprived of a lot of anxieties which arise from an excess of requirements by a human mind which knows no restraints. Egotistical and callous people who do not know the need of love of one's neighbour, are free of a number of anxieties which they attain if they participate in the fate of their neighbours. People who do not possess a refined taste for art or poetry, can live happily in an environment where they cannot possibly attain such pleasures. If this

[70]   M. V. Lomonosov (1711-65), famous Russian scientist and founder of Moscow University in 1755.

argument were driven to its logical conclusion, we would have to acknowledge that animals devoid of higher human reason, enjoy a far greater existence. They do not for example, fear death, as do the majority of people, since they do not even anticipate it and are not aware of any danger which threatens them. The state of plants due to extreme meagerness of their psychic life, is probably even more tranquil, since they are incapable even of locomotion. But we would have to acknowledge that the most tranquil existence is that which is of an inorganic nature. Any stone will always be peaceful and undisturbed.

The ideal peace for the hedonists is dead nature, or at best, a vegetative state. It seems to me that the nirvana of which Schopenhauer dreams is of a similar kind. But I do not think that it is necessary to use the refined methods of which Schopenhauer speaks to attain this state. People who desire to attain nirvana have always chosen very simple methods of self-deception, according to L. N. Tolstoy,[71] not only by the use of tobacco, but vodka, opium, and dissipations of various sorts. It is obvious just how compatible this road to happiness is with human dignity. Only by completely stifling this sense of dignity can a person, stupefied by these divers methods, be tranquil, but the question is to what extent is he worthy of the name 'man'?

It should be borne in mind that by stifling one's demands in order to achieve a sense of peace, can hardly be called happiness. It is true that in such a state suffering disappears, but it may be asked whether any pleasure remains? In order to enjoy pleasure one should possess a highly developed consciousness. If however, the work of consciousness is generally stifled, then immunity from suffering and the susceptibility to pleasures are also stifled. Animals, of course, suffer less than man, since their psychic life in general is less intensive. But they undoubtedly enjoy pleasure less than man.

Would it not be better therefore, to renounce life and terminate it by suicide? This question inevitably presents itself to every hedonist. There are also philosophical schools, for example, the Stoics, who had no difficulty in recommending this method as a last resort for escaping life's difficulties. In order to act on this with conviction, one must be certain that after death we can expect nothing but non-being. No one however, can prove this. All the arguments that refute the idea of personal immortality prove only one thing, that we know nothing of such a state, that we cannot describe or even imagine it. No one can prove that there is *no* existence after death. At the same time, there are those for whom the immortality of the soul is the object of an unshakeable intuitive knowledge. It may be that these people are right,

---

[71] L. N. Tolstoy (1828-1910), Russian novelist and writer on religious educational and social questions.

and that a new existence awaits the suicide, in which case such a step would be a very poor preparation.

Moreover, in order to make the decision to terminate one's life, one would have to be completely indifferent to the question of one's moral task, one's vocation and the responsibility incumbent upon a person who has not fulfilled his duty. Moral duty, of course, should not be based on logical arguments. We know that doubts are always possible here. But it is impossible also to refute unconditionally moral duty on logical grounds. Hence, there is also no certainty of its non-existence. The most that is possible is more or less reasoned out doubts. But doubts alone are an insufficient basis for self-destruction. A doubter can always obviously say that he has not exhausted all the means of discovering the value of life, since there are people for whom the positive meaning of life is beyond doubt, and one cannot say that these are the most stupid and irrational people. Many of them, on the contrary, belong to the greatest spiritual forces of mankind. The person who finds himself in a state of great doubts, should simply try to change his life in the spirit of the active good to broaden his personality, and he will undoubtedly sooner or later, dismiss the idea of suicide and find sufficiently positive meaning in life.

The dignity of a man and the higher bliss which is connected with the activity that absorbs man and brings him into contact with cosmic infinity, is especially manifested in the personalities of geniuses. A genius is a man, who does not divorce himself from the task and is capable of devoting all the powers of his being to the accomplishment of some task which has cosmic significance, extra-temporal value. But this is offset by the fact, that the genius suffers more deeply than other people, since he feels more acutely the fetters placed on his limited nature. It does not follow from this that the path to moral dignity is accessible only to geniuses. Unfavourable conditions of life can block man's path to the various specialized forms of higher spiritual activity. Not everyone has the capacities necessary for this. Active love of one's neighbour is accessible to all people, with the sole exception of those unfortunates who have completely lost the light of human reason, or have succumbed to imbecility or madness. Some peasant like Akim [72] or Platon Karatayev [73] as well as many of Dostoyevsky's characters, show clearly that light also shines in darkness, that the active force of love may be manifested in people under all conditions, even under those most unfavourable for cultural development. Similarly, we encounter indifferent and loveless people in all layers of society, even among the most intelligent and educated people. From a moral point

[72] A character in L. N. Tolstoy's *The Power of Darkness*.
[73] A character in L. N. Tolstoy's *War and Peace*.

of view such people do not deserve full approbation, in spite of all their talents and genius in other areas. LOVE is higher than all other spiritual capacities. And grace and sublimity of human nature are incomplete if they are not vitalized and motivated by the spirit of love, which is equally accessible to all people from the greatest to the smallest. It is Christianity's great universal task to proclaim this truth.

I shall repeat once more, that it is impossible to prove with absolute certainty that man should place his dignity above all else. He who does not understand this cannot be convinced by any arguments. But it can be said to the doubter that the oppoiste also cannot be proven, i.e., that man has no cosmic significance, that there is no positive meaning in life. The person who ignores the commanding inner voice of his vocation risks a great deal. But he must extricate himself from this situation by a free act of will. People cannot penetrate the secret of the universe except by this inner voice which beckons us upwards to the stars. Man's moral merit consists in the fact that he follows his inner voice despite the great difficulties involved in it and without receiving an unconditional guarantee that he is right. The moral law must be autonomously imposed by man, and only then is he actually a moral being. Herein lies the inner meaning and truth of Kant's third formula of the categorical imperative: the idea that the will of a rational being is to be regarded as the will of the universal law.

This then is the element of risk and mystery which is inherent in the moral law and which moral philosophy has so often pointed out. Kant speaks of the "incomprehensibility" of the moral imperative [74] which turns out to be the only thing we do comprehend in morality. This idea is expressed with variations, by such thinkers as James,[75] Renouvier,[76] and others. There is a profound riddle in the moral personality of man, but there are methods in practical reason for its adequate solution by those who are not deaf to the voice of this reason.

[74] See Kant's *Grundlegung zur Metaphysik der Sitten*.
[75] William James (1842-1910), American philosopher and psychologist.
[76] Renouvier, Charles (1818-1903), French philosopher, whose philosophy has been called "phenomenological neo-criticism".

SELECTED GENERAL BIBLIOGRAPHY
OF WORKS ON RUSSIAN SOCIAL
AND PHILOSOPHIC THOUGHT

The purpose of this selected bibliography is to offer suggestions for further reading on topics treated in this volume. Transliteration of Russian names has been left as it appears in the books and articles cited even when it differs from that used in the present volume. This bibliography lays no claim to being either complete or exhaustive.

Berdyaev, N. A., *The Russian Idea*, translated by R. M. French (London, 1947).

Billington, James H., *Mikhailovsky and Russian Populism* (London, 1958).

Black, Cyril E. (ed.), *The Transformation of Russian Society* (Cambridge, Mass., 1960).

Christoff, P. K., *An Introduction to Nineteenth-Century Russian Slavophilism*, Volume 1: A. S. Xomjakov ('s-Gravenhage, Mouton & Co., 1961).

Fedotov, George P., *The Russian Religious Mind* (Cambridge, Mass., 1946).

Fischer, George, *Russian Liberalism* (Cambridge, Mass., 1958).

Hare, Richard, *Pioneers of Russian Social Thought*, second edition (New York, 1964), Paperback Vintage book.

Kohn, Hans, *Pan Slavism: Its History and Ideology* (Notre Dame, Ind., 1953).

——, *Prophets and Peoples. Studies in Nineteenth Century Nationalism* (New York, 1946) (Ch. 5 on Dostoevsky).

—— (ed.), *The Mind of Modern Russia. Historical and Political Thought of Russia's Great Age* (New Brunswick, N.J., (1955).

Lampert, E., *Studies in Rebellion* (London, 1957).

——, *Sons Against Fathers* (London, 1965).

Lossky, N. O., *History of Russian Philosophy* (London and New York, 1951).

Massaryk, Thomas G., *The Spirit of Russia: Studies in History, Literature and Philosophy*, translated by E. and C. Paul, two volumes (New York, 195?).

Maynard, Sir John, *Russia in Flux* (New York, 1948).

McLean, Malia, Fischer (eds.), *Russian Thought and Politics*, Volume IV (Cambridge, Mass., Harvard Slavic Studies, 1957).

Miliukov, Paul, *Outlines of Russian Culture*, translated by Valentie Ughet and Eleanor Davis (Philadelphia, 1948).

Simmons, E. J. (ed.), *Continuity and Change in Russian and Soviet Thought* (Cambridge, Mass., 1955).
Spet, Gustav G., *Ocherk razvitiya russkoj filosofii* [An Outline of the Development of Russian Philosophy] (Moscow, 1922).
Tompkins, Stuart Ramsay, *The Russian Mind. From Peter the Great Through The Enlightenment* (Norman, Okla., 1953).
Utechin, S. V., *Russian Political Thought* (New York and London, Praeger Press, 1964).
Weidle, Wladimir, *Russia Absent and Present*, translated by A. Gordon Smith (London and New York, 1952).
Zenkovsky, V. V., *A History of Russian Philosophy*, translated by George L. Kline, two volumes (London and New York, 1953).
Zernov, Nicolas, *The Russian Religious Renaissance* (London, 1963).

SUPPLEMENTARY BIBLIOGRAPHY

Selected Works

Baron, Samuel H., *Plekhanov: the Father of Russian Marxism.*
Belinsky, V. G., *Selected Philosophical Works* (Moscow, 1956).
Chernyshevsky, N. G., *Selected Philosophical Essays* (Moscow, 1953).
Chmielewski, Edward, *Tribune of the Slavophiles: Konstantin Aksakov.*
Clardy, Jesse V., *The Philosophical Ideas of Alexander Radischev.*
Dobrolyubov, N. A., *Selected Philosophical Essays* (Foreign Languages Publishing House, Moscow, 1956).
Edie, Scanlan, Zeldin (ed.), *Russian Philosophy*, three volumes (Chicago, 1965).
Grunwald, Constantin de, *Saints of Russia* (London, 1960).
Herzen, Alexander, *Selected Philosophical Works* (Foreign Languages Publishing House, Moscow, 1956).
Malia, Martin, *Alexander Herzen and the Birth of Russian Socialism* (Cambridge, Mass., 1961).
McConnell, Allen, *A Russian Philosopher: Alexander Radischev 1749-1802.*
Payne, Robert, *The Holy Fire* (London, 1958).
Pisarev, Dmitry, *Selected Philosophical, Social and Political Essays* (Moscow, 1958).
Plekhanov, G., *Selected Philosophical Works*, Volume one (Moscow).
Poggioli, Renato, *Rozanov* (New York, 1962).
Radischev, A. N., *A Journey from St. Petersburg to Moscow*, translated by Leo Wiener (Cambridge, Mass., 1958).
Riha, Thomas (ed.), *Readings in Russian Civilization*, three volumes (Chicago and London, 1964).
Zernov, Nicolas, *The Russians and their Church* (London, 1945).

WORKS BY RUSSIAN PHILOSOPHERS INCLUDED IN THIS BOOK

Askol'dov, Sergei Alekseyevich, *Mysl i deistvitelnost* [Thought and Reality] (Moscow, 1914).
——, *Osnovnyie problemy theori poznaniya i ontologi* [Fundamental Problems of Theory of Knowledge and Ontology] (Moscow, 1900).
——, *A. A. Kozlov* (Moscow, 1912).

Askol'dov, Sergei Alekseyevich, "V zashchitu chudesnovo" [In Defence of the Miraculous], *Voprosy fil. i psikh*, No. 71 (1904).
——, "Myshlenniye, kak obektivno obuslovleny protsess" [Thinking as an Objectively Conditioned Process], *Voprosy*, No. 66 (1903).
——, "Vnutrenni krizis trantscendentalnovo idealizma" [The Inner Crisis of Transcendental Idealism], *Voprosy*, No. 125 (1914).
——, "Vremya i yevo religiozny smysl'" [Time and Its Religious Significance], *Voprosy*, No. 117 (1913).
——, "Analogiya, kak osnovnoi metod poznaniya" [Analogy as the Basic Method of Cognition], *Mysl*, No. 1 (Petrograd, 1922).
——, "Vremya i yevo preodoleniya" [The Overcoming of Time], *Mysl*, No. 3.
——, "Ideya spravedlivosti v khristianstve" [The Idea of Justice in Christianity], *Philosophic Miscellany in Honour of L. M. Lopatin* (1911).
Berdyaev, Nicolai, *Subjektivism i Individualism v Obschestvennoi Filosofii* [Subjectivism and Individualism in Social Philosophy] (St. Petersburg, Popov, 1901).
——, *Problemy Idealizma* [Problems of Idealism] (Moscow, Moscow Psychological Society, 1903).
——, *Sub Specie Aeternitatis* (St. Petersburg, Pirozhkov, 1907).
——, *Novoe Religioznoe Soznanie i Obschestvennost* [The New Religious Consciousness and Society] (St. Petersburg, Pirozhkov, 1907).
——, *Dukhovni Krisis Intelligentsii* [The Spriritual Crisis of the Intelligentsia] (St. Petersburg, Obschestvennaya Polza, 1910).
——, *Filosofia Svobody* [The Philosophy of Freedom] (Moscow, Put, 1911).
——, *Alexei Stepanovitch Khomiakov* [A. S. Khomiakoff] (Moscow, Put, 1912).
——, *Sudba Rosii* [The Fate of Russia] (Moscow, Leman & Sacharov, 1918).
——, *Filosofia Neravenstva* [The Philosophy of Inequality], (Berlin, Obelisk, 1923).
——, *The Beginning and the End*, translated by R. M. French (London, 1952).
——, *Bourgeois Mind and Other Essays* (London, 1934).
——, *Christianity and Class War*, translated by Donald Attwater (London, 1932).
——, *The Destiny of Man* (London, 1945).
——, *The Divine and the Human* (London, 1949).
——, *Dostoyevsky*, translated by Donald Attwater (New York, 1957).
——, *Dream and Reality*, translated by Katharine Lampert (London, 1950).
——, *The End of Our Time*, translated by D. Attwater (London, 1933).
——, *The Fate of Man in the Modern World*, translated by Donald A. Lowrie (London, 1935).
——, *Freedom and Spirit*, translated by O. F. Clarke (London, 1935).
——, *The Meaning of History*, translated by George Reavey (London, 1936).
——, *The Meaning of the Creative Act*, translated by D. A. Lowrie (New York, 1955).
——, *The Origin of Russian Communism*, translated by R. M. French (London, 1937).
——, *The Realm of Spirit and the Realm of Caesar*, translated by D. A. Lowrie (London, 1952).
——, *The Russian Idea*, translated by R. M. French (London, 1947).
——, *The Russian Revolution* (Michigan University, Ann Arbor, 1961).
——, *Slavery and Freedom*, translated by R. M. French (New York, 1944).
——, *Solitude and Society*, translated by George Reavey (London, 1947).
——, *Spirit and Reality*, translated by George Reavey (London, 1939).
——, *Truth and Revelation*, translated by R. M. French (London, 1953).
Bugayev, N. V., "Matematika i Nauchno-Filosofskoye Mirosozertsaniy" [Mathe-

matics and a Scientific-Philosophic World-View], *Voprosy*, Volume 9. Book 45), 697-717.

Bugayev, N. V., *Matematika, kak orudie nauchnoye i pedagogicheskoye* [Mathematics as a Scientific and Pedagogical Instrument], translated into French, *Des Mathematiques Considérées Comme Instrument Scientifique et Pédagogique* (Paris, 1872).

Chelpanov, G. I., *Problema vospriyatiya prostranstva* [The Problem of the Perception of Space], two volumes (Kiev, 18983.

——, *O Pamyati i mnemonike* [On Memory and Menmosis], second edition (St. Petersburg, 1903).

——, *Vvedenie v filosofii* [Introduction to Philosophy] (Kiev, 1905).

——, *Uchebnik psikhologii* [Psychology] (Riga, 1924).

——, *Mozg i dusha* [Brain and Psyche], fourth edition (Kiev, 1907).

——, *Vvedenie v eksperimentalnyuy psikhologiyu* [Introduction to Experimental Psychology], third edition (Moscow, 1924).

——, *Ocherki psikhologii* [Outlines of Psychology] (Moscow, 1926).

——, *Obzor noveishei literatury po voprosu o vospriatii prostranstva* [Review of the Latest Literature on the Question of the Perception of Space] (Kiev, 1896).

——, *Sbornik statei* [Collected Articles] (Moscow, 1912).

——, "Ocherk sovremennykh uchenii o dushe" [Outline of Contemporary Doctrines on the Psyche], *Voprosy*, Volume 11, Books 52, 53.

——, "Ob apriorkhnykh elementakh poznaniya" [On a priori Elements of Cognition], *Voprosy*, Volume 12, Books 59, 60.

Chicherin, B. N., *Istoriya politicheskikh uchenii* [A History of Political Doctrines], five volumes. Second edition (Moscow, 1889-1902).

——, *Oblastnyia uchrezhdeniia Rosii v xviii-om veke* [Regional Institutions in Russian in the 18th Century] (Moscow, 1856).

——, *O Narodnom Predstavlenii* [Representative Government and Representation] (Moscow, 1899).

——, *Sobstvennost' i gosudarstvo* [Private property and the State] (Moscow, 1882-83).

——, *Voprosy Politki* [Problems of Politics] (Moscow, 1904).

Chicherin, B. N., *Nauka i religiya* [Science and Religion], second edition (Moscow, 1879).

——, *Mistitsizm v nauke* [Mysticism in Science] (Moscow, 1880).

——, *Polozhitelnaya filosofiya i yedisnstvo nauki* [Positive Philosophy and the Unity of Science] (Moscow, 1894).

——, *Filosofiya prava* [Philosophy of Law] (Moscow, 1900).

Frank, S. L., *Biografia P. B. Struve* [A Biography of P. B. Struve] (New York,. 1956).

——, *Dukhovniya osnovy obschestva: vvedenie v sotsialnuyu filosofiu* [The Spiritual Foundations of Society: An Introduction to Social Philosophy] (Paris, YMCA Press, 1930).

——, *Nepostizhimoye: Ontologicheskoye vvedenie v filosofiu religii* [The Unfathomable: An introduction to the Philosophy of Religion] (Paris, 1939).

——, *Real'nost' i chelovek: metafisika chelovecheskogo bytiya* [Reality and Man: the metaphysics of human existence] (Paris, YMCA Press, 1956).

——, *Religia i nauka: nauchnaia broshiura* [Religion and Science: A scientific brochure] (Frankfurt, Main, 1959).

——, *Svoboda i kul'tura* [Freedom and Culture] (St. Petersburg, 1906).

——, *Svet vo t'me: opyt khristianskoi etiki i sotsial'noi filosofii* [Light and Darkness: An essay on Christian Ethics and Social Philosophy] (Paris, 1949).

Frank, S. L., *Etiudy o Pushkine* [Studies on Pushkin] (Munich, 1957).

——, *Vvedeniye v filosofiu* [An Introduction to Philosophy], second revised edition (Berlin, 1923).

——, *Eres' utopizma* [The Heresy of Utopianism] (San Martin, 1954).

——, *Zhivoye Znanie* [Living Knowledge] (Berlin, 1923).

——, *Krushenie kumirov* [The Downfall of the Idols] (Berlin, 1924).

——, *Lichnaya Zhizn' i sotsial'noye stroitel'stvo* [Personal Life and Social Order] (Paris, 1933).

——, *Materializm kak mirovozzrenie* [Materialism as a world-view] (Paris, Warsaw, 1928).

——, *Osnovy Maksizma* [The foundations of Marxism] (Berlin & Paris, 1926).

——, *Pushkin kak politicheskii myslitel'* [Pushkin as a Political Thinker] (Belgrade, 1937).

——, *Religiozno-istoricheskii smysl russkoi revoliutsii* [The religio-historical meaning of the Russian revolution] (Berlin, 1924).

——, *Filosofia i Zhizn'* [Philosophy and Life], the date of the imprint is mutilated.

——, "Etika nigilizma, k kharakteristike nravstvennago mirovozzreniya russkoi intelligentsii" [The ethics of nihilism, characterization of the moral world-view of the Russian Intelligentsia], in *Vekhi* [Landmarks] (Moscow, 1909).

——, *Predmet Znaniya* [The Object of Knowledge] (Moscow, 1915).

——, *God With Us. Three Mediations*, translated by Natalie Duddington (London, 1946).

——, *A Solovyov Anthology*, translated by Natalie Duddington (London, 1950).

Grot, Nikolai Yakovlevich, *Filosofia i yeya obschiya zadachi. Sbornik statei* [Philosophy and its general tasks, Collected Essays] (Moscow, 1894).

——, *Nravstvenniye idealy nashego vremeni. Friedrich Nietzsche i Lev Tolstoi* [Contemporary moral ideals. Friedrich Nietzsche and Lev Tolstoi] (Moscow, 1894).

——, "O vremeni" [On Time], *Voprosy*, Books 23-25 (Moscow, 1889).

——, "Osnovanie nravstvennago dolga" [Foundations of moral duty], *Voprosy*, Books 12, 15 (Moscow, 1889).

——, "Osnovaniya eksperimentalnoi psikhologii [Foundations of experimental psychology], *Voprosy*, Book 30 (Moscow, 1889).

——, *Osnovniye momenty v razvitii novoi filosofii* [The Main periods in the development of modern philosophy] (Moscow, 1894).

——, *Ocherk filosofii Platona* [Outline of Plato's philosophy] (Moscow, 1896).

——, "Ponyatie o dushe i psikhicheskoi energii v psikhologii [The Concept about the soul and psychic zergy in psychology], *Voprosy*, Books 37, 39 (Moscow, 1889).

Kareyev, Nikolai Ivanovich, "O svobode voli" [On the Freedom of Will], in *Edyudy sotsiologicheskiye i filosofskiye*.

——, *Osnovnyie voprosy filosofii istorii* [Fundamental Problems of the Philosophy of History] (St. Petersburg, 1883).

——, *Besedy o vyrabotke mirosozertsaniya* [Discussions on the developing of a world-view] (St. Petersburg, 1895).

——, *Filosofia cul'turnoi i sotsial'noi istorii novago vremeni* [The Philosophy of modern cultural and social history] (St. Petersburg, 1893).

——, *Istoricheskaya filosofia gr. L. N. Tolstogo v "Voine i mire"* [Philosophy of the historic element of Count L. N. Tolstoi's *War and Peace*].

——, *Istoriko-filosofskiye i sotsiologicheskiye etyudy* [Historico-philosophical and sociological studies] (St. Petersburg, 1895).

Khvostov, V. M., "O pessimistitcheskom Mirovozzrenii" [Concerning a pessimistic World-view], *Voprosy*, Volume 22, Book 108, 187-233.
———, "Pliuralisticheskoye Miroponimaniye" [A Pluralistic World-View], *Voprosy*, Volume 22, Book 109, 361-394.
———, "Nravstvennaya zadacha chelovechestva" [The moral task of humanity], *Voprosy*, Volume 22, Book 110, 437-490; Volume 23, Book 111, 1-33.
———, *K voprosu o Svobode Voli* [On the Question of Freedom of Will], Volume 105, Book 96, 31-54.
———, "Pamyati dorogogo tovarischa Kn. S. N. Trubetskogo" [In memory of a dear friend Prince S. N. Trubetskoi], *Voprosy*, Book 81 (Moscow, 1906).
———, *Zhenshchina nakanune novoi epokhi* [Woman on the Eve of a New Epoch] (Moscow, 1905).
———, *Obshchestvennoye mnenieye i politicheskiye partii* [Social Opinions and Political Parties] (Moscow, 1906).
———, *Etyudy po sovremennoi etike* [Essays on Modern Ethics], Dedicated to S. Trubetskoi, with chapters on Nietzsche, Stirner, Kautsky, and Petrazicki (Moscow, 1908).
———, *Nvrastvennaya lichnost i obshchestvo: Ocherki po etike i sotsiologi* [Moral Personality and Society: Outilines on Ethics and Sociology], Articles and lectures (Moscow, 1911).
———, *Opyt kharakterestiki ponyatii aequitas i aequum jus v rimskoi klassicheskoi yurisprudentsii* [The Concept of aequitas and aequum jus in Roman classical jurisprudence] (Moscow, 1895).
———, *Natural'niya ob'yazatel'stva po rimskomy prava* [Natural obligations in Roman Law] (Moscow, 1898).
———, *Sistema rimskogo prava* [The System of Roman Law] (Moscow, 1902).
———, *Semeinoye i nasledstvennoye pravo* [Family and Hereditary Law] (1900).
———, *Veschnoye pravo* [The Law of Property] (Moscow, 1901).
Lopatin, L. M., "Dekart kak osnovatel' novago filosofskago i nauchnago mirosozrtsaniya [Descartes as the founder of modern philosophic and scientific world-view], *Voprosy* (Moscow, 1896).
———, *Filosofskiya kharacteristiki i rechi* [Philosophical Characterisations and Addresses] (Moscow, 1911),
———, *Lektsii po istorii novoi filosofii* [Lectures on the history of modern philosophy], first edition (Berlin, 1923).
———, "Podvizniya assotsiatsii predstavlenii" [Active association of ideas], *Voprosy*, Book 18 (Moscow, 1893).
———, "Ponyatie o dushe po dannym vnutrenyago opyta [The Concept of the Soul on the Data of Inner Experience], *Voprosy*, Book 32 (Moscow, 1889).
———, "Spiritualizm, kak psikhologicheskaya gipoteza" [Spiritualism as a Psychological Hypothesis], *Voprosy*, Book 38 (Moscow, 1897).
———, "Teoreticheskiya osnovy soznatelnoi nravstvennoi zhizni" [Theoretical Foundations of the Conscious Moral Life], *Voprosy*, Book 5 (Moscow, 1895).
———, "Yavlenie i sushchnost' v zhizni soznaniya" [Appearance and Reality in the Life of Consciousness], *Voprosy*, Book 30 (Moscow, 1895).
———, *Kurs psikhologii* [A Course of Psychology] (Moscow, 1903).
———, *Polozhitel'niya zadachi filosofii* [Positive tasks of Philosophy]. Second edition (Moscow, 1911).
———, "Polozhenie eticheskoi zadachi v sovremennoi filosofii [The State of the Ethical task in Modern Philosophy], *Voprosy*, Book 7 (Moscow).
———, "Kritika empiricheskikh nachal nravstennosti" [Critique of empirical principles of morality], *Voprosy*, Volume 1, Book 3 (Moscow).

Lopatin, L. M., "Nravstennoye uchenie Kanta" [Kant's moral doctrine], *Voprosy*, Volume 1, Book 3 (Moscow).
——, "Vopros o real'nom edinstve soznaiya" [The question of the real unity of consciousness], *Voprosy*, Books 69, 70, 71 (Moscow).
——, *Uchenie o posznanii* [The doctrine of cognition], Volume 6, Book 76.
——, "Aksiomy filosofii" [Axioms of philosophy], *Voprosy*, Volume 16, Book 30 (Moscow).
——, "Pitagorskiye sistemy filosofii" [Pythagorean systems of Philosophy], *Voprosy*, Volume 17, Book 83 (Moscow).
——, *Nastoyascheye i buduscheye filosofii* [The present and future of philosophy].
——, "Pamyati Vladimira Solovyeva" [In memory of Vladimir Solovyov], *Voprosy*, Volume 21, Book 105 (Moscow).
——, "Spiritualizm kak monisticheskaya sistema filosofii" [Spiritualism As a Monistic System of Philosophy], *Voprosy*, Volume 23, Book 115 (Moscow).
——, "Monizm i plyuralizm" [Monism and Pluralism], *Voprosy*, Volume 24, Book 116 (Moscow).
——, "Solovyov i knyaz' E. N. Trubetskoi" [Solovyov and Prince E. N.Trubetskoi], *Voprosy*, Volume 24, Books 119, 120, 123.
——, "Sovremennoye znanie filosofskikh idei knyza S. N. Trubetskogo" [Contemporary knowledge of Prince S. N. Trubetskoi's philosophic ideas], *Voprosy*, Volume 27, Book 131 (Moscow).
——, "Knyaz' S. N. Trubetskoi i ego obscheye filosofskoye mirosozertsanie" [Prince S. N. Trubetskoi and his general philosophic world-view], *Voprosy*, Book 81 (Moscow, 1906).
Lossky, Nicolai O., *Vvedeniye v filosofiyu* [Introduction to Philosophy], second edition (Petrograd, 1918).
——, *Logika* [Logic], second edition (Berlin, 1923).
——, *Obosnovaniye Intuitivizma* [The Intuitive Basis of Knowledge], third edition (Berlin, 1924).
——, *Dialekticheskii materialism v SSSR* [Dialectical materialism in the USSR] (Paris, YMCA Press, 1934).
——, *Gnoseologicheskoye vvedeniye v logiku* [Epistemological introduction to logic] (Charbin, 1921).
——, *Tipy mirovozzrenii* [Types of world views] (Prague, 1924).
——, *Intuitionalism*, translated by N. A. Duddington (1914).
——, *The Limits of Evolution*, translated by N. A. Duddington (1927).
——, *The Chief Characteristics of a System of Logic Based upon Intuitivism in Epistemology and Ideal-realism in Metaphysics* (Oxford University Press, 1931).
——. *The Metaphysics of the Stoics*, translated by N. A. Duddington (1929).
——, *The Philosophy of Vladimir Soloviov*, translated by N. A. Dudington (1923).
——, *The Primitive and Civilized Mind*, translated by N. A. Duddington (London).
——, *The Successors of Vladimir Soloviov*, translated by N. A. Duddington (1924).
——, *Value and Existence*, Part one translated by S. S. Vinokooroff, Part two translated by J. S. Marshall (London, George Allen and Unwin, 1935).
——, *The Intuitive Basis of Knowledge*, translated by N. Duddington (London, 1919).
——, *The World as an Organic Whole*, translated by N. Duddington (London, 1928).
——, *The Fundamental Problems of Epistemology* (1919).
——, *Freedom of Will*, translated by N. A. Duddington (London, 1932).
——, *Sensory, Intellectual and Mystical Intuition* (Paris, 1930).
Solovyov, Vladimir, *War Progress and the End of History: including a Short*

Story of the Antichrist, translated by Alexander Bakshy (London, 1915).
——, *The Justification of the Good: An Essay in Moral Philosophy*, translated by Natalie Duddington (Constable's Russian Library, 1918).
——, *Plato*, translated by Richard Gill (London, 1935).
——, *God, Man and the Church: the Spiritual Foundations of Life*, translated by D. Attwater (London, 1938).
——, *The Meaning of Love*, translated by Jane Marshall (London, 1946).
——, *Lectures on God-Manhood* (London and Dublin, 1948).
——, *Russia and the Universal Church* (London, 1948).
——, *Krizis zapadnoi filosofi* [The Crisis of Western Philosophy] (St. Petersburg, 1911).
——, *Filosofskiye nachala tselnovo znaniya* [The Philosophic Principles of Integral Knowledge] (St. Petersburg, 1877).
——, *Dukhovniya osnovy shizni* [Spiritual foundations of life] (New York, 1958).
——, *Smysl voiny* [The Meaning of War].
——, *Syd'ba Pushkina* [Pushkin's fate] (St. Petersburg, 1899).
——, *Tri razgovora* [Three Conversations] (New York, Chekhov Publishing House, 1954).
——, *Sobranie sochinenii Vladimira Sergeyevicha Solovyova* [Collected Works of Vladimir Sergeyevich Solovyov], nine volumes (St. Petersburg, 1901-1903).
Tsertelev, Dimitry Nikolaeyvich, "The Philosohpy of Schopenhauer" (in Russian) (St. Petersburg, 1880).
——, "Contemporary Pessimism in Germany" (in Russian) (Moscow, 1885).
——, "Schopenhauer's Aesthetics" (in Russian) (St. Petersburg, 1888).
Trubetskoi, Sergei Nikolayevich, *Kurs istorii drevnei filosofii* [A Course on the history of ancient philosophy], two volumes (Moscow, 1910).
——, *Sobranie sochinenii* [Collected Works], 6 volumes (Moscow, 1907-1912).
——, *Istoriya drevenei filosofii* [History of ancient Philosophy] (Moscow, 1906).
——, *O prirode chelovecheskago soznaniya* [On the Nature of Human Consciousness], *Voprosy*, Books 6, 7 (Moscow, 1891).
——, "Osnovaniya idealizma" [Foundations of Idealism], *Voprosy*, Books 31-35 (Moscow, 1896).
——, "Religioznyi ideal yevreyev" [The religious ideal of the Jews], *Voprosy*, Book 43 (Moscow, 1898).
——, "Uchenie o Logose v drevnei filosofii v svyazi s razvitiem idealizma" [The doctrine of the Logos in ancient philosophy in connection with the development of idealism], *Voprosy*, Book 36 (Moscow, 1897).
——, "Filon i ego predshestvenniki" [Philo and his predecessors], *Voprosy*, Books 40, 41 (Moscow, 1897-98).
——, "Filosofii khristianskoi teokratii v pyatom veke" [Philosophies of Christian theocracies in the fifth century], *Voprosy*, Books 9, 10, 13, 14 (Moscow, 1891-92).
——, *Determinizm i nravstennaya svoboda* [Determinism and Moral Freedom], Volume 1 of Collected Works.
——, *Renan i yego filosofiya* [Renan and his Philosophy], Volume II of Collected Works.
——, *Razocharovannyi slavyanofil'* [A Disillusioned Slavophile] (on Leonteyev), in Volume II of Collected Works.
——, "Psikhologicheski determinizm i nravstvennaya svoboda" [Psychological determinism and moral freedom], *Voprosy*, Volume I, Book 25.
——, "Etika i dogmatika" [Ethics and dogmatism], *Voprosy*, Volume VI, Book 29.
——, "Messianicheskii Ideal yevreyev v svyazi s ucheniem o Logose" [The Mes-

sianic ideal of the Jews in connection with the doctrine of the Logos],
Voprosy, Book 43.
——, "Pitagori i Pitagoreitsy" [Pythagoras and the Pythagoreans], *Voprosy*, Book 77.

WORKS ON AUTHORS IN THIS VOLUME

N. O. Lossky

Askol'dov, S., *Novaya gnoseologicheskaya teoriya N. O. Losskavo* [N. O. Lossky's new epistemological theory] (St. Petersburg, 1906).
Bubnov, N. U., *Kultur and Geschichte im russischen Denken der Gegenwart* (Berlin, 1927).
Duddington, N. A., "Philosophy in Russia", *Journal of Phil. Studies*, I, II, IV, VI (1926, 1927, 1929, and 1931).
——, *The Philosophy of N. O. Lossky* (London, Dublin Review, 1933).
Frank, S. L., *Die russische Philosophie der letzten fuenfzehn Jahre* (1926).
Sanborn, Herbert, *L'intuition, la matiere et la vie*, by N. Lossky (Paris, Felix Alcan, 1928).
Tomkieff, S., *The Philosophy of N. O. Lossky* (Durham University, 1923).
Yakovenko, B., *Chetviortyi mezhdunarodnyi kongress po filosofii* [The Fourth international congress of philosophy] (1912).
——, *Desyat' let russkoi filosofii (1914-1924)* [Ten years of Russian Philosophy] (Prague, 1925).
——, *Dreissig Jahre russischer Philosophie (1900-1929)* (1930).
——, *N. Lossky. L'intuition, la Matiere et la Vie* (Paris, Alcan, 1928).
Yershov, M., *Puti razvitiya filosofii v rossii* [The ways in which philosophy developed in Russia] (1922).
Zenkovski, V., *N. O. Lossky. Tipy mirovozzrenii: Vvedeniye v metafiziku, 1931* (Put', 1932).

Vladimir Solovyov

Alis, Adhemar, *The Russian Newman Vladimir Soloviev* (New York, 1933), *Thought*, Volume 8.
Duddington, N., *The Religious Philosophy of Vl. Solovieff*, Volume 15 (Boston, Hibbert Journal, 1917).
Lavrin, Janko, "Vladimir Solovyov", *Slavonic and East European Review* (London), 1930, December 9th, 1931, June 10th.
Lopatin, L. M., "Filosofskoye Mirosozertzanie Vl. Solovieva [Vl. Soloviev's philosophical world-view], *Voprosy* (Moscow, 1901).
Losski, N., "The Philosophy of Vl. Soloviev", *Slavonic Review*, Volume 2 (London, 1923-1924).
Mochoulski, K., *Vladimir Soloviev, Zhizn i Outchenie* (Paris, YMCA Press, 1936).
Novgorotzeff, P., "Ideia Prava v Filosofii Vl. S. Solovieva" [The idea of law in Vl. S. Soloviev's philosophy], *Voprosy* (Moscow, 1901).
Radlov, E., "Vl. S. Soloviev Zhizn i Outchenie" [Vl. S. Soloviev, his life and teaching] *Obrazovanie* (St. Petersburg, 1913).
Rappoport, S. J., "The Russian Philosopher V. Solovyev", *Contemporary Review*, Volume 108 (New York, 1913).
Struve, P. B. "Pamiati Vl. Solovieva" [In memory of Vl. Soloviev], *Mir Bozhiy* (St. Petersburg, 1900).

Trubetskoi, S. N., "Osnovnoye nachalo Uchenia V. S. Solovieva" [The fundamental teaching of Vl. S. Soloviev], *Voprosy* (Moscow, 1901).
——, "Smert' Vl. Solovieva" [The death of Vl. Soloviev], *Vestnik Evropy* (St. Petersburg, 1900).
——, "Tri Razgovora" [Three Conversations], *Voprosy* (Moscow), 1900.
Trubetskoi, E. N., "K Voprosu o Mirosozertsanii Vl. S. Solovieva [The problem of V. S. Soloviev's world-view], *Voprosy* (Moscow, 1913).
——, "Krushenie Teokratii v Tvoreniakh Vl. S. Solovieva [The Fall of the theocracy in the works of Vl. S. Soloviev], *Russkaya Mysl'* (Moscow), 1912.
Vvedenski, A., *O Mistitzizme i Krititzizme v Teorii Poznania V. S. Solovieva* [Mysticism and criticism in V. S. Soloviev's theory of knowledge].
Zernov, N. M., *Three Russian Prophets: Khomyakov, Dostoyevsky, Soloviev* (London, 1944).

REFERENCES TO ORIGINAL RUSSIAN SOURCES
USED IN THIS VOLUME

Selections from Voprosy

G. I. Chelpanov, "Ob apriornykh elementakh poznaniya" [A Priori Elements of Cognition], *Voprosy*, Volume 12, Book 59, pp. 529-559.
S. N. Trubetskoi, "O prirode chelovecheskogo soznaniya" [On the Nature of Human Consciousness], *Voprosy*, Book 6, No. 2, pp. 132-156 and Book 7, pp. 21-56.
V. S. Solovev, "Pervoye nachalo teoreticheskoi filosofii" [The First Principle of Theoretical Philosophy], *Voprosy*, Volume 8, Book 40, pp. 667-915.
S. A. Askol'dov, "Vnutrennii krizis transtzendental'nogo idealizma" [The Inner Crisis of Transcendental Idealism], *Voprosy*, Book 125, pp. 781-796.
N. V. Bugayev, "Osnovnyya nachala evoliutsionnoi monadologii" [Basic Principles of Evolutionary Monadology], *Voprosy*, Book 2 (17), pp. 28-44.
B. N. Chicherin, "Metafizika est' li nauka?" [Is Metaphysics a Science?], *Voprosy*, Volume 11, Book 54, pp. 460-657.
L. M. Lopatin, "Monizm i pliuralizm" [Monism and Pluralism], *Voprosy*, Volume 6, No. 116, pp. 68-92.
D. N. Tsertelev, "Prostranstvo i vremya, kak formy yavlenii" [Space and Time as Forms of Phenomena], *Voprosy*, Volume 5, Book 23, pp. 235-247.
N. Ya. Grot, "Osnovaniya nravstvennago dolga" [The Foundation of Moral Duty], *Voprosy*, Volume 3, Book 12, pp. 146-164.
N. I. Kareyev, "K voprosu o svobode voli s tochki zreniya teorii istoricheskago protzesa" [On the Question of Free Will From the Point of View of the Theory of the Historical Process], *Voprosy*, Volume 2, Book 8, pp. 113-142.
V. M. Khvostov, "Evdemonisticheskoye znachenia nravstvennago dopra" [The Eudaemonistic Significance of the Moral Good], *Voprosy*, Volume 22, Book 110, pp. 187-233.
N. A. Berdyaev, "Subyektivizm i obyektivizm". Chapter I of *Subyektivizm i Individualizm v Obschestvennoi Filosofii* [Subjectivism and Objectivism, Chapter I of Subjectivism and Individualism in Social Philosophy] (St. Petersburg, 1902), pp. 16-141.
N. O. Lossky, "Osnovnyya svoistva tsennosti, Chapter 3, in *Tsennost' i bytiye* [The Fundamental Characteristics of Values, Chapter 3 in Value and Being] (YMCA Press, Paris, 1931), pp. 78-121.

INDEX